FOOD BIOCHEMISTRY

C. ALAIS
G. LINDEN
both Professors of Biochemistry
University of Nancy, France

Translation Editor
I. MORTON

Translator
A. WHITEHEAD

ELLIS HORWOOD
NEW YORK   LONDON   TORONTO   SYDNEY   TOKYO   SINGAPORE

This English edition first published in 1991 by
ELLIS HORWOOD LIMITED
Market Cross House, Cooper Street,
Chichester, West Sussex, PO19 1EB, England

A division of
Simon & Schuster International Group
A Paramount Communications Company

This English edition is translated from the original French edition *Abrégé de biochimie alimentaire*, published in 1987 by Masson éditeur, © the copyright holders
© English Edition, Ellis Horwood 1991

Typeset in Times by Ellis Horwood Limited
Printed and bound in Great Britain
by Hartnolls, Bodmin, Cornwall

**Exclusive distribution by Van Nostrand Reinhold (International),
an imprint of Chapman & Hall, 2–6 Boundary Row, London SE1 8HN**

Chapman & Hall, 2–6 Boundary Row, London SE1 8HN, England

Van Nostrand Reinhold Inc., 115 5th Avenue, New York, NY10003, USA

Nelson Canada, 1120 Birchmont Road, Scarborough, Ontario M1K 5G4, Canada

Chapman & Hall Japan, Thomson Publishing Japan, Hirakawacho Nemoto Building, 7F, 1-7-11 Hirakawa-cho, Chiyoda-ku, Tokyo 102, Japan

Chapman & Hall Australia, Thomas Nelson Australia, 102 Dodds Street, South Melbourne, Victoria 3205, Australia

Chapman & Hall India, R. Seshadri, 32 Second Main Road, CIT East, Madras 600 035, India

Rest of the world:
Thomson International Publishing, 10 Davis Drive, Belmont, California 94002, USA

British Library Cataloguing-in-Publication Data

Alais, Charles
Food biochemistry. —
(Ellis Horwood series in food science and technology)
I. Title   II. Linden, Guy   III. Series
574.19
ISBN 0–7476–0056–2 (Library Edn.)
ISBN 0–7476–0061–9 (Student Edn.)

Library of Congress Cataloging-in-Publication Data

Alais, Charles.
[Abarégé de biochimie alimentaire, English]
Food biochemistry / C. Alais, G. Linden: translator, A. Whitehead.
p. cm. — (Ellis Horwood series in food science and technology)
Translation of: Abrégé de biochimie alimentaire.
Includes bibliographical references and index.
ISBN 0–7476–0056–2 (Library Edn.)
ISBN 0–7476–0061–9 (Student Edn.)
1. Food — Composition. 2. Biochemistry. I. Linden, G. II. Series.
TX545.A4213   1991
664–dc20
91–23024
CIP

Table of contents

Preface

What I have said will go to prove that true science is the one which teaches us to increase our satisfaction by drawing out the best from nature's productions.

M. Henri Braconnot
Nancy, 4th April 1830

(Extract from the *Note on Casein and Milk*, Annales de Chimie et de Physique (1830) **43**, 351.)

The main objective of this work is to provide a biochemical approach for students of food science and technology. It may also be useful to biologists generally and to biochemists in particular in providing a source of reference to help resolve some of their problems. Finally, professionals in the food industry will find here detailed information on aspects of biotechnology.

With the continuing development of teaching in this field in the mainstream courses of Instituts Universitaires de Technologie†, Universities and Grandes Ecoles‡ in France, the need for an *Abrégé* (Essential Guide) has become urgent. Students have to refer to various specialist works, which are considerable in number, expensive and often out of date.

The authors were faced with the task of selecting material and presenting it in such a way that the finished book would be reduced to a size in keeping with the spirit of the *Abrégé* collection.

This book concentrates on biochemistry, as such; microbiological aspects have not been taken into account. General ideas about the mechanism of life will not be considered here; it will be assumed that the reader knows about them; but it must be said that our book will cover some of the metabolic aspects.

† Universities concentrating on technological subjects.
‡ Specialist schools with competitive national entry.

For easy reference the subject matter has been divided into two sections. The first section comprises a review of the constitution of food substances. The second section outlines the biochemical properties of main human foods in this part of the world.

Part I
The constituents of foodstuffs

1

General observations on the composition of foodstuffs

I. ANALYTICAL VALUES

Most human foods are complex substances of animal and vegetable origin. A summary of their average composition in the unrefined state is given in Tables 1.1(a) and 1.1(b), where vitamins are not taken into account. These substances are often called *nutrients*.

Two special cases must be added:

— substances produced by micro-organisms, still not very widespread in the western world, but of growing importance.
— pure products, almost 100% pure, obtained by the food production industry or by a chemical process. Ordinary 'sugar' or sucrose, is the main example of this. Extra-cellular water cannot be considered as a food, for reasons which we will explain later (Chapter 7).

The following comments arise from reading Table 1.1:

(1) The water content of fresh products, with the exception of grains and cereals, varies from 55 to 93 percent. It is lower in meat (55–75 percent) than in fish (60–80 percent) and especially lower than in most vegetable products (74–94 percent).
(2) Substances listed in columns 2–6/7 are complex and less evenly distributed than the water content:
   • Proteins are quite abundant and sometimes dominant in animal products, whilst carbohydrates are found in small quantities.
   • Carbohydrates predominate in vegetable products, except in those high in amino acids, like soya, or those containing oil.

Table 1.1 — Average composition of main foodstuffs (g per 100 g edible portion)

(a) *Animal foods*

	Water	Proteins	Lipids	Carbo-hydrates	Minerals	Calories[a]
	(1)	(2)	(3)	(4)	(5)	(6)
Meats, medium fat						
— beef, mutton	60	17	20	0.5	1.3	250
— pork	55	16	25	0.5	1.2	290
Meats, lean						
— horse	75	21	2	1.0	1.0	110
— fillet of beef	67	20	10	0.7	1.3	180
— chicken	70	21	8		1.4	150
Hens' eggs[b]	74	13	12	0.6	0.9	160
Fish, freshwater (carp)	78	18	2		1.4	100
Fish, marine, lean (cod)	80	17	2		1.6	90
Fish, marine, fatty (tuna)	60	26	13		1.6	220
Oysters	80	10	1.8	6.0	c	80
Offal						
— calf's liver	70	20	4	3.0	1.7	120
— calf's brain	78	10	9	2.0	1.5	130
Cooked meats						
— black pudding	30	28	41		c	480
— cooked ham	48	22	22		c	300
— salami	30	24	35		c	400
Cow's milk	87.5	3.5	3.9	4.8	0.8	68
Cheese						
— Camembert	55	20	23	1.0	0.9	310
— Gruyère	34	30	30	1.5	2.6[d]	390

[a] For kilojoule value, multiply by 4.18.
[b] Unit weight 60 g.
[c] Salt content (NaCl) of 1–10%.
[d] Ca: 1.0.

Note: The water loss during the cooking of meats (even by boiling) is about 25%.
         Loss of other constituents in the boiling of meat is variable.

- In meat, eggs and milk, the lipid level equals the protein level, but it is low in vegetables (except oil-producing plants).
- Minerals are not present in great quantity in most foodstuffs.

(3) The calorific power, or energy value, varies considerably. Generally it is inversely proportional to the water content and proportional to the lipid content of foods. The lowest value is found in very hydrated vegetables at around 20 calories, and the maximum value rises to around 900 calories in fatty tissues.

(4) *Fibre* is not included in these tables; it comprises a large category of substances almost or completely insoluble in water: cereal bran is a traditional source of

Table 1.1 — Average composition of main foodstuffs (g per 100 g edible portion)

(b)   *Vegetable foods*

	Water	Proteins	Lipids	Carbo-hydrates (soluble)	Cellu-lose (fibres)	Minerals	Calories
	(1)	(2)	(3)	(4)	(5)	(6)	(7)
Fresh vegetables							
— lettuce	94	1.2	0.2	3	0.6	0.75	18
— tomato	93	1.0	0.3	4	0.6	0.60	22
— green beans	89	2.4	0.2	7	1.4	0.50	40
— peas	74	6.0	0.4	16	2.2	0.50	90
Dried vegetables							
— haricot beans	12	19.0	1.5	60	4.0	3.0	330
— soya beans	8	35.0	18.0	30	5.0	4.9[a]	420
Cereal products							
— soft wheat	14	11.5	1.5	68	2.0	1.75[a]	330
— flour (75% bran sifted)	12	9.5	1.2	75		0.60[a]	350
— polished rice	12	7.5	1.7	77	0.2		350
— pasta, uncooked	8	13.0	1.4	76	0.4		375
— pasta, cooked	61	5.0	0.6	32	0.2		150
— white bread	35	7.0	0.8	55	0.3	2.3[b]	255
Fresh fruits							
— cherry	80	1.2	0.5	17	0.3		77
— orange	87	1.0	0.2	9	0.8		44
— banana	75	1.4	0.5	20			90
— chestnut	52	4.0	2.6	40	2.0		200
Dried fruits							
— fig	27	4.0	1.0	62	3.5		275
— walnut	4	15.0	60.0	15			660
Fruit jam	30	0.5	0.1	70[c]		0.2	280
Honey	20	0.5	0.2	76[c]		0.3	300

[a] Mg: 0.25 in soya; 0.15 in wheat and flour.
[b] NaCl: 0.8.
[c] Jam: equal quantities of fructose, glucose and sucrose. Honey: fructose and glucose (little sucrose).

Note: The water content of vegetables is little affected by cooking in water, but this process greatly reduces their carbohydrate and salt content.

fibre; but other plant sources are being studied (fibre from apple, beetroot, chicory, pea, tomato, cocoa beans, etc.).

In the past, fibre was eaten mainly by people with intestinal ailments. These days, it is considered to be a vital constituent of diet (Chapter 10, §II). The substances making up fibre are essentially long carbohydrate polymers in the form of micro-fibrils. They are mainly situated in the external part of seeds, in the bran.

In this first section we will examine the biochemical properties of food constituents.

In the second section, we will look at the principal foods and the effect of the main treatments.

II.   NUTRITIONAL VALUES

An outline is given below of the generally accepted norms in terms of daily energy and protein requirements for men and women in different circumstances.

You will notice one fact which may come as a surprise. The requirements of the adolescent girl reach a maximum (2490 calories and 75 g of protein) at 13–15 years, which is not the case for males.

1.   Energy requirements (daily)

	Requirement coverage in 1 g		Balanced portion % of total energy contribution	
	kcal	kJ		
Carbohydrates	4	17	50–55	
Lipids	9	38	30–35	(maximum)
Proteins	4	17	12	(half as animal protein)

	Men		Women	
	kcal	kcal	kcal	kcal
Physical activity				
— below average	2 100	8 800	1 800	7 500
— normal	2 700	11 300	2 000	8 400
— above average	3 000	12 500	2 200	9 200
— heavy labour	3 500	14 600		
Adolescents				
— 10 to 12 years	2 600	10 900	2 350	9 800
— 13 to 15 years	2 900	12 100	2 490	10 400
— 16 to 19 years	3 070	12 800	2 310	9 700
Children (both sexes)				
— 1 to 3 years	1 360	5 700		
— 4 to 6 years	1 830	7 600		
— 7 to 9 years	2 190	9 200		

Data provided by CNERNA Commission.

2. Protein requirements (daily)

	Men (g)	Women (g)
Physical activity		
— below average	63	54
— normal	81	60
— above average	90	66
— heavy labour	105	
Adolescents		
— 10 to 12 years	78	71
— 13 to 15 years	87	75
— 16 to 19 years	92	69
Children (both sexes)		
— 1 year	22	
— 3 years	40	
— 5 years	55	
— 8 years	66	
— 11 years	78	

Data provided by CNERNA Commission.

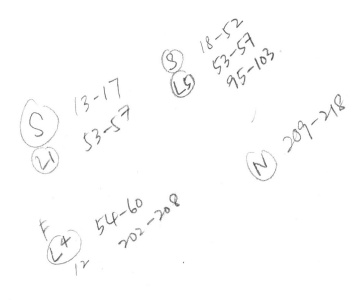

2

Simple carbohydrates and derived products

I. STRUCTURE AND ISOMERISM

Fig. 2.1 lists the various natural forms of carbohydrates. The most common forms of 'sugar' belong to the monosaccharides (not changed by hydrolysis) and the disaccharides. The majority of substances in the other carbohydrate categories have little or no sweetening capacity (ability to give a sugary taste).

Fig. 2.2 summarizes the derivation of the aldoses and ketoses with 3 to 6 carbon atoms in the D series, which is by far the most important. This is defined by the location of the OH group in the penultimate position on the chain to the right (using the Fischer formula). Apart from arabinose, it is rare to find L monosaccharides in nature, and they are not fermented by ordinary yeasts.

It should be noted that no relationship exists between the D and L forms and the direction of rotation of polarized light in monosaccharides containing more than 4 carbons. There exist, for example, some D hexoses ($+$) which rotate the light to the right and some D hexoses ($-$) which are laevorotatory.

In Table 2.1 the different isomers are presented in order of ascending complexity. Types 4 and 5 do not appear in Fig. 2.2, because they are linked to the spatial structure.

There is tautomerism in type 4. In the pentoses the *furanose ring* (5-sided) is the most common. Normally the *pyranose* (6-sided) occurs in the hexoses. We find both these forms in some monosaccharides, with possible interchange between the forms. As an example, fructofuranose is to be found in condensation products, whereas in the free state and in solution fructopyranose is the more stable and forms progressively after hydrolysis.

A state of equilibrium exists between the α and β anomers in aqueous solution just as there is a similar equilibrium between conformers. In practice, changes in equilibrium are important:

— the α form has the highest rotatory power among the D series of hexoses; when it is dissolved in water a gradual reduction to the value found in concentrations at

(A) **Definition**: carbonyl substances formed from one or several units of polyhydroxy-aldehyde or ketones.

The term 'hydrate of carbon' should not be used since $C_n(H_2O)_n$ is not valid for all carbohydrates. A number of these substances are not 'sugars'. The term 'saccharides' should disappear.

(B) **Classification**:

(1) *Monosaccharides*: simple sugars, not changeable by hydrolytic processes; reducing agents; generally with 3–7 carbon atoms.

    (1.1) *aldoses*: the carbonyl (CO) is in position 1.

    (1.2) *ketoses*: the carbonyl is in position 2.

(2) *Glycosides*: complex sugars, capable of change through hydrolysis; the carbonyl group is linked with another compound, X.

    (2.1) *Saccharide*: X is another monosaccharide.

        (2.1.1) *Oligosaccharides*: a small number of monosaccharide residues, generally 2–6 units.

        (2.1.2) *Polysaccharides*: large number of monosaccharide residues.

            (2.1.2.1) *Homopolysaccharides*: a single monosaccharide occurring X times (glycogen or animal starch, cellulose).

            (2.1.2.2) *Heteropolysaccharides*: several monosaccharides interlinked according to a certain pattern (gums).

    (2.2) *Glycosides*: X is not a monosaccharide (aglycone).

        (2.2.1) *O-glycosides* (alcohol, phenol).

        (2.2.2) *N-glycosides* (nucleoside bases).

        (2.2.3) *S-glycosides* (thiol).

(3) *Derived monosaccharides*: often combined in glycosides or in polysaccharides.

    (3.1) *Deoxy sugars*: CH_2 replaces CHOH, CH_3 replaces CH_2OH.

    (3.2) *Amino sugars*: NH_2 replaces an OH, usually in position C_2 of the aldoses.

    (3.3) *Uronic acid*: COOH replaces the CH_2OH, carried on the last carbon.

    (3.4) *Glycones*: simple composition (chitin) or composite (mucopolysaccharides).

(4) *Monosaccharide esters*

    (4.1) *Simple phosphoric* (forms active in metabolism).

    (4.2) *Nucleoside-diphosphate*: UDP (forms active in condensations).

    (4.3) *Sulphuric* (substances from algae and lichen).

    (4.4) *Uronic acids* (pectins).

Fig. 2.1 — Carbohydrates.

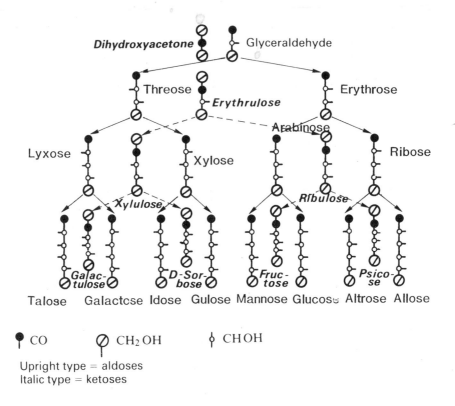

Fig. 2.2 — Monosaccharides in the D series.

equilibrium α→β is observed. This is the process of mutarotation of sugars, which is speeded up in alkaline medium;
— the form C-1, in the chair form, is the most stable in view of its favourable energy level, but it does not permit the formation of carbohydrate chains linked by water abstraction. The form 1-C, however, does allow this, assisted by dehydration (Table 2.1, type 5).

N.B.   For easy written reference, abbreviated symbols, of three to six letters, have been proposed:

Glc:	glucose	Rha:	rhamnose
Gal:	galactose	GlcNac:	N-acetylglucosamine
Man:	mannose	NeuNac:	N-acetylneuraminic acid
Ara:	arabinose	MurNac:	N-acetylmuramic acid
Fuc:	fucose	GlcAu:	glucuronic acid

Table 2.1 — Isomerization of carbohydrates

Type of isomerization	Examples	Observations
1. *Isomerization of position*: Of –CO–	(1) – – – CHOH–CHO – – – CO–CH$_2$OH (2)	Aldoses transforming into ketones
2. *Enantiomers*: Optical isomerism	H–C≡O H–C≡O $\quad\vert$ $\qquad\qquad\vert$ H–C–OH HO–C–H $\quad\vert$ $\qquad\qquad\vert$ CH$_2$OH CH$_2$OH (D series) (L series)	Mirror image formula (according to Fischer)
3. *Epimers*: Isomerism which only selects one asymmetric C from several	Mannose ↔ glucose (C$_2$) Galactose ↔ glucose (C$_4$)	No mirror image
4. *Anomers*: In the hemiacetal form, with the position of the –OH bond in relation to the plane	 (α) (β)	Form in solution (Haworth formula)
5. *Conformers*: Change from the boat form into the 'chair' form (favourable energy level)	 (C–1) (1–C)	Result of substitution modification

II. PENTOSES

We will only look at two of the aldoses: arabinose and xylose. Ribose is a component of nucleic acids and of certain co-enzymes which are present in all cells, but in very small proportions. Lyxose is not a natural monosaccharide. The two ketoses, ribulose and xylulose only appear, in phosphorylated form, in biosynthesis.

1. Arabinose

This is one of the rare examples of widely distributed D and L forms; the cyclic structure is furanose:

— the D form is found mainly in the mixed sugars, as for example in that of the aloe where a D-arabinose is linked to an anthraquinone;
— the L form is more widespread. It can be found in the free state, in relatively small quantities, in certain fruits and bulbs; e.g. plum, cherry, onion, etc. It is not metabolized in humans because of the absence of a specific kinase and it is eliminated by the renal process. Eating a large quantity of fruit may cause sugar to appear in the urine, resembling sugar diabetes if the analysis is not carried out by specific methods (reducing power). In the combined state, this L form is predominant in arabans, found in acacia gums.

2. Xylose

The D form, with a pyranose structure, seems to be the only one found in nature. Little of this monosaccharide is found in the free state. Small quantities are to be found in fruits, like apricots — in this respect much the same as for arabinose.

Xylose is abundant in the condensed form in straw and wood hydrolysis products. It is found in xylans and vegetable araboxylans.

The β-glucosidase enzyme also hydrolyses xylosides because of the spatial structural relationship existing between xylose and glucose (the first 4 carbon atoms have the same spatial configuration).

III. HEXOSES

Only three of eight aldohexoses in the D series (Fig. 2.2) play an important role in food biochemistry. These are glucose, galactose, and mannose, of these only galactose sometimes occurs in the L form. Of the four hexoketoses, fructose (in the D form) is the most widespread. The other hexoses are either not found in nature or else occur in the form of derivatives, like iduronic and guluronic acids (see Chapter 3, §VI). Note that allose is found in the form of derivatives which have been dehydroxylated several times, for example digitoxose, 2,6-didesoxy-D-allose, which forms glucosides with sterols, which have cardio-active properties.

1. Glucose (D)

In both the free state and the combined state this monosaccharide is undoubtedly the most widespread in plants and animals. Its importance is reinforced by the fact that in analytical chemistry we still often express all the reduced sugars as glucose (except in milk).

It is usually found in the β-pyranose form: it is a white powder, very water-soluble (85 g per 100 ml). In solution there are two forms of stable equilibrium at 20°C: α— 35% and β — 65%.

It is glucose which provides the start of the Meyerhof-Embden cycle, which is the main channel for breakdown of the monosaccharides in muscles and in microbial fermentations to the level of pyruvic acid. Other hexoses have to be isomerized to glucose, in the form of 1-phosphoric ester, before entering this cycle.

Many glucose derivatives are found in the natural state (formulas in Fig. 2.3):

— Glucosamine (formerly chitosamine), deoxyamino acid at C_2 and almost always N-acetylated, as with most of the sugar amines. It is found in higher sugars (human milk), in polysaccharides (chitin) and in glycoproteins.
— One diamine monosaccharide corresponding to glucose, in C_2 and C_6, the neosamine-C, and one amino-monosaccharide bearing the NH_2 on the C_3 grouping, kanosamine, have been found in antibiotics.
— Deoxy-6-D-glucose, or quinovose, is found in various plants.
— Glucuronic acid is the only uronic acid often found in animals. It has an important biological role, the fermentation of a glucuronoside through linkage between the reducing group and the OH, SH or NH_2 group of another compound. This *glucurono-combination* permits the urinary elimination of substances not usually found in the animal organism. An example of this can be seen in the elimination by humans of derived toxic products, hormones and bile pigments, etc.

2.   D-Mannose and L-rhamnose

Mannose is rarely found in the free state in animal and plant cells. It does not form higher sugars. On the other hand it is often a constituent of homogenous polycarbohydrates, mannans and heterogenous galactomannans, etc. It is also present in animal glycoproteins.

It is a rare thing among the heteropolysaccharides, but a glycerol mannoside may act as a carbohydrate reservoir in algae. Streptomycin B contains a residue of mannose.

The solubility of this monosaccharide is very high in water (250 g per 100 ml), whereas it is low in alcohol.

Mannosamine linked with pyruvic acid forms neuraminic acid which is to be found in various animal substances and in particular in the glycoproteins.

The deoxy-6-L-mannose is rhamnose and this derivative belonging to the L series is sometimes found in the free state in plants (*Rhus toxicodendron*) and much more often in numerous heterosugars, particularly those which contain cardio-active substances, such as ouabain.

Rhamnose is also a component of polysaccharides (pectins for example).

3.   Galactose

The L form of galactose is found in nature (it is less abundant than the D form) and is one of the components of gelose found in algae, linseed mucilage, etc. The 6 deoxy derivative is *fucose*, which is the major natural monosaccharide in the L series. It is found in oligo- and poly-holosugars (*Fucus* algae) and in glycoproteins. D fructose also exists in the form of plant heterosugars.

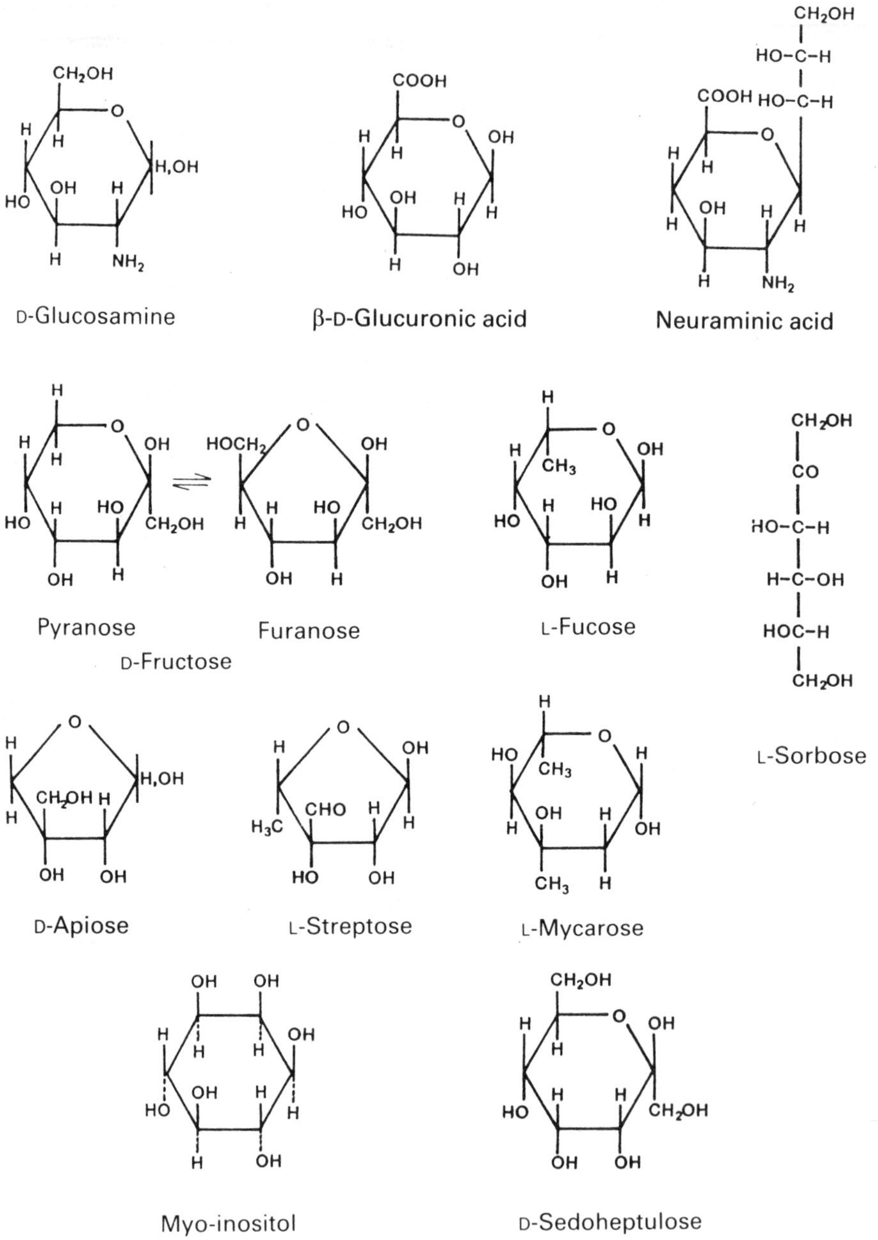

D-Glucosamine   β-D-Glucuronic acid   Neuraminic acid

Pyranose   Furanose   L-Fucose

D-Fructose

L-Sorbose

D-Apiose   L-Streptose   L-Mycarose

Myo-inositol   D-Sedoheptulose

Fig. 2.3 — Formulae of monosaccharides, neuraminic acid and sugar alcohols.

After glucose, D galactose is the most common monosaccharide. Not much of it is to be found in the free state (e.g. blood, normal urine) but, as we shall see later, it is frequently present combined with other compounds; for example in disaccharides (milk lactose), in polysugars (galactans) and in heterosugars (e.g. solanine). Among the complex lipids it is the most important widespread monosaccharide. The pyranose structure is the most common, but you find the furanose structure more often than with glucose.

Galactosamine is a constituent of the *mucopolysaccharides*. Galacturonic acid is found in pectins, in sulphuric esters of galactose and in carrageenan (see Chapter 3, §IX).

4. D-Fructose
This is the ketose which corresponds both to glucose and to mannose. Its former name was *laevulose*, which described its strong laevorotatory optical activity ($-93°$ at the 15°C equilibrium). It is abundant in the free state in vegetables and, as its present name suggests, in fruit. In bee's honey it is found in equal quantities to glucose, which tends to suggest that it is sucrose in origin. It is only found in very small quantities in animal cells, except in seminal fluid, where, in concentrations of 2–3 g per litre, it is the main energy source for spermatozoa.

It is also frequently encountered in the combined state: in oligosaccharide, especially plant (sugar, gentianose, raffinose), polysaccharide (inulin, laevans).

In practice, fructose has two interesting properties: its sweetening capacity is high (114, as against 100 for sucrose) and it has very high water solubility (Table 2.2). It is difficult to crystallize, and when present in mixtures inhibits the crystallization of other sugars, giving a honey-like consistency. It is easier to obtain sweetened products with a good consistency from honey and *invert sugar* than from sucrose.

Table 2.2 — Sweetening capacity of the main sugars and their alcohols[a]

D-Fructose	114	D-Galactose	63
Xylitol	102	D-Mannose	59
Sucrose[b]	100	D-Sorbitol	51
Invert sugar	95	Maltose	46
D-Glucose	69	Lactose	16
D-Mannitol	69	Raffinose	22
D-Xylose	67		

[a] In solution of 10 g/100 ml.
[b] Depending on which authority is followed, the sucrose reference is equal either to 1 or to 100 (cf. Table 17.1).

Fructose is currently produced industrially from sugarbeet, using two particular processes: hydrolysis and isomerization.

5. L-Sorbose
This monosaccharide is rare in the natural state — it is found in the juice of rowan berries and in passion flower pectin. It is above all of historical interest. It is formed

by the dehydrogenation of sorbitol by the 'sorbose bacterium' (*Acetobacter xylinum*). It so happens that it is the C_5 of D-sorbitol which is transformed into carbonyl and, as this should be written in position 2, so we must turn the formula around and thus place it in the L series!

Note: Where a chain is of more than 6 atoms, very little monosaccharide is present. However, let us mention two examples of ketoses with 7 carbons. These are to be found in the plant world, they are only partially metabolized by rats and their names stem from the extended hexoses:

— altroheptulose or sedoheptulose (found in *Sedum*) which is an intermediary substance in photosynthesis;
— mannoheptulose which accumulates in the fruit of the avocado tree (avocado pear).

IV. ATYPICAL MONOSACCHARIDES

In the plant world, and especially in the Actinomyces family, we note branched monosaccharides which carry a tertiary alcohol function or several carbonyl groups (Fig. 2.3). For example:

— *D-Apiose*: a sugar with 5 carbons in the series $C_n(H_2O)_n$ where a second CH_2OH is found branched on the C_3. This is one of the constituents of numerous plant glycosides, notably in parsley, rubber trees, etc.
— *Streptose*: a hexose having a second aldehyde function branched on the C_3 and a deoxylated form on the C_5. It is found in furanose form in streptomycin A, an antibiotic produced by *Streptomyces griseus*.
— *Mycarose*: substance found in spiramycin, which is an extreme example with 3 carbon atoms deoxylated from a total of 7.

These last two substances are typical examples of Actinomycetes antibiotics. They are related to the sugars and their action is due to the blocking of the enzyme system by a substance which is not transformable but is analogous to a monosaccharide.

V. SUGAR ALCOHOLS

1. Alditols

We must remember that these are not monosaccharides, because there are no carbonyl groups. However, they are interesting because they are monosaccharide derivatives through hydrogenation and are found in fruits and in various groups of plants.

The reduction of the CO group by chemical means is an easy process (sodium borohydride, hydrogen using a catalyst, sodium amalgam). It is more interesting to use a biological process. We know which oxido-reducing enzymes provoke reaction in one direction or another (oxidation of the polyol, in a monosaccharide). Certain alditols, derived from aldoses which are commonly found in the plant world, probably come from aldoses corresponding through enzyme reduction to NAD or NADP.

Figure 2.2 shows that as many alditols as aldohexoses exist and twice as many as ketohexoses. The reduction of the latter produces a mixture of two alditols which carry the OH on the left or right of C_2 in the conventional written form.

It should be noted that in contrast to the monosaccharides, these substances are rarely combined. However, we do find mannitol glucoside in some algae. The scientific name is that of the aldohexose with the suffix *itol*; but simple names, usually designating the plant where it was initially discovered, are often used for those known for a long time.

Recent interest in these substances stems from their particular physicochemical properties (e.g. water fixation) and also their special biological properties, notably the non-dependence of insulin and the non-cariogenic effect, which explains their use in dietetic foods.

1.1   *D-Sorbitol*
This, with its isomer mannitol, is the most widespread alditol:

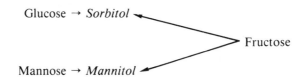

D-Sorbitol is an important constituent of many natural foods, such as the common edible fruits, but on the other hand it is rare in mammalian tissue. In humans it is metabolized and is better than glucose for diabetics whilst giving the same amount of energy (about 400 calories). In view of this, sorbitol is used in the production of food for diabetics. It has another property which enhances its use, in that it is non-fermentable by yeasts.

From the technological point of view, sorbitol has other characteristics which have contributed to its use as an important auxiliary substance in the food production industry, especially in jam products, where it often replaces *invert sugar* (produced by the *invertase* enzyme). These features are summarized below:

— High level of water binding. Water is in part responsible for its honey-like texture. It can only evaporate slowly in the presence of a sufficient quantity of sorbitol.
— Heat resistance (using the invertase enzyme process it is not possible to cook at more than 70°C).
— Delaying effect on the crystallization of sucrose and glucose; the crystals remain small and are not detectable in the mouth.

— Little sweetening (about half that of sucrose). Humans can eat more of it without being adversely affected.
— Relatively low viscosity of its syrups, making for easier handling.
— Ease in chelating heavy metals, which helps to improve the conservation of fatty products.

It does have a drawback, in that too much sorbitol at any one time does have a laxative effect.

Sorbitol used in the food industry is not an extracted product. It is manufactured through hydrogenation of glucose and is generally used as a 70% concentrated syrup.

1.2 Mannitol

Mannitol, also, is abundant in plants. In certain mushrooms there is more of it present than monosaccharides. Its metabolism differs little from that of sorbitol after diffusion across the intestinal wall. Mannitol is oxidized to fructose by mannitol dehydrogenase. Mannitol is 50% excreted in the faeces and urine and the residue is oxidized in the liver.

Owing to its poor assimilation, mannitol assists diuresis. There is a process for examining kidney function involving 'clearance' using mannitol, which is based on the way mannitol moves across the glomerulus.

1.3 Xylitol

This is found in weak concentration in many fruits and plant products. It is extracted from hemicellulose in wood and is a new sweetening agent, which has the same energy value, looks the same and has about the same sweetening capacity as sucrose; but it has in addition a very interesting property; xylitol is incapable of taking any part in the normal process of deterioration of teeth. For this reason it has for 15 years been recommended as a 'non-cariogenic sugar' in the food industry, despite its high price (15 times that of sucrose). In higher organisms, xylitol can be changed into glucose, the level varying between 20% and 80%. This takes place in the liver and depends on the need of the body for glucose. The transformation is slow and this means that xylitol can be of interest for diabetics. The human body has a high tolerance of it (up to 200 g per day).

2.   Cyclitols

More especially in the plant kingdom, but also in the animal kingdom, penta- or hexa-alcohol natural derivatives of cyclohexane abound. They do not correspond to a monosaccharide, but we usually place them alongside the alditols.

The hexahydroxylic cyclitols are interesting: there are 9 stereo-isomers (7 inactive, 1 dextrorotatory and 1 laevorotatory) corresponding to the formula $C_6H_{12}O_6$. Among the inactive isomers is found the sugary substance extracted from muscle extract which has been given various names: inosite, i-inositol, myo-inositol, meso-inositol (Fig. 2.3). It is the one most frequently found in animals, either in the free state or combined, and is present in various tissues: liver, muscle, blood, urine and especially in sperm. It was considered to be a vitamin in the past (B_7). Whilst in man no visible signs of spontaneous deficiency of it have ever been observed, deficiency of it has been manifested in rats by skin problems, loss of fur (alopecia) and asthaenia.

In the combined state we find myo-inositol linked with monosaccharides (with galactose in sugar-beet galactinol) and with phosphoric acid. Mono- di- or tri-phosphoric esters form the inositolphospholipids. The hexaphosphoric ester is *phytic acid,* which carries as many P as C atoms (P=28% and C=11%). It is the most strongly phosphorylated of plant constituents. In edible seeds it may represent 80% to 90% of the total phosphorous content. Phytic acid constitutes an exception in the living world, where phosphorylated polyesters are rare. Moreover *in vitro* studies show how unequal are its acidic groups; there are six strong acid functions (pK=1.8), but only two weak ones (pK=6.3); the other four functions are only revealed at pH=9.7, probably because of hydrogen links between neighbouring radicals. Phytic acid, like oxalic acid, lowers man's absorption of calcium as a result of the formation of insoluble salts. Phytin is a complex salt, made up of calcium and magnesium, found in many plants. It is mainly extracted from *corn steep liquor* (soluble part of maize grains).

VI.   SUGAR LINKAGE

This involves the participation of at least one reducing group of a monosaccharide and of another group which may be –OH, –NH or –SH. A disaccharide is formed if the –OH group belongs to another monosaccharide. A glycoside is formed if it belongs to an alcohol group, a phenol or sterol, or is –NH and –SH.

Sugar linkage with a cyclized monosaccharide results in an acetal. The reducing power disappears.

The anomer form is combined, either as in α (above) or in β. The existence of one carbon atom between two oxygen atoms differentiates this linkage from the ether linkage; it does not possess the latter's resistance to limited acid hydrolysis.

If the linkage involves two reducing groups of monosaccharides, the disaccharide is no longer reducing. It is said to be of the 'trehalose' variety; it has no mutarotation and cannot give rise to a new glycosidic linkage (though it can be so affected). By contrast, if the disaccharide comprises two different residues (as with sucrose) there are two possibilities of hydrolysis by the specific hydrolases.

VII.   GLUCOSE DISACCHARIDES

Table 2.3 shows the seven glucosyl-glucoside disaccharides. In nature, *trehalose* is certainly the most common form. It is the main sugar of insect haemolymph and is also a constituent of some mushrooms and algae. It is also the sugar of a toxic glycolipid — the 'cord factor'. A hydrolytic enzyme exists — namely trehalase —

which has great specificity: it only splits the glycoside linkage in trehalose. It is found in mammal intestines, in insects and in micro-organisms.

Table 2.3 — Glucosyl-glucoside disaccharides

Position	Anomer	Name	Source
1→1	α-α'	Trehalose	Haemolymph of insects, mushrooms, algae
1→2	β	Sophorose	Plant glycosides (Stevia, Sophora)
1→3	β	Laminaribiose	Enzyme hydrolysis of laminaria (algae)
1→4 {	α	Maltose	Enzyme hydrolysis of starches
	β	Cellubiose	Enzyme hydrolysis of cellulose
1→6 {	α	Isomaltose	Enzyme hydrolysis of amylopectin and microbial dextrans
	β	Gentiobiose	Plant glycosides (gentian, amygdalin)

Sophorose and *gentiobiose* are found in glycosides. The high sweetening capacity of Stevia has attracted the attention of researchers. The other four disaccharides exist only in very condensed form, making up molecules of starch, cellulose and laminarin. Note that these disaccharides are obtained directly by enzyme hydrolysis of the natural polymers, which does not usually give the end-result of monosaccharides. The 1→4 linkage is the most frequent. In its predominant form, which is the anomer β-maltose, it is a strongly dextrorotatory disaccharide (+136°).

VIII.   SUCROSE

This is ordinary sugar, from sugarbeet or sugarcane. It is made up of a glucose and a fructose residue. The scientific name shows this precisely :

α-D-glucopyranosyl (1→2) β-D-fructofuranoside

It is non-reducing and hydrolyses easily in acid medium. Enzyme hydrolysis is achieved through two glycosidic processes: the α-glucosidase process and the a β-fructosidase process. The latter has been called 'invertase' because the monosaccharide mixture, because of the strong laevorotatory character of fructose, retains this property (−20°). Furthermore, the mixture is always referred to as 'invert sugar'. Invertase is very commonly found, notably in human intestines.

Sucrose is very abundant in nature. It has been found in all chlorophyll plants, since it is the main product of photosynthesis. Later we shall be considering its oligosaccharide derivatives. A number of polysaccharides are made up with one unit of sucrose at the start of the chain.

For people living in developed countries, sucrose is a carbohydrate foodstuff of great importance. Actually it is the one human food which is pure and in crystalline form, and it is rapidly utilized in the organism.

Sucrose is also involved in the composition of caramelized products through aromatization. Here it is interesting to note that since — as with other sugars — the partial solubility of glucose and sucrose is additive in mixed solutions, so it becomes possible to obtain concentrations of up to 75%, which is much higher than when just one of these sugars is used alone. In this way syrups can be prevented from crystallization and fermentation (Fig. 2.4).

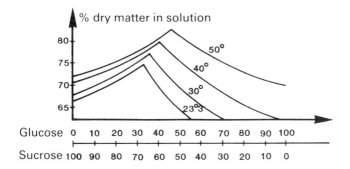

Fig. 2.4 — Saturation points of glucose–sucrose mixtures.

The chlorination of sucrose enables an increase in sweetening capacity of 800 times, which is twice as much as saccharin and nearly four times more than aspartame, whilst the calorific value is very low. However, unlike these two sweeteners, this compound, called sucralose, is thermally very stable (see Chapter 17, §III.2).

Industrial *invert sugar* is obtained through the action of an acid on sucrose. Traces of the acid always remain, being trapped in the process, which means that the pH of a 10% solution is 3.5 on average. This sugar is used in the ice cream and jam-making industries because of its potential for texturization and its anti-crystallization properties.

Honey is a natural invert sugar: in fact a sugar invertase (β-fructosidase) is trapped in the pouch of bees and this transforms the excess of sucrose in the nectar; its pH (4.0) is a little higher than that of industrial invert sugar.

The *sucroglycerides* are industrial derivatives of sucrose, used as non-ionic surface agents. These stem from the cross-esterification of a natural triglyceride (e.g. tallow, palm-oil) with sucrose, in which a mixture is formed, made up of mono-acid diesters of sucrose and of mono- and di-glycerides. These substances are used as emulsifiers: for example, in reinforced milks (with added tallows or suets) for calves, or for other foodstuffs which are neutral or low in acid. They lead to an important lowering of both surface and interfacial tension. They are non-toxic and can be assimilated.

A new product, derived from sucrose, is coming onto the market: *sucrose polyester*. This synthetic molecule contains 6 or 8 ester groups of fatty acids. The usefulness and the non-toxic nature of this substance have been shown: weight loss (200 g per day) in obese persons, reduction of the cholesterol level in the blood (by 20%), reduction in the absorption level of cholesterol contained in foods; does not pass into the blood, has no marked secondary effects, apart from a slight loss in vitamin E. This fat 'look-alike', which looks and tastes the same and has the same consistency as vegetable oil, may replace up to 25% of fats used in the home, and 75% of those used in catering.

Note: Some sucrose isomers are known which are clearly reducing agents. An example is *leucrose* (α-glucose 1→5 fructopyranose) which is formed by the action of dextran sucrase.

IX.   LACTOSE

This is 'milk sugar'; it occurs in no other substances. It is a reducing agent:

β-D-galactopyranosyl (1→4) D-glucopyranoside α *or* β

It occurs very predominantly in the milk of ruminants, e.g. 5% in cow's milk (see Chapter 13). In human milk it forms half of the dry matter — 6.5%. Its level in the very fatty milk of cetaceans is very low — about 1%.

The two forms, α and β, have very different properties (Table 2.4) and both are of practical interest. The α form crystallized with a molecule of water is common lactose, which can be dehydrated. The β form crystallizes, without water fixation, from a concentrated solution, above 94°C, which is a critical temperature for crystallization; no hydrate of the β form is known.

Table 2.4 — Properties of the lactose isomers

	α(H₂O)	β	Equilibrium (20°C)
Rotatory power $[α]_D^{20}$	+89.4	+35	+55
Melting point	202	252	—
Solubility[a]			
— 15°C	7.3	50	17
— 100°C	70	95	—
Concentration in 20% solution	38	62	(β/α=1.63)
Sweetening power (sucrose=100)			16

[a] g per 100 g water.

Lactose is only slightly soluble, about ten times less in equilibrium than sucrose at ambient temperature (180 g per 100 g). The difference is less at 100°C because the solubility of lactose is much increased. It is thus a disaccharide which is quite easy to separate by crystallization; but of course it is not possible to obtain thick syrups or jams from lactose. Moreover, it has little sweetening capacity (1/6 in relation to sucrose); milk is not very 'sweet' and milky diets are tolerable because they do not nauseate.

Lactose is an interesting example of crystalline polymorphism; in slow crystallization various forms are seen, which end up as elongated, complex, hard crystals. Certain substances inhibit crystallization; an example is riboflavin (vitamin B_2) but at a higher concentration than that which exists in milk. Chemical hydrolysis is more difficult than for sucrose; it is necessary to treat it hot with an acid; here there is no inversion.

Enzymatic hydrolysis presents problems. β-Galactosidase (or lactase) is not widely found, though some rare yeasts do contain it (*Kluyveromyces fragilis* is used in industry). It is secreted at the level of the jejunum in infant intestines, and after that it disappears at varying rates according to different human races. In the coloured races the loss occurs early, sometimes at about 3 years; in white people we find a proportion of individuals who are 'persistently lactase positive' at a high level. In the USA only 15% of white adults are 'alactasic' as against 75% of blacks.

Another serious form of intolerance exists in children who do not possess the enzyme which permits the epimerization of galactose into glucose, i.e. hexose-1-phosphate-uridyltransferase. Here the absorption of milk leads to galactosaemia. This metabolic disorder is rare. On the subject of abnormalities, let us point out that the ingestion of high doses of galactose may be the origin of cataracts.

We must remember that galactose must be transformed into glucose in order to enter the biological cycles (anaerobic glycolysis and the pentose-phosphate cycle).

X. PLANT OLIGOSACCHARIDES DERIVED FROM SUCROSE

1. α-Galactosides

These are the reserve substances which make up one or several α-D-galactoses linked through the bonding 1→6 glucose to sucrose, or through the same linkage between them; they are all non-reducing:

α-D-glucose 1→2 β-D-fructose-sucrose

α-D-galactose 1→6 ——————— -Raffinose

α-D-galactose 1→6 —— —— ——————— -Stachyose

α-D-galactose 1→6 —— —— —— ——————— -Verbascose

α-D-galactose 1→6 —— —— —— —— ——————— -Ajugose

The most important ones contain between 3 to 6 residues of monosaccharide, but some are known to contain 8 residues. These are found in various plants.

Raffinose is always associated with sucrose; it is eliminated from molasses in the purification of beet sugar. A lot of yeasts contain no α-galactosidases. They only ferment ⅓ of the fructose from the molecule and melibiose is the residual disaccharide (galactosyl-glucoside). There is a property, about which a little will be said in the second section of this book: raffinose inhibits the crystallization of sucrose in the final phase of the production of beet sugar. A fall in yield occurs where raffinose is polarimetrically treated with the sucrose at the start of operations.

The alcohol-soluble sugars of seeds, flowers and leguminous plants all incorporate these α-galactosides, soya being the richest (8% on average). Human beings cannot digest these substances; it is wise to get rid of them as far as possible by an appropriate treatment.

2.   Trisaccharides

These are made up from a monosaccharide lengthened on one side or the other by another monosaccharide residue. Four examples are give in the diagram below. Their names derive from the plants in which they have been found; planteose comes from plantain seeds, and is the symmetrical derivative of raffinose; melezitose is the sugary substance exuded by plants following insect stings — lime honeydew, meleze manna; etc.

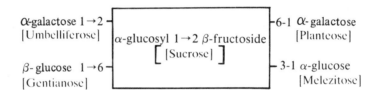

```
α-galactose 1→2 ─┐                                  ┌─ 6-1  α-galactose
[Umbelliferose]  │ α-glucosyl 1→2 β-fructoside │        [Planteose]
                 │        [ [Sucrose] ]        │
β-glucose  1→6 ──┘                                  └─ 3-1  α-glucose
[Gentianose]                                           [Melezitose]
```

XI.   ANIMAL OLIGOSACCHARIDES

Many oligosaccharides ending with a lactose residue (Gal β 1→4 Glc) are found in the milk of mammals with one stomach. It seems that galactose, L-fucose, N-acetylglucosamine and N-acetylneuraminic acid (sialic acid) occur in varying sequence. More than 30, with molecular mass from 1000 to 3000 (5 to 15 residues of monosaccharide), representing a level of 1% to 2%, have been isolated in the human female. Their origin and biological role remain controversial.

Little of these substances (0.1%) is found in the milk of ruminants.

Oligosaccharides are found in urine, especially of sick human beings, with N-acetylglucosamine at each end. Let us take as an example a three-branched sugar made up of 7 residues of just 2 monosaccharides:

```
β-GlcNac (1→2) -α-Man (1→3) --
                                 --
         βGlcNac (1→4) ------------> β-Man (1→4) GlcNac
                                 --
β-GlcNac (1→2) -α-Man (1→6) --
```

XII. *O*-GLYCOSIDES

These are essentially plant material. They form the reserve substances localized in the cell vacuoles; but they can be considered as waste substances, possessing a role comparable with the glucuronides in larger animals. Many substances in this group have pharmaceutical properties. The following four groups can be distinguished.

1. Alcohol glycosides

The cyanogetic glycosides are formed from α-glucose (sometimes substituted by another monosaccharide) linked with an alcoholic nitrile. Enzyme hydrolysis releases hydrocyanic acid, which is a violent poison. For example: the *amygdalin* of bitter almonds and of other fruit kernels is composed of gentiobiose linked with phenylglycolic nitrile (characteristic of the Rosaceae family); hydrolysis produces successively glucose, HCN and benzaldehyde; an enzyme which ensures this transformation is emulsin — this can be toxic for human beings.

amygdalin

2. Phenolic glycosides

These are very numerous in plant tissue. One very interesting series is the one where the poisonous part derives from the chromane family and where a certain number possess a vitamin activity for blood capillaries, the skin, etc. *Hesperidin* is made up of trihydroxy-methoxy-flavanone (chromane linked with a benzene ring) associated with rhamnoglucoside; this is the dominant flavonoid in oranges and lemons.

Hesperidin   Vicin

Toxic glycosides derived from pyriminidinone, such as *vicin* from leguminous plants (*Vicia sativa*) which is responsible for 'broad bean disease' (haemolytic anaemia), can be linked here.

3. Sterol glycosides

These are equally numerous to, and doubtless more important from the point of view of human health than, the previous groups. Here are two examples:

— *Solanine*: toxic substance of the solanaceous plants (e.g. potatoes, tomatoes); used as an insecticide.

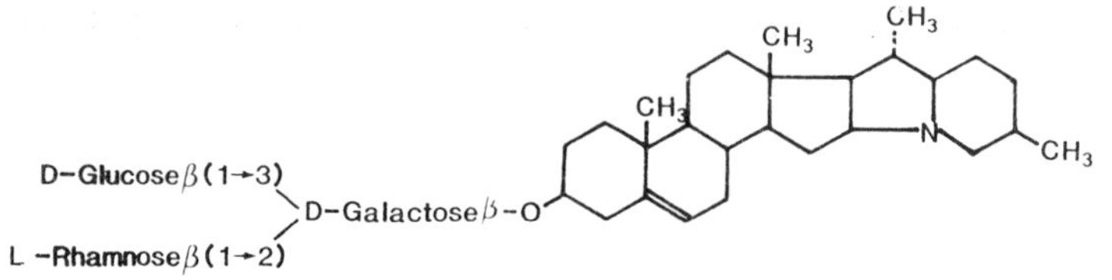

CH3
CH3
CH3
N
CH3
D-Glucose β(1→3)
D-Galactose β-O
L-Rhamnose β(1→2)

— *Digitonin*: a medicine beneficial to the heart, with slow and protracted action (derived from digitalis).

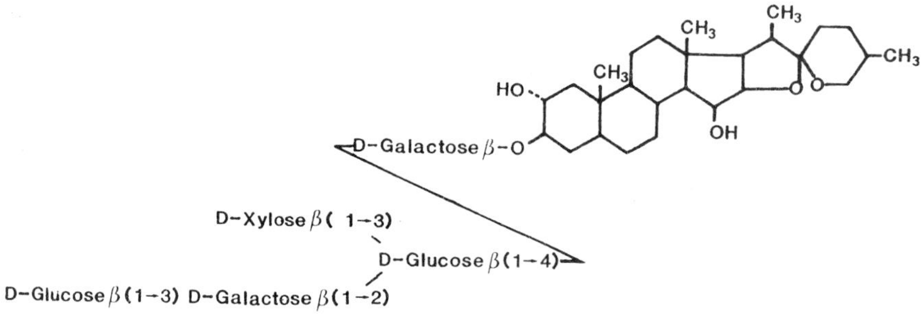

CH3
CH3
CH3
CH3
HO
O
O
OH
D-Galactose β-O
D-Xylose β(1→3)
D-Glucose β(1→4)
D-Glucose β(1→3) D-Galactose β(1→2)

4. Antibiotic glycosides

The first discovered of these is streptomycin. The aglycone part is diguanidoscylloinositol; the sugar part is made up of two atypical monosaccharides, streptose and *N*-methyl-L-glucosamine. This antibiotic is produced by *Streptomyces griseus*, a type of soil Actinomyces.

HN=C-NH2
NH
NH
HN-C=NH2
OH
OH
O
CHO
O
H3C
HO
OH
O
O
OH
CH2OH
H3C-NH
OH

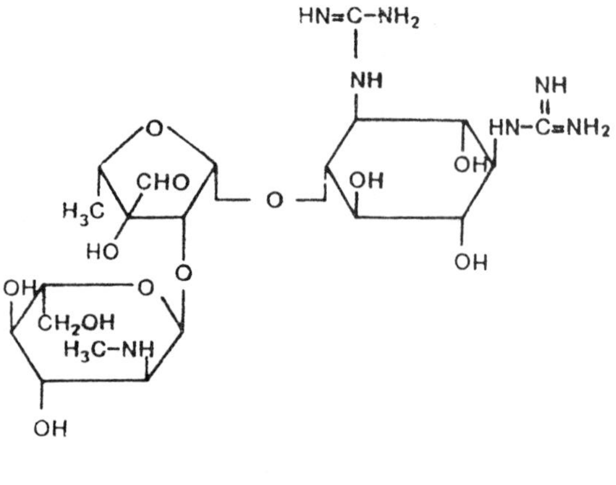

Note: The S-glycosides are much less important, occurring mainly in Cruciferous plants.

The N-glycosides are derived from ribose or deoxyribose linked to bases to form a nucleoside, present in all cells (RNA and DNA); they play no part in food.

3

Polysaccharides

I. GENERAL REMARKS

Polysaccharides or glucans (homo- or hetero-) are large molecules made up of several hundreds or several thousands of residues of various monosaccharides, linked to each other by different types of bond (α or β; 1→4, 1→6, 1→3, etc.). Polysaccharides of average molecular weight, where between 10 and 250 monosaccharides are incorporated (molecular weight between 2000 and 35 000), are not found in the natural state and so there is a break in the size scale not seen with proteins. However, their variety is limited by the fact that a pattern of one or two monosaccharides is repeated X times and generally one or two bonds predominate.

The polysaccharides are of great importance for several reasons:

(1) They comprise dietary substances most consumed in the West: amylose and amylopectin, constituents of the *starch* grains of cereals, leguminous plants, etc., for which they are the form of carbohydrate reserve.
(2) In animals, glycogen (animal starch) provides the reserve of monosaccharides.
(3) They are the raw materials for enzyme or chemical transformation, mainly by hydrolysis.
(4) They are important agents in technological processes, as thickeners, gelling agents, etc.
(5) They comprise the substances responsible for the cellular walls in plants (cellulose) and for the skeleton of arthropods (chitin).
(6) The glucosamino-glucurono-glycans, often called simply glucosaminoglycans and formerly mucopolysaccharides, are constituents of the conjuctiva and fluids of the animal organism.

We will study in turn the food polysaccharides (starch, glycogen, inulin), cellulose and chitin, thickening hydrocolloids, which are rarely, if ever, assimilated by humans, and finally the glucosaminoglycans.

II. STARCHES AND GLYCOGEN

All the starches are made up of α-D-glucopyranose in linear chains with the bond α (1→4), as with amylose, or in chains branched by the α (1→6) bond on α (1→4) chains as with amylopectin and glycogen. The natural state of those cereals will be studied in Chapter 10.

1. Amylose

Amylose is the least abundant constituent and its molecule is the most simple and the smallest (molecular weight from 150 000 to 600 000). The glucose α (1→4) chain is linear, but not straight; the monosaccharide residues are arranged in a helix pattern, with possibly 6 residues per turn; the whole arrangement forms a type of slack tube. It is thought that the particular reaction of iodine with starch, which gives an intense blue colour, is due to the penetration of the iodine into the centre of the helix structure; it thus acquires special physical properties, such as a high absorption of light (Fig. 3.1).

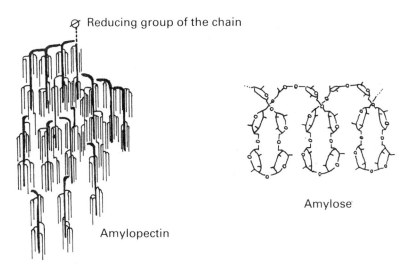

Ø Reducing group of the chain

Amylose

Amylopectin

Fig. 3.1 — Structure of amylose and amylopectin.

The most well known starches in Europe, those of wheat and potato, are relatively rich in amylose, 20–30%.

2. Amylopectin

Amylopectin is much more abundant than amylose; the 'waxy' or 'glutenous' starches such as rice, maize and sorghum, contain up to 95–97% of amylopectin.

Amylopectin has the same structure as amylose, except that the molecule has a bushy appearance because of the branching on a –CH$_2$OH at intervals of approximately 25 residues and the molecular weight is much higher (several millions). Note that the side chains have the same structure as the main chains (Fig. 3.1).

3. Glycogen

Glycogen has a structure very close to that of amylopectin, but is differentiated from it by the following characteristics:

- it is the form most usually found in carbohydrates in the animal organism;
- it has more frequent branching, approximately every 10 to 14 residues;
- it is water-soluble at ambient temperatures;
- it forms a brown colour with iodine.
- resistant to concentrated alkalis.

4. Physical properties of starches

The hydrogen bonds which are established between chains by the hydroxyl groups influence both the physical resistance and the solubility of the molecules. They allow the formation of quite compact masses which have a certain degree of crystallinity, which is to say a regular spatial structure. These bonds can be broken by the use of an appropriate reaction agent or through heating; in this way the solubility is raised and the crystallinity reduced.

Starch in seeds is actually almost insoluble in cold water. When the mixture is heated a dispersion process occurs, which forms a sort of 'paste' and produces an increase in viscosity. There is a critical temperature which varies with the structure of the starch; above it, the thickening is irreversible; below it, the thickening is reversible. This temperature is between 60°C and 85°C.

Retrogradation of starch is an important phenomenon. It corresponds to the formation of inter-chain links (inter-reactions) between the aligned molecules. The result is the syneresis phenomenon, with possible exudation of liquid and a fall in viscosity. In addition enzyme hydrolysis becomes difficult. Retrogradation of starch has important consequences in various areas: a cake not well risen, cream separated, bread hardened (gone stale) without being dry, runny pastes and glues.

The higher the proportion of linear amylose, the more rapid the retrogradation process. This amylose is more susceptible to reaction agents than amylopectin. For example, by using epichlorhydrin the paste is rendered less viscous and its retrogradation less than might have been possible, even using an autoclave.

5. Functional properties of starches

Now better understood, the functional properties of starches are increasingly exploited in the food industry, where they replace other plant or microbial bio-polymers which are more expensive. Such starches are more or less modified in the following ways:

— *sometimes in the composition proportions* of the two essential constituents, and which give rise to opposing effects (amylose favours gelling on cooling; amylopectin yields thick liquids which do not gel on cooling);

— *sometimes through pre-cooking or* pre-gelatinization, which favours their incorporation in cold foods (starch then becomes dispersible at a lower temperature and has a swelling effect in cold water);
— *sometimes by grafting on radicals* through a chemical treatment which yields products of variable viscosity.

Through this last method, 'dextrin' liquid starches are obtained, used in the making of gums in confectionery. Another modification is called 'reticulation', where bridges are created between glucose molecules, strengthening the network; creamy textured starches are obtained. These special starches are used to replace part of the fat substance in the so-called 'low-fat' products since they are miscible with lipids and yield soft mixtures. It must be added, however, that natural amylaceous substances such as tapioca are also used in low-fat products.

III.   STARCH HYDROLYSIS

1.   Enzyme hydrolysis

The glucosyl hydrolases may be classified into 3 groups designated by the heading E.C.3.2.1. (glucosidases) in the official nomenclature for enzymes:

- enzymes specific for bonds α $(1 \rightarrow 4)$
- enzymes specific for bonds α $(1 \rightarrow 6)$
- enzymes specific for bonds α $(1 \rightarrow 4)$, α $(1 \rightarrow 6)$.

1.1   α-amylase
This enzyme, which can be of animal, plant or microbial origin, randomly hydrolyses the α $(1 \rightarrow 4)$ bonds of amylose and amylopectin chains. It is also called *endo-amylase* and *liquifying* or *dextrinizing* amylase.

The main product formed is an oligosaccharide of 6 or 7 residues, together with maltose. Note that this enzyme also attacks starch in granular form.

According to its origin, the optimal pH for its activities varies between 4.7 and 5.9 and the optimal temperature between 50°C and 55°C.

1.2   β-amylase
This enzyme, which can be extracted from plants and from certain strains of microorganisms, hydrolyses the starch chains from their non-reducing end, freeing β-maltose (from this we get the name β-amylase, which does not describe the specificity of the cut-off point). This is called the 'saccharifying' enzyme. The hydrolysis is blocked by the 1→6 branching. Because of this, it only reacts on the external parts of the amylopectin macromolecule. About half of the amylopectin exists in the form of *limit dextrins*. β-Amylase has no action on the native starch grain if this remains intact.

1.3   Specific enzymes of bond α (1→6)
These enzymes, also called debranching enzymes, hydrolyse α $(1 \rightarrow 6)$ bonds whilst preserving the branching in the amylopectin chains and in glycogens.

They are of plant origin (enzyme R) or of microbial origin. Pullulanase and isoamylase are the two debranching enzymes which have been the most studied. Both are of bacterial origin and their action depends essentially on the ease with which the enzyme is able to penetrate the macromolecular network of the substrate.

1.4   Amyloglucosidase

This enzyme, also called glucoamylase, hydrolyses α (1→4) and α (1→6) bonds of amylose and amylopectin, freeing D-glucose. It is extracted from moulds of the genus *Rhizopus* and *Aspergillus*. It acts more rapidly on long chains than on short chains and hydrolyses α (1→4) bonds more rapidly than α (1→6) bonds.

Amylases have many industrial uses, notably in brewing and bread-making. They are also used to prepare manufactured sugar products, either in the form of 70% syrup or sugars of varied molecular size (glucose, maltose, triose, tetrose, etc.), or in powdered form (92–94% reducing sugar). Note here that these syrups may be hydrogenated: they are then marketed under the name of lycasins and have some technological advantages in that they allow thermal treatments in confectionery and give rise to more elasticity in chewing gums.

The isomerization of glucose into fructose, at least partially, by passing a syrup down a column containing isomerase immobilized on granules, has become an industrial operation, like that of invert sugar, in view of its varied applications, such as for making soft sweets.

1.5   Cyclodextrin glycosyl-transferase

Slightly hydrolysed starch may be broken down by cyclodextrin glycosyl-transferases (CGTases), synthesized by several micro-organisms such as *Bacillus macerans* and *Bacillus subtilis*. This enzymatic degradation produces large rings of 6 to 8 glucose units: the cyclodextrins. Since these molecules have a central hydrophobic cavity and a hydrophilic exterior layer, it would seem that they may be very useful to the food industry: e.g. for protection against oxidation, elimination of unwanted taste and bitterness, improvement of solubility, stability and complexing of hydrophobic substances (flavours and cholesterol).

2.   Chemical hydrolysis

Hydrolysis by dilute acids is progressive. First come dextrins which do not produce a paste and are coloured by iodine first violet, then red, after which come dextrins which do not colour, then maltose and, finally, glucose.

The advantage of this procedure is the fast and complete hydrolysis to glucose. Disadvantages are colour and taste defects and an increase in salt content after neutralization, unless the acid is removed (sulphuric acid plus lime).

IV.   INULIN

This is the carbohydrate reserve of plants which do not accumulate starch, such as the Jerusalem artichoke, dahlia, sweet potato, etc. In fact, these are *levans* made up of quite short, unbranched chains of at least 40 to 100 residues of fructose in the furanose form with the bond β (2→1). The presence of a residue of glucose may be seen at the beginning of the chain (glucosidopolyfructoside). It seems that one sucrose molecule may be the 'initiating source' onto which a sucrase transfers a fructose residue taken from another sucrose molecule.

Inulin is directly water-soluble, without forming a paste, and is not coloured by iodine. Inulase is a very widespread hydrolytic enzyme.

Note: Levans with the structure β (2→6) exist in the plant world and in certain bacteria (*Bacillus subtilis*, *Aerobacter levanicum*, etc.).

V.   CELLULOSE

Cellulose results from the exclusively linear condensation of glucose units which are linked by β (1→4) bonds. Chitin has this same structure, formed from joining *N*-acetyl-β-D-glucosamine residues.

1.   Cellulose

Cellulose is almost exclusively limited to the plant kingdom, where it is responsible for the cellular wall structure. Human beings cannot digest it since they have no cellulase (or cytase). Micro-organisms, on the other hand, possess this enzyme and are the reason for the utilization of cellulose by ruminants, snails and various xylophagic insects. Procedures have been devised to render wood, cotton, etc., edible through acid hydrolysis under pressure, purification of the hydrolysis product and, possibly, culture by micro-organisms.

In the seminal fibres of Gossypium (cotton), the cellulose is almost pure (98%); the chains contain about 3000 units of glucose (molecular weight 500 000); this makes for a molecule of 1.5 μm; it is not quite straight, but is quite rigid. In wood, the molecules are arranged in parallel in a very ordered *microcrystalline* fashion in certain regions called *micelles* which alternate with less well-ordered areas.

Cellulose is chemically very inert; it is hydrophilic in character, although practically insoluble in water and other usual solvents; it is resistant to dilute acids. It is soluble, but partially hydrolyses, in a concentrated solution of zinc chloride; the hydrocellulose formed takes on a blue colour with iodine.

2.   Cellulose derivatives

Cellulose derivatives with one, two or three alcoholic groups in the glucose residue, more or less soluble products, can be formed, of which some are used for food. Among the principal cellulose derivatives used in the food industry the following should be noted:

- sodium carboxymethlcellulose (CMC)
- hydroxypropylcellulose (HPC)
- methyl hydroxypropylcellulose (MHPC).

The *Carboxymethylcelluloses* or *CMC*, which are completely water-soluble, are ethers formed by the reaction of monochloroacetate in alkaline condition. The degree of substitution in food is equal to or less than 1. It is used as a dispersion agent in fruit juice, to improve the structure of ice cream, to preserve flours (1–2%), to combat dyspepsia, etc.

$$CH_2-O-CH_2-COONa$$

The other derivatives are non-ionic and show, in contrast to CMC, a difference of solubility in hot water. Thus MC and MHC, which are soluble in cold water, gel at water temperatures between 50°C and 90°C according to the degree of substitution in the cellulose chain. HPC behaves in similar fashion, precipitating when the water temperature reaches 40°–50°C. This explains the use of these derivatives in bakery products, since they enable adjustments to dough consistency, improvements in water retention, reduction in the rate at which some cakes go stale and lengthening of shelf life. At the same time, the gelling effect at high temperature may be useful in some applications (the manufacture of doughnuts, breadcrumb coatings and reconstituted foods).

Some other derivatives are of importance in various industries, notably cellulose acetate, prepared with acetic anhydride, for the production of films, magnetic tapes, dialysis membranes, etc.

Note: The *xylans*, homoglycans with the same structure as cellulose, but formed from xylopyranose, are other constituents of lignified tissues, as in the cellular walls of algae which have no cellulose.

VI. HYDROCOLLOIDS AND GELLING AGENTS

Table 3.1 summarizes the substances used, or proposed for use in this capacity, in the food industry, generally in low dosage. The following technological aims are pursued:

Table 3.1 — Thickening and gelling substances

Substance	Composition
I. PLANT	
1.1 *Gums (true)*: gum arabic, karaya gum, tragacanth gum	Complex galacto arabans, very branched
1.2 *Seed 'gums'*: guar, carob	Galactomannans, little branching
1.3 *Pectins* (cellular walls)	Galacturonides
1.4 *Marine algae extracts*:	
1.4.1 Brown algae (Phaeophyceae)	
— alginates	Polyuronides
— laminarans	Dextrans ($1 \rightarrow 3$)
— fucoidans	Complex polysaccharides
1.4.2 Red algae (Rhodophyceae)	
— carrageenans	Sulphur galactans
— furcellarans	Sulphur galactans
— agar-agar	Galactans and galactomannans
1.5 *Amylaceous*: starch, dextrin	Dextrans $\alpha(1 \rightarrow 4)$
1.6 *Cellulose* (chemical derivatives)	Dextrans $\beta a(1 \rightarrow 4)$
II. MICROBIAL.	Complex structure
2.1 *Xanthan* (Xanthomonas)	
III. ANIMAL	
3.1 *Gelatine* (degraded skin or bone collagen)	Proteins
3.2 *Casein* (milk)	Proteins
3.3 *Glycosaminoglycans*	Polyuronides and sugar amines
3.4 Chïtin (degraded)	Polysaccharide

(1) Stabilizing capacity: preventing the flocculation of a product, the crystallization of a constituent or the separation of insoluble parts (cocoa). This is also called the suspensoid property.
(2) Thickening capacity: producing a considerable increase in viscosity, due to swelling of strongly hydrophilic molecules; the density of the product is little altered.

(3) Gelling capacity: allowing water binding and preventing syneresis (retraction with exudation of the product).

The effects described above are in relation to the concentration of the additives; but certain substances lend themselves better to producing one effect than another. For example, gums are used to thicken a liquid (too great a quantity would be required to obtain a gel) and k-carrageenans is used for gelling.

Secondary effects are sometimes obtained: smoothness, creamy structure, cracking effect, rubbery gels, brittle gels.

The properties of the additive may be modified by various treatments; in the case of acid materials, change of cation, esterification, modification of structure (alkaline heating of certain carrageenans to obtain the 'anhydrous' form), etc. This happens mainly where economic conditions are unfavourable for a given product.

VII.   GUMS

1.   Tree gums

These form the hydrophilic part of 'gum tree' secretions. Two species of acacia are exploited: *Acacia verek* and *Acacia seyal* or *arabica*; the former is used most, yielding gum arabic or 'Senegalese gum'. The *Karaya* is an Indian tree which yields a similar sort of gum. It replaces Tragacanth gum, which comes from a bush found in semi-desert regions, which is more costly and has a different chemical structure.

Acacia gums are neutral or slightly acid salts of polysugars, with a very complex branched structure, made up of 5 monosaccharides in variable proportion, as represented in Fig. 3.2. It is possible to distinguish a simple and regular principal chain, made up of galactose residues (within the squares) and branchings which all begin from a galactose; two main ones are drawn. Moreover the cation linked to the –COOH groups of galacturonic acid is also variable: Ca^{2+}, Mg^{2+}, K^+. On removal of the cation we get 'arabic acid', which is relatively strong, with a pK of about 3.8.

2.   Seed gums

These are not true gums: they do not exude, they do not yield salts, and they are of a simpler structure. They are extracted from seeds crushed to flour.

Carob comes from the seeds of the carob tree, a tree of the *Leguminosae* family from the Mediterranean region. The structure is made up of one polymannose β (1→4) chain with branching at the single galactose residue every 4 or 5 residues of mannose. There are also traces of arabinose present.

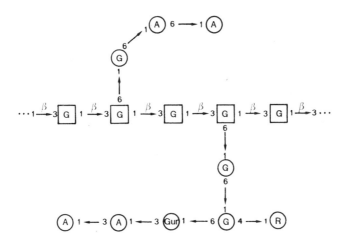

G   =D-galactose 45%
A   =L-arabinofuranose 25%
R   =L-rhamnose 15%
Gur=D-galacturonic acid 15%
        (and its 4-methoxy derivative)

Fig. 3.2 — Average structure and composition of *Acacia verek* gum.

The relationship between galactose and mannose has implications for the physical properties of the gum. The short branchings are not regular, but situated in zones.

Guar gum is very similar to carob and, being cheaper, tends to be used in its place. It comes from a plant native to India and Pakistan (*Cyamopsis tetragonolobus*), which is nowadays cultivated in Texas. The structure is the same as for carob, with more branching coming in at all the first or second chains in a regular manner. On average, it consists of 60% mannose and 40% galactose. Guar flour, which is marketed for use in food production, paper production and textile industry, has the following composition: water 9%; sugars 88%; minerals 1%; lipids 1%.

Tara gum has the same structure, with a galactose/mannose ratio of 1:3. It is more viscous on account of its high molecular weight. It is used in South America.

VIII. PECTINS

These are polygalacturonides methylated to varying degrees, in linear chains, and are constituents of plant cell walls. They have a relatively simple structure, with regular

α (1→4) bonds; but it must be stressed that their properties depend on the degree of methylation, which is the number of methyl groups expressed as a percentage of the number of –COOH groups.

High methoxyl pectins (about 70%) form gels in a very sugary and acid medium.

Low methoxyl pectins (less than 50%) may yield a gel in a medium low in sugar and acid, but with the presence of calcium or another divalent cation.

Pectins may be modified by alkaline demethylation with NH_3, thus obtaining a polyamide. The latter yields less brittle gels with less risk of syneresis.

Pectin acids are totally demethylated products; they are insoluble in water, except in the form of an alkaline salt.

Obviously, the universal presence of pectin in all plants means that there must be many enzyme systems capable of breaking them down. The pectolytic enzymes fall into two large groups: the pectinesterases and the depolymerases. These enzymes are used in the extraction of juice from certain soft fruits (strawberries, raspberries), for the clarification of some fruit and vegetable extracts and for maceration (e.g. baby foods, nectars).

IX.   SUBSTANCES FROM MARINE ALGAE

1.   Carrageenans

At present, the carrageenans are the marine algae products most used in the food industry. They are extracted from algae, treated with a hot water process, and then the purified products are treated with alcohol.

The structure is always linear and made up of galactose molecules substituted to some degree. It has some similarity to pectins, but the bonds forming the chain are more complex. It is useful to single out one unit of *carrabiose* comprising two galactose residues linked β (1→4). These units are linked together by an α (1→3) bond. Moreover, the monosaccharide residues are either esterified by sulphuric acid, or have an oxygen bridge between carbons 3 and 6 (anhydrogalactose). The presence of sulphated groups gives carrageenans a marked acid character; but it must be pointed out that carrageenic acid itself has never yet been isolated.

Several types of carrageenans exist; the most important are formed by a long chain of κ- and λ-carrabiose.

K−carrabiose   λ−carrabiose

Other types exist which seem to be the fore-runners of these two. Since κ-carrabiose is very prone to gel formation (whereas λ-carrabiose is incapable of producing a gel) research has been carried out as to why and how this occurs. Anhydrogalactose 3–6 results from sulphate removal from a cyclic disulphate by an enzyme in the plant or by hot soda treatment. It is probably this form which explains its peculiar characteristics held in high regard in stereochemistry (Fig. 3.3). We should point out the existence of two forms of the cyclic compound, that on the right of κ-carrabiose, we write as the 'chair' form; the C_1 form is the stable form, as the carbon atom substitution is in the equatorial position. The closing of the 3–6 linkage forces the chair back plane 3–4–5 to close down, which in turn causes the 1–2–0 plane to be raised; we then get the 1-C form where the substitution is axial (perpendicular to the main plane). The chair back plane, 3–4–5, must pivot on its axis in order to make the 1→3 bond with the next ring. In this way a spiral to the left is produced, leaving all the sulphate groups outside on the same side, a process which allows the coalescence of parallel chains. There is no swinging movement in the case of λ-carrabiose; rotation of the second ring serves no useful purpose and a hydrogen bond may establish itself between neighbouring residues. Here the sulphate groups, which are very large and charged, are scattered round the skeleton, which stops gel formation.

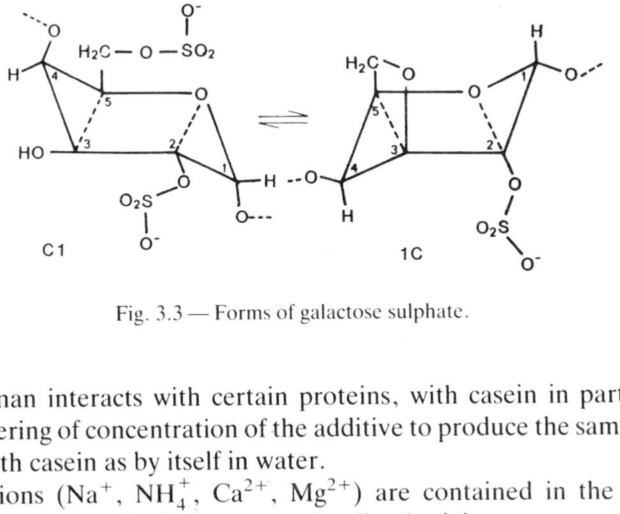

Fig. 3.3 — Forms of galactose sulphate.

κ-Carrageenan interacts with certain proteins, with casein in particular. This results in a lowering of concentration of the additive to produce the same gel rigidity (0.6–1.2%), with casein as by itself in water.

Several cations (Na^+, NH_4^+, Ca^{2+}, Mg^{2+}) are contained in the commercial product: a temperature of 60–70°C is needed to dissolve it in water; coagulation takes place during cooling, at about 45°C (only the sodium salt is directly soluble in cold water). In acid medium and without heat, no coagulation is produced: but in heat and at a pH less than 5.0, rapid degradation occurs with a loss of viscosity and gelling capacity.

Note: Similar substances, but less sulphated, exist in some red algae, in particular *gelose* (or Japanese agar) and *furcellarans* (or Danish agar). 3–6 Anhydro-L-galactose has been identified in agarose.

2. Alginates

Alginates come from brown algae, and their structure is different from that of the carrageenan. Because of their precipitation in acid medium and also where calcium is present, they are less used than the carrageenans. They are not suitable for sole use in dairy products.

Like pectins, alginates are polyuronides. However their acid component is either D-mannuronic acid with the β (1→4) bond, or L-guluronic acid (epimer at C_5 of the first) with the α (1→4) bond, or both of these together (co-polymers). Except for the usual presence of the sodium ion and secondarily, potassium, there is no substitution.

Attempts have been made to improve the potential of alginates; in particular, esterification with propylene glycol reduces their sensitivity to metals and widens their usage.

X. GLUCOSAMINOGLYCANS (OR MUCOPOLYSACCHARIDES)

These are large linear molecules made up in a double pattern from a distribution of one uronic acid and one N-acetyl sugar amine, to some degree sulphated, thus giving a very acid character (except for the first example quoted). These substances are constituents of conjunctiva or support structures and of fluids in animals. They are often bound to proteins or lipids. The structures of the main examples are detailed below:

Hyaluronic acid:
　　[D-glucuronic acid β (1→3) N-acetylglucosamine] β (1→4)
Chondroitin sulphate A:
　　[D-glucuronic acid β (1→3) N-acetylgalactosamine-4-sulphate] β (1→4)
Chondroitin sulphate B:
　　[D-iduronic acid β (1→3) N-acetylgalactosamine-4-sulphate] β (1→4)
Chondroitin sulphate C:
　　[D-glucuronic acid β (1→3) N-acetylgalactosamine-6-sulphate] β (1→4)
Heparin:
　　D-glucuronic acid α (1→4) N-acetylglucosamine-N-sulphate] β (1→4).
　　　　　　　　　　　　　　　⟶ 2-sulphate

Hyaluronic acid is not sulphated. Its molecular weight is very high, amounting to several millions. It is a very viscous polysaccharide, yielding a stiff gel at 0.5% concentration. It is present in all human tissues and fluids, responsible for assuring water retention and is an important factor in cell permeability.

The chondroitin sulphuric acids are similar to each other; the only difference between A and C is the carbon atom used for esterification. They are the main carbohydrate constituents of cartilage, skin, tendons, bones, etc. Their molecular weights are relatively low, in the region of 50000.

Heparin has a less regular structure than the others; whereas sulphamidation ($-NH-O-SO_2-O-$) is regular, esterification with the C_2 of glucuronic acid is not. This is a very acid material, widely distributed, which has anti-coagulant properties in blood.

Note: Mucins are also present in certain foods. They yield very viscous solutions. Submaxillary mucin contains a carbohydrate part made up essentially of a double pattern: N-acetyl-neuraminic acid linked to α (2→6) N- acetylgalactosamine, with a molecular weight of about 350 000.

XI. POLYSACCHARIDES AND THE GELLING PROCESS

As with other types of organic macromolecules, primary, tertiary or higher order structures can be defined for polysaccharides. The primary structure corresponds to the sequence of sugars in the monosaccharide chains (nature of the sugars, position in the chain, modes of bonding, etc.). The secondary structure is defined by the spatial formation of the monosaccharide chains: spirals, ribbons, etc. The tertiary structure corresponds with the way in which the chains join up or cluster and construct stable entities.

Gel formation is one of the very characteristic properties of polysaccharides, that is, the formation of huge molecular networks of a particular texture in the mesh of which other molecules and the solvent can lodge (Fig. 3.4).

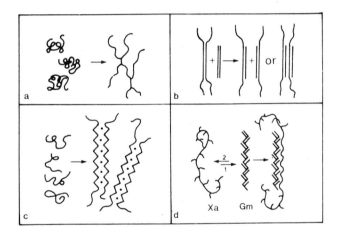

Fig. 3.4 — Gelling properties of polysaccharides. (a) Passage from polysaccharide solution to gel (few junctions; e.g. starch gel). (b) Incorporation of new segments in a chain with spiral junction at the level of zone structures (formation of dimers or aggregation; e.g. carrageenan gels). (c) Association of sequences of polyuronates by calcium Ca^{2+} chelation (black spots). Formation of a molecular network with 'egg-box' structure (e.g. alginates, pectins). (d) Formation, by cooling, of a mixed gel obtained from xanthans (Xa) and galactomannans (Gm).

When a solid polymer is placed in a small quantity of solvent, the first stage of the interaction is solvation with *gel* formation. The gel then disperses to a *sol* in the presence of excess solvent:

Polysaccharide → gel → sol .

The formation of a gel is due to interactions between chains through hydrogen bonds and salt linkages. If these bridges internally and between the chains are not chemical, gel formation depends mainly on the concentration of the polymer and on the temperature (the hydrogen bonds being few at weak concentrations and stable at low temperatures).

The molecules take a new form and the stability of the gel is determined by the number of these bonds. One of the most notable features of a gel is that whilst it has the appearance of a solid, its composition approaches that of a pure liquid state. For example an agar solution may contain 99.9% water and yet be capable of holding a defined and stable shape.

In this way, polysaccharides can form three-dimensional networks in space. Two or more chains may be attracted by the interconnecting regions or 'junction zones'. They produce either homogeneous gels, formed by a single type of molecule, or heterogeneous gels, made up from the association of several polysaccharides. Certain ions have a determinant role in the establishment of inter-chain reactions. This is the case with calcium. Through chelation it establishes bridges which are repeated regularly and make up clusters with a shape similar to an 'egg-box'. Moreover regular regions are formed in polysaccharides through the lateral association of chains. This phenomenon is helped by the existence of long repetition sequences in the chains.

In summary, the phenomenon of gelling and association may be provoked by simple physico-chemical modifications of the medium (e.g. pH, ionic concentration, temperature). A large mass of the solvent may be completely modified by a very small quantity of monosaccharide chains.

4

Lipids

I. GENERAL REMARKS

The lipid group, as defined nowadays, is a more heterogeneous group than that of carbohydrates and the proteins. It may be subdivided into:

(1) Lipids proper (esters or amides of a fatty acid — carboxylic acid formed from at least 4 carbon atoms — and an alcohol and an amine)
   (1.1) Glycerolipids (glycerides and glycerophospholipids)
   (1.2) Sphingolipids
   (1.3) Waxes
   (1.4) Steroids
   (1.5) Esters
      • Glycerol esters
      • Sphingosine amides
      • Esters with an alcohol of high molecular weight
      • Sterol esters
      • Acid-alcohol esters
(2) Lipoids (substances which have the same solubility characteristics as lipids)
   (2.1) Isoprenic lipids (carotenoids and quinones)
   (2.2) Free sterols
   (2.3) Hydrocarbons.

Firstly we will look at the properties of fatty acids. Then we will study the two categories of true lipids, (1.1) and (1.2). Finally we will examine the isoprenic lipids and sterols. It must be said at once that the glyceride category is strongly predominant in fatty foods.

N.B. The words *fat* and *oil* refer solely to the solid or liquid state of lipids; they have no relationship to any other property; the structure does not change.

II FATTY ACIDS
1. Classification
All have the grouping —COOH at the end of a varied chain:

(1) Non-polar side chain
    (1.1) Saturated
        (1.1.1) Linear chain   — soluble (C_4–C_{10})
                                        — insoluble (C_{12} and over)
        (1.1.2) Branched chain — iso
                                          — anteiso
                                        — others
        (1.1.3) Cyclic chain
    (1.2) Unsaturated (or desaturated)
        (1.2.1) Monoenoic
        (1.2.2) Polyenoic conjugated or non-conjugated

(2) Polar side chain
    (2.1) Hydroxyl acids
    (2.2) Keto acids
    (2.3) Other acids.

2. Occurrence
Here again in animal and plant fatty foods the great predominance of some fatty acids is to be seen. Let us mention particularly the four most abundant, with an even number of carbon atoms:

— palmitic acid: saturated, C_{16}
       CH_3–$(CH_2)_{14}$–COOH

— stearic acid: saturated, C_{18}
       CH_3–$(CH_2)_{16}$–COOH

— oleic acid: monoene in C_{18} (*cis* form)
       CH_3–$(CH_2)_7$–CH=CH–$(CH_2)_7$–COOH

— linoleic acid: diene in C_{18} (*cis* form)
       CH_3–$(CH_2)_4$–CH=CH–CH_2–CH=CH–$(CH_2)_7$–COOH

It must be stressed, however, that increasing use of physical methods of analysis (ultraviolet and infrared spectrophotometry, mass spectrometry and especially gas liquid chromatography) has permitted the discovery of more than 150 naturally occurring fatty acids.

In microbial lipids, which are not exactly foods, the most common fatty acids are often acids with an odd number of carbon atoms, which are only found in very small quantities in animal and plant fat bodies. For example, in the lipids synthesized by yeasts cultivated on alkanes, the dominant fatty acid is heptadecenoic acid — $C_{17:1}\Delta^9$ (20% of total).

3.   Proportions

The proportions of fatty acids in fatty foods may vary widely. Table 4.1 shows the average composition of 7 fatty plant foods and of 5 fatty animal foods. It can be seen that in the two kingdoms the total of saturated and unsaturated acids is of about the same order of magnitude (minor fatty acids are not included).

Oils are naturally very rich in unsaturated acids, which are liquid (in the *cis* form) at room temperature, whereas fats are richer in saturated acids, and their melting point is higher with the same number of carbon atoms.

III.   PHYSICAL PROPERTIES OF FATTY ACIDS

1.   Configuration

The configuration of the saturated hydrocarbon chains is probably in an elongated form, with a valence angle of 110° which corresponds to the minimum energy level (Fig. 4.1 (a)). However, this is a hypothetical situation, since in theory an infinite number of different configurations might occur because of the free rotation round single bonds.

Double bonds introduce a rigid structure to unsaturated chains. The *trans* configuration more or less preserves the linear structure; but this form is only rarely found in the natural state (vaccenic acid $C_{18:1}\Delta^{11}$). By contrast, the *cis* configuration, which is much more widespread, has an angle of about 30° (Fig. 4.1 (b) and (c)) in the chain.

2.   Melting point

This is an important value. It is about the same for the fatty acid and for the homogeneous saturated triglyceride (with the three fatty acids the same). Important considerations are as follows.

- For a given type, the melting point of the fatty acid increases according to the length of the hydrocarbon chain. For example, in the saturated acid series, the increase varies from between 6.5 and 9.5°C for every two additional carbon atoms:

lauric acid (C_{12}): 44.3°C	stearic acid (C_{18}): 69.6°C
myristic acid (C_{14}): 53.9°C	arachidic acid (C_{20}): 76.5°C
palmitic acid (C_{16}): 63.1°C	lignoceric acid (C_{22}): 86.0°C

- For a given chain length, the melting point is lowered with increase in the number of double bonds: the reduction is greater for the *cis* form than for the *trans* form (rare):

$C_{18.0}$ stearic acid	69.6°C
$C_{18.1}$ vaccenic acid (*trans*)	44.0°C
$C_{18.1}$ oleic acid (*cis*)	13.4°C
$C_{18.2}$ linoleic acid (*cis*)	−5°C
$C_{18.3}$ linolenic acid (*cis*)	−11°C

Table 4.1 — Composition of fats. Average values as a percentage of the total principal fatty acids (where >1%)

Fatty acids	Plant fats and oils — Oils						Plant fats and oils — Fats			Animal fats — Cow's milk Butter	Animal fats — Body fat			Whale oil
	Olive	Peanut	Soya	Rape Classic	Rape New	Lucerne	Palm	Copra	Cocoa	Butter	Beef	Pork	Man	
1. Saturated														
C_4 to C_{10}[a]	—	—	—	—	—	—	8	15	—	9	—	—	—	—
C_{12} lauric	—	—	—	—	—	—	50	46	—	3	—	12	—	—
C_{14} myristic	1	—	—	—	—	2	15	18	—	10	13	14	3	5
C_{16} palmitic	10	8	9	3.5	5	22	8	9	24	30	65	6	24	15
C_{18} stearic	2	4	3	1.5	2	1	2	3	34	10	1	10	8	1
Others	1	6	—	—	—	2	—	—	2	2	—	2	—	1
(Total saturated)	(14)	(18)	(12)	(5)	(7)	(27)	(83)	(91)	(60)	(64)	(79)	(44)	(35)	(22)
2. Unsaturated														
$C_{16:1}\,\Delta9$ palmitoleic	—	—	0.5	—	—	—	—	—	—	2	—	—	5	15
$C_{18:1}\,\Delta9$ oleic	75	57	33	25	55	5	15	8	38	30	20	43	47	36
$C_{18:2}\,\Delta9,12$ linoleic	8	25	48	19	20	20	1	1	—	2	—	10	10	—
$C_{18:3}\,\Delta9,12,15$ linolenic	—	—	6.5	3	8	48	—	—	—	—	—	—	—	—
$C_{20:4}\,\Delta5,8,11,14$ arachidonic	—	—	—	—	—	—	—	—	—	—	—	—	—	14
Others	3	—	—	—[b]	10	—	—	—	2	2	1	3	3	13[c]
(Total unsaturated)	(86)	(82)	(88)	(95)	(93)	(73)	(16)	(9)	(40)	(36)	(21)	(56)	(65)	(78)

[a] Butyric acids: C_4-butyric, C_6-caproic, C_8-caprylic, C_{10}-capric.

[b] Erucic acid, $C_{22:1}\,\Delta13$.

[c] Of which 8% is clupanodonic acid $C_{22:5}$.

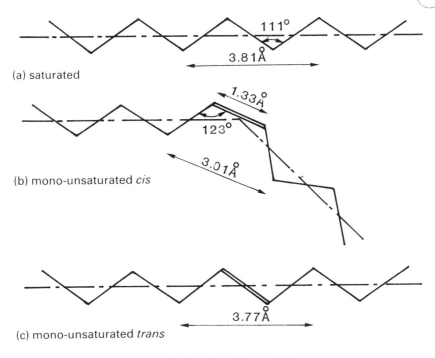

(a) saturated

(b) mono-unsaturated *cis*

(c) mono-unsaturated *trans*

Fig. 4.1 — Configuration of fatty acid chains.

- Catalytic hydrogenation (using reduced nickel) of unsaturated fatty acids hardens the fat. In the food industry this is an important method for the transformation of plant oils to fats, following treatment of the oleic series to give stearic acid: manufacture of margarine, shortenings, etc. (See Chapter 16.)

3. Polar structure

The structure is polar in view of the presence of the carboxyl group, but the hydrocarbon chain is hydrophobic. We must consider two current ideas in relation to fatty acids:

- the hydrophobic nature increases in relation to the number of carbon atoms;
- the COOH dissociation decreases with increase in the number of carbon atoms.

Consequently, the hydrophobic nature of the chain has a greater effect than the hydrophilic nature of the carboxyl group. Only fatty acids with a short chain (butyric acids and the C_4 to C_{10} acids) may be called volatile, i.e. carried in steam, and only the first two (C_4 and C_6) are water-soluble. For the others, the properties linked with the hydrophobic nature predominate, in particular insolubility in water.

Fatty acids with short chains are characteristic of butter from ruminants and of vegetable fats, palm kernel and copra (Table 4.1). There is sometimes fraudulent addition of palm and copra fat to butter. These acids melt at about 25°C to 30°C, about the same as butter: but the chemist knows well how to recognise this adulteration, either by the short chain fatty acid indices or by gas–liquid chromatography.

IV.   UNSATURATED FATTY ACIDS
1.   Position of the double bond

This is written, in simplified formulae, in two ways:

- in relation to the carboxyl group: $C_{18:2}\Delta^{9,12}$ (chemist's notation)
- in relation to the CH_3: $C_{18:2}\omega^{6,9}$ (physiologist's notation).

Types can be defined thus: all the fatty acids which have, similar to linoleic acid, a double bond at the 6 carbon from the methyl group, form part of the n-6 family.

Oleic acid predominates in animal fats and in the oils and fats produced by seeds and fruits. The lipids from green plants contain mostly corresponding acids with 2 or 3 double bonds: linoleic and linolenic. These polyenoic acids are of the 'methylene interrupted' type:

$$-CH=CH-CH_2-CH=CH$$

Some also exist in the 'conjugated' form: $-CH=CH-CH=CH-$, but in smaller quantities. These fatty acids are more reactive, particularly as regards to oxidation (cf. IX of this chapter). Conjugated fatty acids have a high rate of absorption at 230 nm, which allows their measurement. Moreover it is possible to isomerize the 'methylene interrupted' acids to conjugated acids by alkaline treatment and thus permitting a new spectrometric measurement. Two isomers are obtained from linoleic acid:

$$- CH = \overset{6}{CH} - CH_2 - CH = \overset{9}{CH} -$$
$$- CH = CH - CH = CH - CH_2$$
$$- CH_2 - CH = CH - CH = CH -$$

No allenic structure $-CH=C=CH-$ has been found. In contrast, some acetylenic fatty acids are found in nature, but they are very rare; an example is tariric acid (fat from *Picramia tariri*) $C_{18:1}a^6$, which is a form of a reduced acid in parsley, from petroselinic acid $C_{18:1}\Delta_6$.

It should be noted that a long-chain mono-unsaturated acid, erucic acid (Table 4.1) is very abundant in the oils from standard Cruciferous plants. This is important because it is toxic to laboratory animals, in whom it promotes a myocardial lesion; though its toxicity to humans is doubtful. However, plant breeding research has been carried out from the point of view of strain selection: oils from the new strains of rape which are almost entirely free of erucic acid (canbra oil or canola oil).

2.   Essential nature of polyunsaturated fatty acids

This is well known. Linoleic acid or 18:2 (n-6), which is the most important, has specific characteristics but it only reacts when it is the precursor of other fatty acids in the (n-6) series, such as arachidonic 20:4 (n-6) or dihomogammalinolenic acid 20:3 (n-6). (See Table 4.2.) These two fatty acids are in fact the departure points for the first series of prostaglandins.

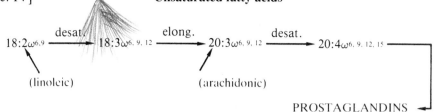

$$18{:}2\omega^{6,9} \xrightarrow{\text{desat.}} 18{:}3\omega^{6,\,9,\,12} \xrightarrow{\text{elong.}} 20{:}3\omega^{6,\,9,\,12} \xrightarrow{\text{desat.}} 20{:}4\omega^{6,\,9,\,12,\,15}$$

(linoleic)   (arachidonic)

PROSTAGLANDINS

The importance of linolenic acid has long been underestimated. Signs of linoleic acid deficiency were much more noticeable (stunted growth, skin disorders) and for a long time these masked the effects of the linolenic acid. It is now well established that linolenic acid is essential for the normal functioning of the retina. Other studies have shown that the (n-3) fatty acids, of which linolenic acid is the prime example, are essential during certain periods in life for some tissues, eg. for the formation of nerve cells.

Dietary fatty acids, in addition to those of endogenous origin, may undergo successive desaturation and elongation within the organism. It is shown in Table 4.2 that the same enzymes from Δ6 desaturase are capable of reacting with ingested linoleic and linolenic acids, yielding the (n-6) and (n-3) types. There is thus competition between these different substrates for the same enzymes. Δ6 Desaturase, which is the key enzyme in these metabolic processes, shows high affinity for the most unsaturated substrates such as linolenic acid. In other words, too much linolenic acid in the diet may inhibit the transformation of linoleic acid into arachidonic acid. To achieve a balanced diet, both these types of fatty acids must be present. It is considered at the moment that the relationship between linoleic acid and linolenic acid must lie between 5 and 10, linoleic acid representing 3% to 5% of the total calorie input and linolenic acid 0.5% to 1%.

Without going into details, it is possible, but not yet totally proven, that the activity of the Δ6 desaturase falls off as the person gets older. If this is the case, there would be an advantage in eating fatty foods containing acids going beyond the Δ6 desaturase. Some oils of this type are now appearing on the market (oils of evening primrose, borage and blackcurrant pips). Certain animal fats, fish in particular, are good sources of these long chain polyunsaturated fatty acids.

The desaturases ('desat.') and the elongating enzyme ('elong.') have high specificity only when the double bond exists as ω^6 in the molecule. Where there is a deficiency of linoleic acid, the oleic acid may be transformed; the acid $20{:}3\,\omega^{9,12,15}$ accumulates without the formation of prostaglandins. External symptoms (dermatitis) appear when the proportion of the latter to arachidonic acid exceeds 0.4. This happens when linoleic acid constitutes less than 1.5% of the dietary calories in the new-born infant; cow's milk comes into this category (see Chapter 13).

3. Iodine value
This is an analytical value for halogen addition to the double bond. This old concept has withstood the process of development in methodology. Theoretically, at least, the higher the iodine value of a fatty material the higher its unsaturated fatty acid content. In fact the iodine binding is not complete when the double bond is close to the −COOH group:

Table 4.2 — Principal biosynthesis pathways of polyunsaturated fatty acids

	Polyunsaturated fatty acids											Type
Food	18:3 Δ9,12,15	△	18:4 Δ6,9,12,15	⇒	20:4 Δ8,11,14,17	△	20:5 Δ5,8,11,14,17	⇒	22:5 Δ7,10,13,16,19	△	22:6 Δ4,7,10,13,16,19	n-3
	18:2 Δ9,12	△	18:3 Δ6,9,12	⇒	20:3 Δ8,11,14	△	20:4 Δ5,8,11,14	⇒	22:4 Δ7,10,13,16	△	22:5 Δ4,7,10,13,16	n-6
De novo synthesis by the organism	18:0	△	18:1 Δ9	△	18:2 Δ6,9	⇒	20:2 Δ8,11	△	20:3 Δ5,8,11			n-9
	16:0	△	16:1 Δ9	△	16:2 Δ6,9	⇒	18:2 Δ8,11	△	18:3 Δ5,8,11	⇒	20:3 Δ7,10,13 △ 20:4 Δ4,7,10,13	n-7

△ Desaturase.
⇒ Elongation enzyme.

— oleic acid $C_{18:1}\Delta^9$, iodine value 89.5 (in theory, 90)
— oleic acid $C_{18:1}\Delta^3$, iodine value 16 ⎫
— hypogeic acid $C_{18:1}\Delta^2$, iodine value 9 ⎭ (rare acids) .

4. Fish oils

These have a characteristic fatty acid composition. They contain long chain polyun-saturates, such as clupanodonic acid, which influence the blood lipids in two ways. They lead to a lowering of the cholesterol level accompanied by a fall in the triglyceride level, both of which are factors for good health.

V. GLYCERIDES
1. Triglycerides

The triglycerides are largely predominant. The di- and monoglycerides are only present usually at less than 2% of the total lipid.

The three positions on the glycerol molecule are not identical, since two are primary and one secondary. In addition, the two primary positions are not exactly equivalent; the carbon atom numbering is shown in the following diagram:

$$\text{(1)}\ CH_2 - O - CO - R_1$$
$$R_2 - OC - O - CH\ \text{(2)}$$
$$\text{(3)}\ CH_2 - O - CO - R_3$$

Stereo-specific numbering
(Sn-glycerol)

The substitution of the 2 carbon atom becomes assymmetrical where R_1 is different from R_3. However, optically active glycerides have never been observed in natural products.

There has been a great deal of discussion about the distribution of fatty acids on the three positions of glycerol. It seems that maximum heterogeneity might be an approximate principle (regular distribution), according to Hilditch. A fatty acid is as widely distributed as possible among the different glycerides; a homogeneous triglyceride appears only where one fatty acid represents two-thirds of the total fatty acids. However, many exceptions are observed, for example the presence of homogeneous triglycerides in fatty materials which contain less than 66.6% of a given fatty acid.

2. Direct analysis

Direct analysis of triglycerides is very useful. It permits the establishment of a relationship between the physical properties and the composition of fatty materials. Nowadays it is practised alongside the determination of individual fatty acids.

In the fat content for cow's milk, which is one of the most complex known, the number of carbon atoms per glyceride ranges from 34 to 56. The short chain fatty acids are bonded mainly in position 3 and the long chain fatty acids in position 1.

3. Lipolysis

In organisms, lipolysis stems from catalysis by a lipase. In mammals, food glycerides have to be hydrolysed to fatty acids and 2-monoglycerides, which are then able to penetrate the cells of the intestinal membrane, with the help of the pancreatic lipase (E.C.3.1.1.3):

$$
\begin{array}{l}
CH_2 - O - CO - R_1 \\
| \\
CH - O - CO - R_2 + 2\,H_2O \xrightarrow{\ \text{lipase}\ } R_1 - COOH + R_3 - COOH + \\
| \\
CH_2 - O - CO - R_3
\end{array}
$$

Glycerides

$$
\begin{array}{l}
CH_2OH \\
| \\
CH - O - CO - R_2 \\
| \\
CH_2OH
\end{array}
$$

The 2-monoglycerides may isomerize into 1-monoglycerides, which then can hydrolyse.

Lipase is a carboxylesterase, but is practically inactive in water. It becomes active at the interface between oil and water in a micellar emulsion. It is a hydrolase with active serine.

4.   Reactions of the ester bond

Apart from lipolysis, these reactions are principally as follows. (See also Fig. 4.2.)

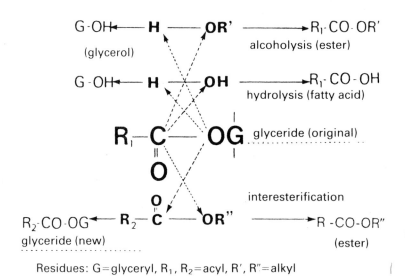

Residues: G=glyceryl, R_1, R_2=acyl, R', R"=alkyl

Fig. 4.2 — Reactions of the ester bond.

- Water hydrolysis is slow and incomplete, even with pressurized steam. The neutralization of the free fatty acid accelerates the reaction; this is *saponification* which produces R–CO–ONa (soap).
- Alcoholization also produces hydrolysis; but with the formation of an ester of the fatty acid and the alcohol used: R–CO–OR'. This means that the mixture from the reaction will contain both glycerol esters (glycerides) and alcohol esters. The

equilibrium is slow to establish: the use of alkaline alcoholate (R′–ONa) speeds up the reaction.

- Interesterification is the reaction of a glyceride with another simple ester. In the presence of an appropriate catalyst (alloy of sodium and potassium or sodium methylate) a random rearrangement of the acyl and alkyl residues is produced. It is then possible to modify the natural triglycerides; for example, in the reaction of methyl butyrate with the triglycerides of the fatty material from milk.

VI.   PHOSPHOLIPIDS

This is a large family in biochemistry, found in all cells and particularly in cellular membranes and subcellular structures, such as the mitochondria. These compounds are very widespread, but they are generally found in small quantity, except in egg' yolk and nervous tissue. Two types can be distinguished, which are often associated in living matter (Fig. 4.3).

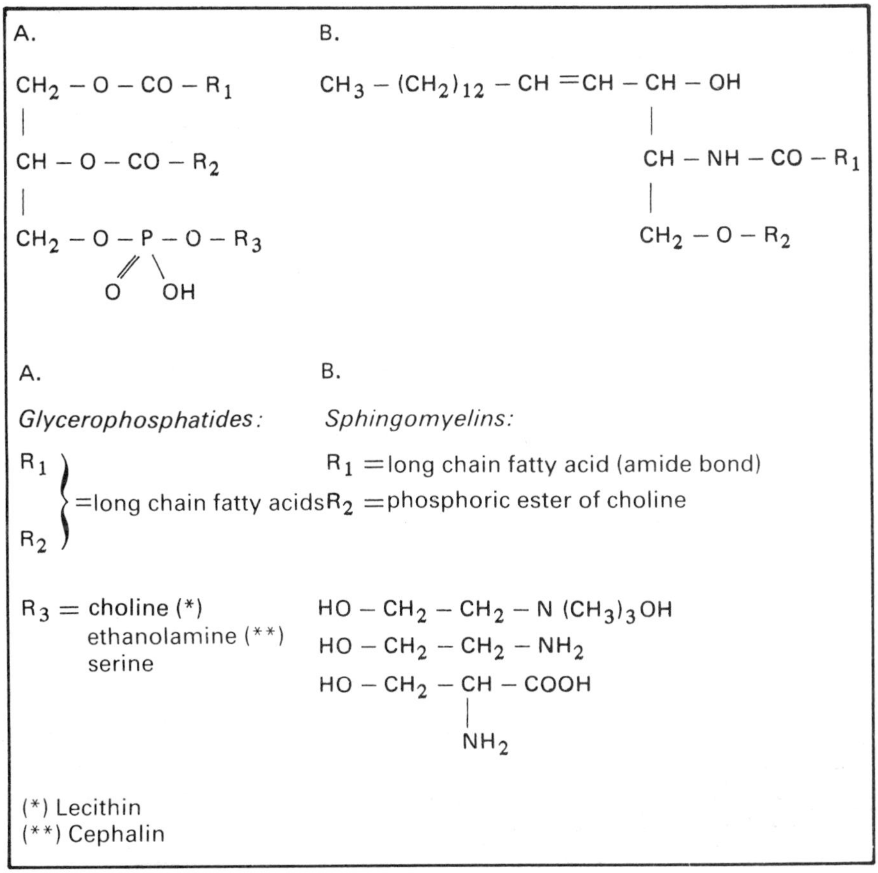

A.

$$CH_2 - O - CO - R_1$$
$$|$$
$$CH - O - CO - R_2$$
$$|$$
$$CH_2 - O - P - O - R_3$$
$$\diagup\diagdown$$
$$O \quad OH$$

B.

$$CH_3 - (CH_2)_{12} - CH = CH - CH - OH$$
$$|$$
$$CH - NH - CO - R_1$$
$$|$$
$$CH_2 - O - R_2$$

A.

Glycerophosphatides:

$$\left.\begin{array}{c}R_1\\\\R_2\end{array}\right\} = \text{long chain fatty acids}$$

R_3 = choline (*)
     ethanolamine (**)
     serine

B.

Sphingomyelins:

R_1 = long chain fatty acid (amide bond)
R_2 = phosphoric ester of choline

$$HO - CH_2 - CH_2 - N\,(CH_3)_3\,OH$$
$$HO - CH_2 - CH_2 - NH_2$$
$$HO - CH_2 - CH - COOH$$
$$|$$
$$NH_2$$

(*) Lecithin
(**) Cephalin

Fig. 4.3 — Structure of phospholipids.

1. Glycerophospholipids

These are the 1,2-diglycerides, with, at position 3, a phosphoric acid residue, itself linked to a hydroxylamino acid (serine) or a hydroxyl amine (choline, ethanolamine). The fatty acids are always long chain, often with stearic acid in position 1 and oleic acid in position 2.

They are broadly classified under the term *lecithin*, despite the fact that this is more specifically applied to the phosphatidyl-choline group. The other two categories are called *cephalins*.

In contrast to the triglycerides, these are polar substances with two dissociated functions: acid and amine. It is this which explains their essential properties in that they are strongly hydrophilic although fatty by nature. They constitute a bridge between the fatty and the aqueous phases and they have a great facility for forming (cellular) lipoproteins in thin layers, constituents of membranes. Lecithins are used industrially as emulsifying agents.

The glycerophosphatides are soluble in many organic solvents; but they are not soluble in acetone, a property which is related to the second portion of the molecule.

2. Sphingomyelins

Here it is an amide bond which joins the fatty acid to the material which corresponds to the glyceride. There are, however, two OH groups in the molecule, but one of these is never substituted (secondary alcohol), whilst the other is linked to the phosphoric ester and choline, as in lecithin (Fig. 4.3(B)). The compound which bears the amide bond is sphingosine, which is an unsaturated di-alcohol amine with 18 carbon atoms.

These substances are comparable to lecithins, with which they are linked.

N.B. Other natural non-phosphorylated derivatives of sphingosine exist; namely the glycolipids which have glycosylated residues at position R 2 (cerebrosides, gangliosides and phytoglycolipids).

VII. WAXES

These are the monoesters of a fatty acid and an alcohol, both long chain (up to 40 carbon atoms). The two parts of a molecule are usually of unequal length. The fatty acids are generally saturated, rarely unsaturated and very rarely hydroxylated.

They are found in all kingdoms. They are nearly always solid at ambient temperature. Unlike certain insects, higher animals do not metabolize waxes. Three examples are given below.

— Whale blubber is an almost pure wax. It contains more than 90% cetyl palmitate, which is an example of saturated constituents of equal length ($C_{15}H_{31}COOH$, $C_{16}H_{33}OH$).

— Beeswax, on the other hand, is of complex composition. The predominant wax is myricyl palmitate ($C_{15}H_{31}COOH$, $C_{30}H_{61}OH$), and there is also present the ester of an unsaturated fatty acid ($C_{16:1}\Delta^2$), myricyl hypogeate.

— In bacteria, particular properties are imparted by molecules which are analogous through their make-up; thus trehalose dimycolate, a constituent of the *cord factor* is responsible for the toxic character, as well as the acid resistance, of *Mycobacterium tuberculosis*.

American Indians use a fatty product, Jojoba oil, in reality a plant wax, as a body rub; it is now also used in body shampoos.

VIII. LIPOSOLUBLE CAROTENOIDS AND STEROLS

We now consider the group of substances which accompany lipids in nature, but which possess neither acid nor amide bonds or ester linkages. It is their water-insolubility and their solubility in fatty substances which are responsible for their reactions.

1.   Carotenoids

The carotenoids are strongly unsaturated hydrocarbons, formed from isoprene units linked end to end, or their oxygenated derivatives. They have a common biochemical origin with fatty acids, but here the acetyl-coenzyme A undergoes condensation with branching.

They are always of plant origin, but can also be found in animals, since the oxygenated half-molecule of α-, β- and γ-carotene is vitamin A, found in milk, eggs and liver.

Their biosynthesis is summarized in Fig. 4.4. The phytoene, which is colourless, has 9 double bonds (8 from the isoprene units and one created from the head-to-tail union of geranyl-geranyl phosphate). Red colouring results from tetradehydrogenation, as the conjugated double bonds together produce a pigment. Of these the most stable is lycopene, tomato colouring, which is all *trans* in form. The cyclization of the two extremities of the chain of 40 carbons yields the carotenes: these are split with oxidation by carotenase. This produces retinol (vitamin A_1) with an alcohol function on carbon 15. The vitamin activity depends on the structure of the final ring — a double bond must be between carbons 5 and 6 (β-ionone ring).

Retinol has vitamin activity for growth. However, it is essential for the chemical phenomenon of vision. Rhodopsin, the photosensitive pigment, is made up of a protein, opsin, and retinol in the ll-*cis* form. Light triggers the break- up of the complex and then a return to the retinol ll-*trans* form. This photoisomerization stimulates nervous excitation and the rhodopsin is regenerated in the dark.

The xanthophylls are hydroxylated derivatives at carbon 3 in the para-position to the chain carotenes and are also found in animals.

2.   Sterols

The sterols are also derived in the biochemical chain from active isoprene. They are related to squalene (abundant in the liver of certain fish) which results from the combination of two farnesyl phosphate molecules (Fig. 4.4); they thus have 30 carbon atoms. The essential chemical characteristic is the presence of an OH or O substitution on carbon 3. In Fig. 4.4, the existence of a planar structure means these are isomers, and if the substituent is below the plane the bond is shown dotted.

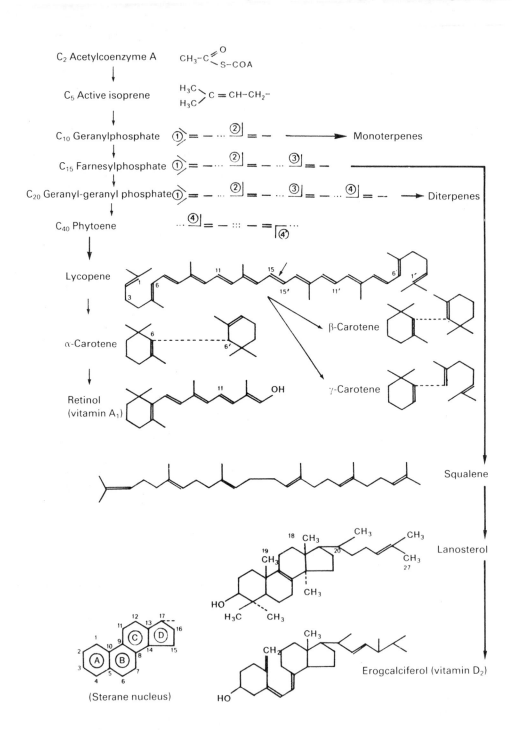

C$_2$ Acetylcoenzyme A

C$_5$ Active isoprene

C$_{10}$ Geranylphosphate ———————→ Monoterpenes

C$_{15}$ Farnesylphosphate

C$_{20}$ Geranyl-geranyl phosphate ———→ Diterpenes

C$_{40}$ Phytoene

Lycopene

β-Carotene

α-Carotene

γ-Carotene

Retinol
(vitamin A$_1$)

Squalene

Lanosterol

Erogcalciferol (vitamin D$_2$)

(Sterane nucleus)

Fig. 4.4 — Biosynthesis and structure of carotenoids and steroids.

The compounds with vitamin activity possess an alcohol group, and those with a hormonal action possess the ketone group (with a reduction in length), as in the male and female sex hormones.

Several isomers are D vitamins; ergocalciferol D_2 has been prepared synthetically. These vitamins regulate the phosphorous–calcium metabolism: deficiency causes rickets in children and osteomalacia (softening of the bones) in adults (Chapter 8).

Cholesterol is linked with proteins in serum lipoproteins, especially the low density type (LDL) which contain up to 45–50% cholesterol and which provide a means of transport of cholesterol from the liver to tissues. When the level of LDL is high in relation to the HDL (high density lipoproteins) there is a high risk of coronary disease (LDL/HDL above 4.0).

IX. LIPID OXIDATION

Oxidation reactions in lipids involve the formation of foul-smelling volatile compounds. These reactions may occur even in foods with less than 1% lipid content. The main substrates for oxidation are the unsaturated fatty acids, which generally oxidize faster in the free state than when they form part of a triglyceride or phospholipid. Some other unsaturated substrates may undergo oxidation reactions, as for example, vitamins A and E, carotenoid pigments and certain hydrocarbons present in oils.

1. General mechanism

Three types of reaction (Fig. 4.5(a)) may be distinguished in the oxidation of lipids:

— *initiation* reactions, which, from unsaturated fatty acids, lead to the formation of free radicals or lipid peroxides. These reactions have a high activation energy and the ease with which they occur is influenced not only by high temperatures but more especially by light and by trace metals. When the peroxide content increases, the so-called secondary initiation can be seen, which results essentially in the decomposition of the peroxides.

— *propagation* reactions, which constitute the oxidation stage of unsaturated lipids by gaseous oxygen. They are characterized by an accumulation of lipid peroxides and require the intervention of free radicals which, in the case of pure lipids, may lead to the formation of 10–100 molecules of peroxide. The activation energy of these reactions is very low.

— *termination* reactions, where free radicals associate to yield a wide variety of non-radical compounds.

2. Consequences of oxidation reactions

Oxidation reactions give rise to many compounds. The main types of molecule obtained after oxidation of a mono-unsaturated fatty acid such as oleic acid are shown in Fig. 4.5(b).

It is fitting to mention first of all the aldehydes and ketones of low molecular weight which are responsible for the rancid smell which accompanies lipid oxidation.

REACTION MECHANISM

● *Initiation*

Primary $RH \longrightarrow R. + H.$
alkyl
radical

$$RH + O_2 \rightarrow ROO. + H.$$
peroxy
radical

$$RH + M^{+n} \rightarrow R. + H^+ + M^{+(n-1)}$$

Secondary $ROOH \rightarrow RO. + .OH$
alkoxy
radical

$$ROOH \rightarrow R. + HO_2.$$

$$ROOH + M^{+n} \rightarrow ROO. + H^+ + M^{+(n-1)}$$
metal

$$ROOH + M^{+(n-1)} \rightarrow RO. + OH^- + M^{+n}$$

$$ROOH + ROOH \rightarrow ROOH \xrightarrow{M^{+n}} ROO. + RO. + H_2O$$
HOOR
hydrogen
bond

———————

● *Propagation*

$$R_1. + O_2 \rightarrow R_1OO.$$
$$R_1OO. + R_2H \rightarrow R_1OOH + R_2.$$

———————

● *Termination*

$ROO. + ROO. \rightarrow$
$ROO. + R. \rightarrow$ } non-radical components
$R. + R. \rightarrow$

Fig. 4.5(a) — General mechanism of oxidation reactions of lipids.

OLEIC ACID

- *Initiation*

$$R_1 - CH_2 - CH = CH - CH_2 - R_2$$

$$R_1 - \overset{\cdot}{C}H - CH = CH - CH_2 - R_2 \quad \text{or} \quad R_1 - CH_2 - CH = CH - \overset{\cdot}{C}H - R_2$$

$$\text{or} \quad R_1 - CH = CH - \overset{\cdot}{C}H - CH_2 - R_2 \quad \text{or} \quad R_1 - CH_2 - \overset{\cdot}{C}H - CH = CH - R_2$$

$$\downarrow O_2$$

$$ROO^{\cdot}$$

$$\downarrow$$

$$ROOH$$

$$R' - \underset{|}{CH} - R'' \rightarrow R' - \underset{|}{CH} - R'' + \cdot OH$$
$$\qquad OOH \qquad\qquad O.$$

- *Propagation*

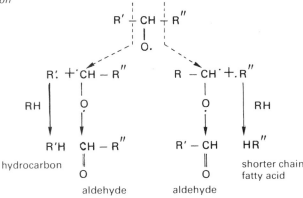

$$R' \dashv CH \vdash R''$$
$$\qquad |$$
$$\qquad O.$$

$$R'. + \overset{\cdot}{C}H - R'' \qquad\qquad R - \overset{\cdot}{C}H + .R''$$
$$\qquad\quad |\qquad\qquad\qquad\qquad\qquad |$$
$$\qquad\quad O \qquad\qquad\qquad\qquad\qquad O$$
$$\qquad\quad \cdot \qquad\qquad\qquad\qquad\qquad \cdot$$

RH   RH

$$R'H \quad \underset{\parallel}{CH} - R'' \qquad\qquad R' - \underset{\parallel}{CH} \quad HR''$$
$$\qquad\qquad O \qquad\qquad\qquad\qquad\qquad O$$

hydrocarbon   shorter chain fatty acid

aldehyde   aldehyde

- *Termination*

$$R' - \underset{|}{CH} - R'' + R. \quad \rightarrow \quad R' - \underset{\parallel}{C} - R'' + RH$$
$$\qquad O. \qquad\qquad\qquad\qquad\qquad\quad O \quad \text{ketone}$$

$$R' - \underset{|}{CH} - R'' + RO. \quad \rightarrow \quad R' - \underset{\parallel}{C} - R'' + ROH$$
$$\qquad O. \qquad\qquad\qquad\qquad\qquad\quad O \qquad \text{alcohol}$$

$$R'. + R''. \rightarrow R' - R'' \qquad\qquad\qquad R'O. + R'' \rightarrow R'OR''$$
$$\qquad\text{polymerized hydrocarbon} \qquad\qquad\qquad\qquad \text{ether}$$

$$R'O. + R''O. \rightarrow R'O - O - O - R''$$
$$\qquad\qquad \text{internal peroxide}$$

Fig. 4.5(b) — Modifications and products obtained from the oxidation of oleic acid.

This is the change which is observed first, despite the fact that some of these compounds (hexanal, 2-decenal) are present in very low concentration, of the order of micrograms per litre.

Additionally, carbonyl compounds may react with proteins or take part in non-enzymatic browning. The presence of lipids may also result in the secondary oxidation of various aromas.

Lipid oxidation also involves loss of vitamin activity and colour. Oxidation of essential fatty acids lowers their nutritional value.

3.   Factors influencing oxidation
The behaviour of lipids with regard to oxidation is very varied and these variations may be explained by the influence of different factors.

In the initial stage, oxidation is retarded by a reduction in the contact *oxygen pressure*, and factors which facilitate the conservation of oxygen are responsible for the defects associated with oxidation.

The presence of *prooxidants*, such as metals, myoglobin protein (similar to haemoglobin) and lipoxygenases, is a further factor. These enzymes, also called lipoxydases, are present in plant tissue and catalyse the oxidation of fatty acids, such as linoleic acid, which have a well-defined type of double bond.

Some foods also contain *antioxidants*. Among the natural antioxidants agents are tocopherol, ascorbic acid, certain amino acids and proteins, and other substances which may chelate metals. Competition may sometimes be seen between a pro-oxidizing and an anti-oxidizing effect.

Among the other factors affecting the oxidation of food lipids, *water activity* must be mentioned. The catalytic action of metals (see Chapter 7) depends on this in particular, as do the *nature* and *degree of dispersion* of the lipids.

5

Proteins

Peptides and proteins are more characteristic of animal or plant tissue than lipids and carbohydrates. General properties only will be examined in this chapter. Particular descriptions for each foodstuff are given in the second part of this book.

I AMINO ACIDS

(1) The α-amino acids making up proteins are shown in Fig. 5.1. With the addition of the two diacid amides there is a total of 20 compounds. All these amino acids can be transferred by ribonucleic acid (RNA) and take part in protein biosynthesis. Their combinations, in varied order, end up in a great number of molecules, ranging from one amino acid to peptides and proteins, all of which play important roles in living organisms.

(2) There are gaps in Fig. 5.1 for the 3–6 carbon series. It is strange to find there is no neutral amino acid with 4 carbons and that those with 5 and more carbons are branched. D forms exist in several derivatives (Glu, norvaline; Lys, norleucine). The hydroxyl derivatives are only 3 and 4 carbons long, the diamine derivatives have 6 carbons, and the acid derivatives are of medium-chain length (4–5 carbons).

(3) There are 7 'neutral' acids, tryptophan not being dissociated. There are 3 polar amino acids, which carry an OH; and 2 sulphur amino acids. These diverse compounds influence the properties of proteins:

— The hydrocarbon groupings, $-CH_3$, $-CH_2$, $=CH-$ have a hydrophobic character. Neutral amino acids increase the hydrophobicity, which increases with chain length. In decreasing order, these are Trp, Phe, Ile, Leu, Pro, Val, Met, Ala (methionine, which is a substituted thiol, remains in this category).

— The polar non-dissociated groups, such as $-OH$ (Ser, Thr, Tyr), $-SH$ (Cys) and $-CO-NH_2$ (Asn, Gln) may form hydrogen bonds, particularly with water, owing to their hydrophilic nature. Cysteine has another bonding possibility, due to its oxidizability; it forms one molecule of cystine with an

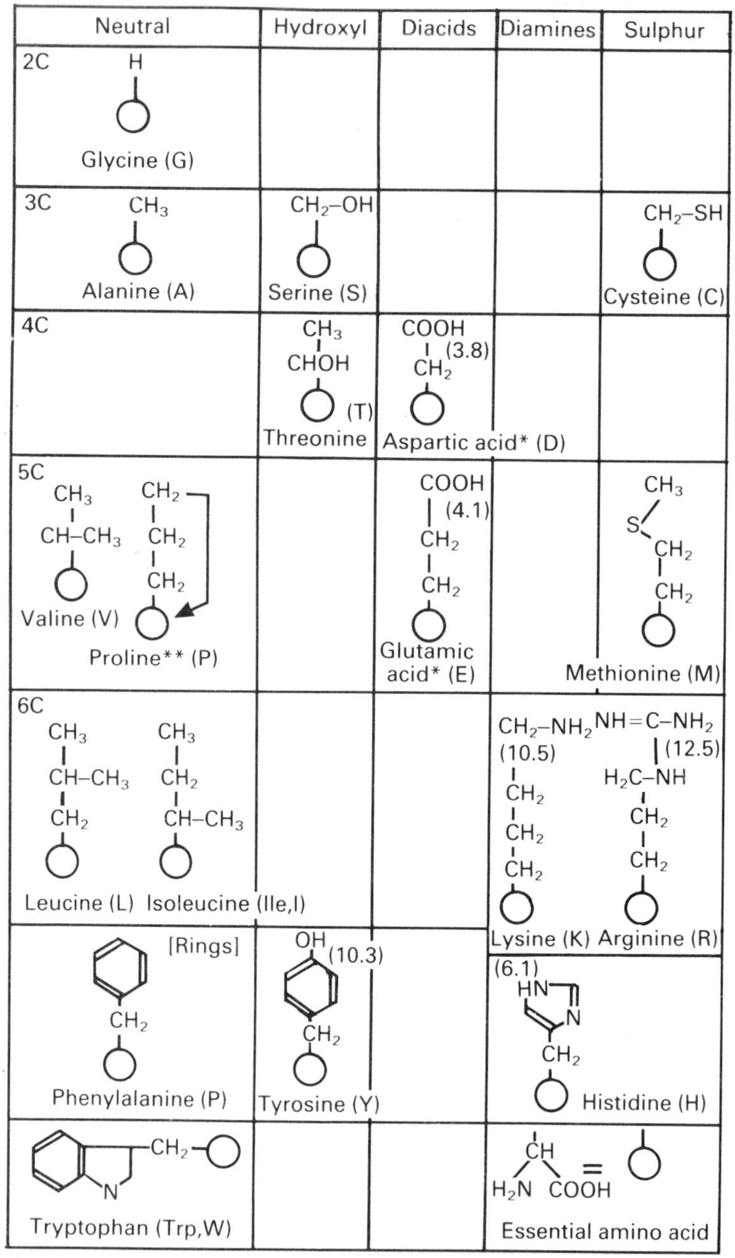

	Neutral	Hydroxyl	Diacids	Diamines	Sulphur
2C	H Glycine (G)				
3C	CH_3 Alanine (A)	CH_2–OH Serine (S)			CH_2–SH Cysteine (C)
4C		CH_3 $CHOH$ (T) Threonine	COOH (3.8) CH_2 Aspartic acid* (D)		
5C	CH_3 CH_2 CH–CH_3 CH_2 CH_2 Valine (V) Proline** (P)		COOH (4.1) CH_2 CH_2 Glutamic acid* (E)		CH_3 S CH_2 CH_2 Methionine (M)
6C	CH_3 CH_3 CH–CH_3 CH_2 CH_2 CH–CH_3 Leucine (L) Isoleucine (Ile,I)			CH_2–NH_2 NH=C–NH_2 (10.5) (12.5) CH_2 H_2C–NH CH_2 CH_2 CH_2 CH_2 Lysine (K) Arginine (R)	
	[Rings] CH_2 Phenylalanine (P)	OH (10.3) CH_2 Tyrosine (Y)		(6.1) HN N CH_2 Histidine (H)	
	–CH_2– N Tryptophan (Trp,W)			CH H_2N COOH Essential amino acid	

* The two diacids exist also in the amide form: asparagine (ASn, N) and glutamine (Gln, Q).

** Proline in the cyclized form of norvaline, a secondary amine.

The figures in brackets give the approximate pH of the supplementary function, which varies according to the environment.

Fig. 5.1 — Principle amino acids (L forms).

−S−S− bond between the −SH from two Cys belonging either in the same molecule, or between two distinct proteins.

— The dissociated groups, such as −COOH (Asp, Glu) and NH_2 or −NH (Lys, Arg, His) accentuate the hydrophilic character and influence the pH of proteins. They lose or accept a proton (H^+) at the pH values indicated in brackets (semi-dissociation of side chain).

(4) Amino acids, with the exception of glycine, have an optical activity due to the presence of an asymmetric carbon. The L form only is found in proteins, which is very characteristic. Sometimes D isomers are found in microbial peptides. Isoleucine and threonine have a second asymmetrical carbon; the 'allo' isomers are not found in the natural state (here −NH_2 and −OH are on the same side).

The three amino acids which possess an aromatic ring absorb ultraviolet light, at the following wavelengths: Phe at 260 nm, Tyr at 275 nm, and Trp at 278 nm. They possess natural fluorescence. These properties are used in analysis.

(5) The 'essential' amino acids are those with a branched chain (or aromatic) (Val, Leu, Ile, Phe, Trp), also with one hydroxyl (Thr), one basic amino acid (Lys) and one sulphur amino acid (Met). They are not synthesized by the majority of higher animals. Tyrosine may replace Phe, and cysteine may replace Met.

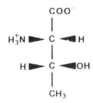

L− Threonine

(6) In addition, nearly 200 'rare' amino acids are known to exist, either in the free state in cells, or combined with other structures, which do not form part of the classic composition of peptides or proteins (examples: 3-methyl-histidine, β-cyano-alanine, azaserine). These amino acids may represent quite a significant percentage (2–5%) of the nitrogen input.

II. PEPTIDES AND PROTEINS

1. Size

A peptide is most often a small protein which is able to dialyse, with no precise lower limit on the dimension. In the past, this was fixed at 10000; nowadays, many chemists consider insulin (MW 5734 D) to be the smallest of the proteins. Biologically active substances are often peptide in nature (antibiotics and toxins) and have special features in their composition, such as unusual amino acids, like the lower homologues of lysine with a free NH_2 group: ornithine (C_5), diamino-butyric acid (C_4) and diamino-propionic acid (C_3). Particular forms are also found in the peptides from bacteria.

Peptides resistant to hydrolysis by the proteases of the intestinal flora and possessing diverse activities, have been shown in the protein sequences of milk, wheat and maize proteins. They may have opiate activity (exorphins), immune-modifying activity, enzyme inhibition, antihypertensive action, antithrombotic action, transport of cations and modulation of digestive hormones.

Some peptides contain isopeptide bonds; there may be either a carboxylic group or an amino group with a side chain which is involved in the bond. Here we note that it is possible, either by enzymatic or chemical means, to graft on, in covalent fashion, amino acids to the side chains of protein skeletons. Experiments with *in vitro* and *in vivo* digestion reveal the usefulness of amino acids attached by the isopeptide bond.

There is no precise upper limit on the size of a protein. Some are known where the molecular weight is over a million. Where the macromolecules are very large, it should be borne in mind that they might be polymers. Table 5.1 gives an idea of the extreme variation in size.

Table 5.1 — Molecular weights of some peptides and proteins

Peptides (<10 000)		Small proteins (10 to 20 000)	
Glutathione	307	Cytochrome C	11 600
Vasopressin	1 060	Ribonuclease	13 500
Tyrocidin	1 270	Lysozyme (egg)	14 400
ACTH	4 500	Myoglobin	16 000
Insulin	5 780	β-Lactoglobulin	18 400
Medium proteins (20 000 to 70 000)		Large proteins (>100 000)	
Casein β	24 000	Hexokinase	96 000
Trypsin	24 000	Collagenase	102 000
Pepsin	34 500	Phosphatase	180 000
Seromucoid α_1	40 000	(milk)	
Ovalbumin	45 000	α_1-Lipoprotein	200 000
Haemoglobin	65 000	Fibrinogen	340 000
		Myosin	475 000
Serum albumin	69 000	α_2-Macroglobulin	820 000

A protein molecule may be formed from a single chain or from several different chains. In the first case, the terminal $-NH_2$ (amino acid No. 1) and carboxyl terminal (amino acid No. x) are singled out. Several proteins are in the latter category. For the biologist, a particular substance may function as a polymer, considered by him to be a molecule. On the other hand, for the biochemist the molecule is the monomer, which is itself a sub-unit for the biologist.

2. Classification
This may be done in several ways:

(a) *Chemical*:   (1) holoproteins (contain only amino acids).
                      — albumins (soluble in pure water, difficult to precipitate with salts)
                      — globulins(less soluble and easier to precipitate)
                      (2) heteroproteins: glyco-, phospho-, metallo-, nucleoproteins.
(b) *Conformation*:   (1) globular
                      (2) scleroproteins, fibrous.
(c) *Function*:   (1) structural proteins
                      (2) plasma proteins and biological liquids (e.g. blood, milk)
                      (3) proteins with biological activity (e.g. enzymes, hormones, transport agents)
                      (4) food proteins (economically viable proteins, easy to digest and tasty, belonging to one of the preceding groups).

III. PRIMARY STRUCTURE AND POLYMORPHISM

1. Primary structure

The primary structure is the sequence of amino acids joined together by a covalent bond, which is the peptide bond, very stable and is itself a substituted form of the amide bond.

$$...NH-CH-CO-NH-\underset{\underset{R_1}{|}}{\overset{\overset{R_2}{|}}{CH}}-CO...$$

The chain configuration is elongated in form, comparable to that of the lipids, with slightly larger valency angles.

The primary structure of a great number of proteins is now known. This is established successively: Firstly, through automatic measuring of the amino acids freed by acid hydrolysis (6N HCl, 110°C, 12–72 hours); Secondly passage through a 'sequencer', also automatic, which allows the determination of the order of the amino acids at the N-terminal residue, according to the degradation method using the PTH (phenylthiohydantoin) derivative for each amino acid.

2. Hereditary polymorphism

Sequence study has revealed, in animal tissues, the existence of 'variants' where the synthesis is governed by the existence of a particular gene in several allelic forms. They only differ by a few residues per chain (usually from one to three) or by the existence of a deletion (absence from a given position). Their properties are very close to those of the normal sequence and they are given the same name.

From the point of view of biological activity, certain variations are associated with abnormalities. Haemoglobin has been the most studied. For example, the beginning of the β chain of human haemoglobin shows a normal sequence and then some abnormalities in positions 6, 7 and 9:

Hb β normal	Val-His-Leu-Thr-Pro-Glu-Glu-Lys-Ser-Ala-. . .
Hb β S (sickle-cell anaemia)	Val-His-Leu-Thr-Pro-Val-Gln-Lys-Ser-Ala-. . .
Hb β C (Georgetown anaemia)	Val-His-Leu-Thr-Pro-Glu-Lys-Lys-Ser-Ala-. . .
Hb β Porto Allegre	Val-His-Leu-Thr-Pro-Glu-Glu-Lys-Cys-Ala-. . .

The S and C variants separate in the course of electrophoresis in alkaline medium; this, however, is not the case with the Porto Allegre variant, which is termed 'silent' and can only be detected by 'peptide mapping' (chromatography of trypsin digested matter).

Such variations have been found in animals, notably in the proteins of cow's milk. Three of the four caseins of cow's milk (casein α_{S1}, β and κ) as well as β-lactoglobulin show a genetic polymorphism in all breeds, that is, several allelic forms or genetic variants (see Chapter 13, §VI). The locus of the β-lactoglobulin has a major effect on the level of this protein in milk and again on the total protein level of whey. These differences are compensated for by inverse differences in the total level of casein. In this case it is no longer possible to talk of abnormalities; there must exist a link between the genes of these proteins and the selection criteria for cattle.

IV. SPATIAL STRUCTURE AND DENATURATION

1. Conformation

The primary structure only partially defines the state of a protein structure. When synthesized by ribosomes the chain is linear; it subsequently undergoes a three-dimensional evolution through the influence of varying forces, attracting or repelling, which manifest themselves all along the chain and which depend on the nature of the side chains, the distance between them and the medium. The end result is a defined conformation, the thermodynamic state of which is characterized by maximal stability and minimum free energy.

The conformation of the native protein, in its biological state, is stabilized by weak energy bonds and structure, and by the disulphide bond or 'disulphide bridge', between two cysteine residues. The formation process has not yet been clearly explained.

Weak energy bonds are of critical importance in biochemistry. They limit the number of possible conformations and they allow the functioning of complex systems. In particular, and outside the protein structures, they regulate the interaction between macromolecules (for example, antigen-antibodies) or between macromolecules and small molecules (for example, enzyme-substrate).

2.   Secondary structure

Here we are concerned with the conformation taken by the polypeptide chain, stabilized by two hydrogen bonds between the skeletal structure, and not the side chains. The important bond here is between the H of $-NH$ and the O of $-C=O$. Two principal forms may exist (Fig. 5.2(a) and (b)).

— *α Helix*: the skeletal structure turns most often to the right with steps of 0.54 nm comprising 3.6–3.7 amino acid residues; the diameter is about 0.6 nm. The side chains are orientated towards the outside. In reality the curve formed is not strictly a helix; it corresponds to a succession of surfaces with an angle of about 80° at the intersection (at the level of the carbon). There is a distance of 0.15 nm between two successive surfaces separating two $-CH-$.

   A molecule wholly constituted from the helix has not been found and the part which does have this structure is very variable, from 0% to 80%.

— *Folded-thin-layer structure (or elongated state) β*: each layer contains twice the four coplanary atoms ($-CO-NH-$) and a hydrogen bond between two chains or two portions of the same peptide chain. The identity spacing is longer than in the former case, at 0.65 nm and the density is weaker. The fold is made on the $-CH-$. The side chains point in a more or less orthogonal direction. The peptide chains are often anti-parallel (the progression is in the opposite direction to the two chains).

— *Other secondary structures*, less frequently found:

   - helix 3_{10}, with 3 residues per turn.
   - helix $π$, with 4.4 residues per turn.
   - helix $μ$, with 5.2 residues per turn.
   - β curvature, allowing the folding of a chain with an angle stabilized by a hydrogen bond, where the sugar chains are most likely to be attached.

The following points should be noted:

(1) In the scleroproteins rich in proline, such as collagen, helical structures exist which do not require the H bond of the polyproline type. These units come together in twisted (coiled) molecules (see Chapter 14).
(2) The statistical 'random coil' shows areas of poorly defined molecules.
(3) Proline cannot be integrated in the helix and folded-layer structures since it causes them to break up.

3.   Tertiary structure

This is really the three-dimensional state which brings together the preceding forms. It is difficult to draw on a two-dimensional surface; yet this structure is of very great

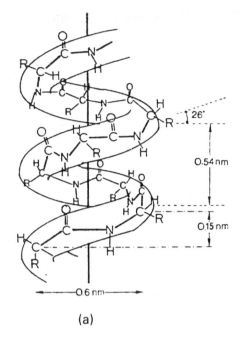

(a)

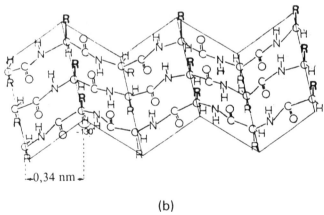

(b)

Fig. 5.2 Secondary structure of proteins. (a) Helicoidal state or α helix. (b) Elongated state or folded-thin-layer structure (β).

importance at the level of protein activity. Through it, residues of amino acids, far away from each other in the sequence, come close together because of the folding of the structure to form 'active sites'.

This structure, established in water medium, tends to push the polar side chains towards the surface, whilst the hydrophobic chains are pushed inside the protein molecule. This last situation implies the existence of 'hydrophobic bonds' (of the type of the Van der Waal's forces) which form principally between the side chains of Ala, Val, Leu, Ile, Phe, Trp.

Note:

(1) The term 'quaternary structure' is used to describe the association of protein molecules which, taken in isolation, do not have biological activity. These molecules may be identical or different. In food biochemistry a good example of this structure is the actomyosin system in muscles (see Chapter 14).
(2) The spatial structures are mainly studied by X-ray diffraction at high resolution (0.2 nm).

4. Denaturation

This is a singular property of proteins which stems from modification of the secondary and tertiary structure with no break-up of the peptide bond, and the primary structure.

Denaturation results from the action of various reagents:

— *physical*: heat, radiation (ultraviolet, ionizing), prolonged agitation, interfacial interaction;
— *chemical*: acids, solutions of heavy metals (deproteinizing agents), certain organic molecules (e.g. urea, solvents, detergents).

It is a most complex phenomenon about which more is still to be known. The starting point is the native conformation. New conformations, sometimes transient, may appear. The end result is often the forming of polypeptide chains which are unfolded or stretched out. In the latter case denaturation is irreversible (as in the case of cooked egg white). However there are apparently cases where denaturation may be reversible, with the reappearance of one or several properties.

The main effects of denaturation are:

● loss of biological activity
● decrease in solubility (exposure of hydrophobic groups)
● increased sensitivity to proteases
● lack of crystallization.

V. PROTEIN–WATER RELATIONSHIP

1. Solubility

Unlike the situation with the other groups, sugars and lipids, great differences are found within the protein group. Three examples may be cited:

● solubility in pure water (albumins, small globulins)

- solubility only in the presence of neutral salts (euglobulins)
- insolubility in water, solubility in alkaline or acid medium (scleroproteins), or in the presence of ethanol (prolamines).

It should be noted that the solubility equilibria of proteins are reached slowly. The solubility appears to depend on the conditions in the medium:

- *Neutral salts* intervene through their ionic forces (concentration and valency of the ions). In practice, are seen:
    - a dissolving effect (salting in) of low ionic force (in general for a concentration of less than 1 M).
    - a precipitating effect, or salting out, at high ionic force.

    These effects are due to increase or decrease in the solvation capacity of the proteins, according to the bell-shaped curve for each protein. At high concentration the water molecules are aligned with the ions.
- *Water miscible solvents* (ethanol, acetone) lower the dielectric constant, which reduces the repulsion forces of proteins and helps their aggregation, leading to precipitation.
- *The pH of the medium* is important, depending on the isoelectric point (pI) of the protein. Here the solubility curve is U-shaped. Solubility is always lower at the pI than at higher values (negative charge) or lower values (positive charge). Certain proteins are practically insoluble at their pI.

Fig. 5.3 shows the solubility of the proteins of fish, soya, whey and casein.

Protein precipitation is a method of preparation which has been much used but it has two drawbacks:

- it rarely yields pure products;
- it quite often results in denaturation; hence the need to work at low temperatures.

2.   Water binding

A dry protein progressively, and more or less rapidly takes up water from the surrounding medium in the following ways:

- binding of water molecules of constitution on specific sites of the protein, through quite strong bonds, such as the hydrogen bond. This water cannot be frozen, is not a solvent and is non-active. There is very little of it (0.06 g/g);
- adsorption of water layers, which do not freeze, but act as a solvent and are reactive: this represents the biggest proportion of the absorbed water in a humid atmosphere;
- retention of water of imbibition or capillary water, physically retained between the protein molecules (in the pores of moist food).

Soluble nitrogen %

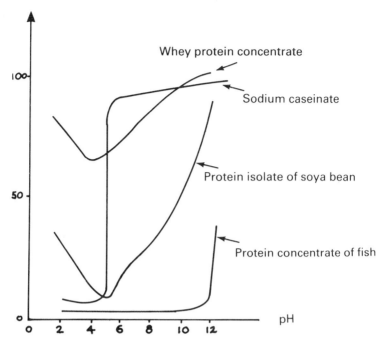

Fig. 5.3 — Solubility of various protein preparations in a 0.15 M NaCl solution, as a function of pH.

The end product of the hydration is either a solution or an enlarged mass, according to the nature of the protein. Some of the factors involved in hydration are: the pH (when it approaches pI the protein–protein interactions are maximal and water fixation minimal), heat (which generally reduces fixation), the atmosphere, the presence of various constituents.

There are no stable relationships between the solubility of a protein and water absorption. Again, there seems to be no strict relationship between the structure of a protein and in its behaviour *vis-à-vis* water, considering proteins as a whole. However, the hydrophobicity calculated according to the abundance of non-polar side groups is important in relation to the functional properties of a protein, as will be seen in the second part of the book.

VI.   SCLEROPROTEINS

There is no exact dividing point between the globular proteins and the scleroproteins, but the most characteristic fibrous proteins possess the following properties:

— axial ratio higher than 10 (length/diameter for a regular molecule);

— repetitive molecular structure, which permits the application of X-ray diffraction study (measurable identity periods);
— insolubility in water, salt solutions, acids, dilute bases, and neutral organic solvents;
— greater or lesser resistance to the action of proteases.

The existence of these properties explains the fibrous character (elastic strands) and the supporting and coating properties.

The properties of three types of scleroproteins are summed up in Table 5.2.

Table 5.2 — Types of scleroproteins

Protein property	Typical protein		
	Fibroin (silk)	α-Keratin (epidermal)	Collagen (muscle)
Spacing period (X-ray) in nm	65–70	51–54	28–29
Amino acid pattern	–Gly–Ala– Gly–Ser– | | |	—	–Gly–Pro– Ala– | | |
Residues % residues	45 28 13	Cys 12 to 20	35 22 10
Secondary structure	Elongated form β (pleated sheet)	Coiled shape (α helix)	Polyproline helix
Interchain bonding	Hydrogen	–S–S– bonding	Hydrogen

The fibroin of the silk-worm and that of the spider are simple proteins because of the heavy predominance of 3 amino acids; in the case of silk, 86% are Gly, Ala and Ser.

Keratins in the α-helix form are the main constituents of the skin epidermis and epidermal derivatives: e.g. body hair, hair, nails, hooves, scales.

Natural fibres have a complex make-up, formed by an association of fibrils in a protofibril, with each fibril itself being formed from twisted helices. Moderate physicochemical treatments allow the transformation of α-keratin into the β form, by the rupture of disulphide bridges. Hairdressers use a reducer, such as thioglycolic acid, for 'perms': the dampened and softened hair is curled, then follows a treatment with an oxidizing salt (persulphate, perborate) which stabilizes a new α structure.

Muscle proteins of the α structure (myosin, fibrinogen) and also collagen, will be examined in Chapter 14.

VII. FUNCTIONAL PROPERTIES OF PROTEINS

Under this new term is gathered some ancient knowledge. Generally the nutritive properties are excluded. Proteins play an extremely important role in food technology. They can be classified according to the following:

(1) organoleptic properties
(2) solubility and related factors; absorptive power, dispersion capacity
(3) water retention; adsorption, thickening, swelling
(4) coagulation, gelation, syneresis
(5) foam formation, expansion (surface property)
(6) emulsification, lipid bonding, film formation
(7) clustering, fibrillation, extrusion, texturizing
(8) various: compatability with additives, absence of unwanted aspects of activity (toxic, allergic, antibiotic), binding of amino acids, etc.

As has just been discussed, properties (2) and (3) depend on the water affinity.

Properties (5) and (6) depend on the 'surface properties'. The reduction in interfacial tension is in relation to the amphiphilic character of the proteins, the molecules of which move with ease towards water/air and water/oil interfaces.

Property (7) is linked with protein–protein interactions; so is property (4), but in in a more complex manner, with modification of the water affinity.

The functional properties depend on both primary structure and the spatial structure of the proteins, but also on medium conditions. These properties can be modified by:

• change of pH
• change of ion concentration
• heat treatment
• contrived hydrolysis (chemical or enzyme)
• chemical modification of the protein (e.g. grafting on of radicals, condensation of amino acids, oxidation).

It must be stressed that the fragility of the spatial structure and the sensitivity of the proteins to external conditions make fundamental studies difficult and make it necessary for there to be many experiments. For example, viscosity is an important factor, but it has no significance unless there is rigorous identification of the measuring conditions, which is difficult to achieve.

In the second part of the book, various problems which the food industry has associated with functional properties will be examined:

— thickening, gelation (aggregation of proteins in an ordered network)
— texturizing, film formation, fibre formation, paste formation
— emulsification (dispersion of two non-miscible substances, of which one forms the continuous phase and the other the dispersed phase)

— foam formation, expansion (dispersion of gas in microbubbles in the liquid or semi-solid phase)

— acquisition and fixation of flavours.

VIII. PROTEOLYSIS

1. Gastro-intestinal

Proteins are foods which are only absorbed following degradation to amino acids. In the human digestive system, proteolytic enzymes act in the stomach and in the intestine (Table 5.3):

Table 5.3 — Proteolytic enzymes of the human digestive system

Name	EC number	MW	pH_0	Specificity (metal)	Observations
Amino-peptidase	3.4.11.1	300 000	8.5	Broad (Zn)	Intestinal
Carboxypeptidase A	3.4.21.2	34 000	7.5	Except Arg, Lys, Pro (Zn)	Pancreatic (zymogen)
Carboxypeptidase B (protaminase)	3.4.21.3	35 000	8.0	Arg, Lys (Zn)	Pancreatic (zymogen)
Dipeptidase	3.4.13.1				Intestinal
Chymotrypsin A, B	3.4.21.1	25 000	8.0	Tyr, Trp, Phe, Leu	Pancreatic (zymogen)
Trypsin	3.4.21.4	24 000	8.0	Arg, Lys	Pancreatic
Elastase	3.4.21.7	25 000	8.0	Except charged and aromatics	Pancreatic
Enterokinase	3.4.21.9	195 000	6.0	Lys-Ile (6-7) of trypsinogen	Intestinal
Pepsin A	3.4.23.1	34 500	2.0	Phe, Leu, Tyr	Of stomach (zymogen)
Pepsin C (gastricsin)	3.4.23.3	31 500	3.0	(more restricted than pepsin A)	Of stomach (zymogen)
Chymosin (rennin)	3.4.23.4	30 700	4.5	Phe, Leu	(Abomasum of young ruminants)
Cathepsin D	3.4.23.5	58 000		(more restricted than pepsin A)	Intracellular protease

(1) The polypeptide chain cleaved into peptides by four main endopeptidases, according to precise specificity rules:

- pepsin A, in the stomach, breaks the —CO—NH— bonds adjacent to a voluminous and rather hydrophobic side chain (Phe, Leu, Tyr) with a very low optimal pH zone (pH 2.0);

- pancreatic trypsin attacks a basic side chain (Arg, Lys) in slightly alkaline medium (pH 8.0);
- pancreatic chymotrypsin attacks a voluminous and hydrophobic side chain (Phe, Leu, Trp, Tyr);
- pancreatic elastase attacks a small non-charged side chain.

In practice, these enzymes are secreted in the form of an inactive enzyme or zymogen. Activation stems from a limited hydrolysis and peptide elimination. In the case of pepsinogen, the activation is spontaneous in acid medium (in the stomach); in the case of the pancreatic zymogens, activation is through enzyme action at the level of the duodenum.

Pepsin is of the type of enzymes in Group 23 of the proteases; the active centre (site for catalytic action) has two residues of aspartic acid.

The three pancreatic enzymes resemble each other closely; they belong to Group 21 the members of which have serine and histidine in the active centre. The differences in the specificities stem from a structural element, the 'pocket', which accepts the side chain of the amino acid attached to the protein.

(2) Some exopeptidases reduce the length of the polypeptide chains, and some dipeptidases cleave the last bond, which is not accessible to other enzymes. Two types of enzymes which attack the chain extremity have been studied:

- carboxypeptidase A and B, in the pancreas, which cleave terminal C-amino acids, with the exception of proline; they are secreted in the state of inactive zymogens; zinc is necessary for their activity;
- intestinal aminopeptidase, which cleaves terminal N-amino acids; zinc is also involved in the function. This is a large molecule (MW 300 000) about 10 times heavier than the preceding enzymes (25 000–35 000).

2. Technique

Proteolysis is a very common process in the food industry. Widely varied enzymes are used:

— *Enzymes, animal in origin*, obtained by extraction from an organ:
   - chymosin (rennin), the fourth stomach (abomasum) extract of young un-weaned ruminants; used in cheese making;
   - pepsin, extract from the stomach of the pig, and more recently, of the bullock; same usage as chymosin and for the production of plastein (see below);
   - 'pancreatin', mixture of animal pancreas proteases; for varied uses.
— *Plant enzymes:* Papain (E.C.3.4.22.2), and ficin and bromelain (which can replace papain) are respectively extracts from the latex of the papaya, the fig and the pineapple stem. All have varied usage: stabilizing beer, tenderizing meats, dry biscuit manufacture, etc. It has been suggested that papain should be used to obtain 'plastein', which is the term for proteins whose composition has been

modified by protease action on a concentrated solution; this rearrangement modifies certain properties.
— *Microbial enzymes.* Three types of enzymes for use in the fermentation industries are prepared from various non-dangerous species:

  • neutral proteases, active at about pH 6.5–7.5, used mainly in tanning (preservation, depilation), brewing, baking, etc. Subtilisin is the neutral protease of *Bacillus subtilis*;
  • alkaline proteases, pH 10.5, much used in the washing powder industry;
  • acid proteases, pH 5.0–6.0, used as an alternative to rennin (*Endothia parasitica, Mucor miehei, Mucor pusillus*).

Note: Most of these enzymes will be discussed again in the second part of the book.

IX.   NON-ENZYMATIC BROWNING — THE MAILLARD REACTION

In various foods a very complex series of reactions may develop, resulting in the formation of black or brown pigments and modifying other organoleptic qualities such as smell and taste. Amino acids and proteins participate in certain of these reactions through the action of free amino groupings. These reactions, called the 'Maillard condensation', are discussed here.

1.   Biochemistry of the reactions

1.1   General scheme of the Maillard condensation
First, sugar and one amino acid yield an addition compound, which is transformed into an *N*-substituted glycosylamine. After an Amadori rearrangement, a molecule of the type 1-amino-1-desoxy-2-ketose is obtained (Fig. 5.4).
     At this stage there are three possible developments:

— A strong dehydration may occur (route 1). This is the most important of the three possibilities, and it gives rise to furfural and dehydrofurfural derivatives, notably 5- hydroxymethylfurfural. The aromas, which are also produced as a result of thermal decomposition of sugars, are not specific to the Maillard reaction.
— A splitting of the molecules into carbonyl compounds of which some lack nitrogen, such as acetol, diacetyl, pyruvaldehyde, may be seen (route 2). The aromas are not specific to these reactions either.
— A more moderate dehydration may take place (route 3). It gives rise to reducing substances which are a mixture of reductones and hydroreductones. These products may react with intact amino acids; they decarboxylate them and transform them into aldehydes which are characteristic of the amino acids involved. Here we have the Strecker degradation, which in this way produces aromas characteristic of the Maillard reaction.

1.2   Reactivity of the different constituents
In the free state, almost all the amino acids show the same behaviour; however, certain experiments have shown that the carboxyl group of the amino acid may have

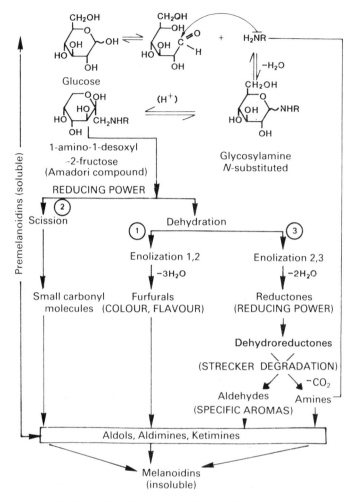

Fig. 5.4 — Simplified scheme of the Maillard reaction.

an inhibiting effect on the reactivity of the amino group, and this effect depends on the distance between the two groups. The peptides and the proteins interact through their free NH_2 groups. Amongst the amino acids included in polypeptide chains, the basic acids, notably lysine with its ε-amino grouping, show strong reactivity.

In the Maillard condensation, the sugars are a more important factor than the amino acids. There is a stronger reactivity with the pentoses compared to the hexoses. The order of decreasing reactivity is:

ribose>xylose>arabinose>mannose>fructose>glucose

The reducing disaccharides (lactose, maltose) are even less reactive than the hexoses. However, the nature of the protein involved is also capable of modifying the sugar reactivity.

To summarize, the behaviour of food products depends essentially on their reactive sugar content and their pH; the most stable may therefore become sensitive to the Maillard reaction by addition of reducing sugars.

1.3   Factors influencing the reaction

Although the reaction is strongly stimulated at high temperatures, heat is not an indispensable condition for the development of the Maillard reaction, which may occur just as easily during storage periods. In a general way, the intensity of the reaction increases with increase in pH, and broadly the pH zone between 6 and 8 presents the best conditions.

Water always retards the development, first by dilution of the medium and, more especially, by the inhibiting role it plays, as it is one of the products formed by the reaction. Relative humidities from about 30% to 70% correspond in general with the best conditions for the Maillard condensation (Chapter 7).

Metals play a significant role: certain cations, such as Mn^{2+} or Sn^{2+}, hinder the reaction; others, however, catalyse it: Cu^{2+} and Fe^{3+}.

2.   Incidence of the Maillard reaction in food technology

There are three main properties of the products formed in the course of the Maillard reaction to be considered:

— colour
— aroma and taste
— reducing power.

2.1   Colour

Although the 1-amino-1-desoxy-2-ketoses (Amadori compounds) are colourless, they are considered to be the colour precursors. Indeed, whichever the route taken by the Maillard reaction, the final result is strong polymerization of the substances formed, to such an extent that insoluble, blackish and sooty molecules — called melanoidins — which constitute the final stage of the Maillard reaction are formed. All the soluble molecules formed during the process of the reaction are broadly called the 'pre-melanoidins'.

It must be pointed out that the thermal degradation of sugars (caramelization) may take place simultaneously with the Maillard reaction and may sometimes give rise to products comparable to those mentioned in Fig. 5.4. Thus the browning may have another origin.

2.2   Aroma and taste

The Maillard reaction induces the formation of two types of aromatic compounds, the furfurals and the reductones, as well as the aldehydes which result from the decomposition of amino acids by the Strecker degradation. The last are specific to the non-enzymatic browning reaction.

The formation of aromas depends on the nature of the amino acids involved in the Maillard reaction, and also on the exact stage reached by the reaction. Each amino acid is capable of imparting numerous flavours, which may be good or bad from the organoleptic point of view. The amino acids are responsible to a large degree, for example, for the flavours of the crust of fresh bread, roasted peanuts, cocoa and certain cheeses.

2.3   The reducing power of the pre-melanoidins

The reducing power appears in the course of a Maillard reaction well before colour formation. It has been demonstrated that at low levels of humidity and before the appearance of browning, the reducing power is due exclusively to the Amadori compounds.

The antioxidant property of the Maillard reaction in relation to plant fats, in particular to linoleic acids, has been shown. Among the amino acids, alanine and proline have shown themselves to be the most efficient.

The Maillard reaction also produces an important variety of acid substances which reduce the pH.

Finally, the pre-melanoidins have a catalytic effect on the Strecker degradation, either by directly initiating the decarboxylation of the amino acid, or by accelerating the formation of reductones, and thus accelerating the degradation process.

6

Minerals

I. IMPORTANT POINTS

Where the mineral constituents of foods are concerned (except for C, N, O, H), the biochemical aspect is of course less. There are however some important points to be considered, whose main characteristics will be seen in Section IV and some applications mentioned in Part II of the book:

(1) quantity: supply, need (expressed either in weight units or in micro-equivalent, mEq)
(2) state: free and exchangeable, linked with proteins and non-exchangeable
(3) role: essential, non-essential, damaging
(4) regulation (mechanism) and deficiency
(5) correlation with some diseases
(6) elimination: urinary, faecal
(7) major elements and trace elements

Trace elements can be distinguished as those which are found in quantities of less than 5 g in the human body.

Table 6.1 gives the composition of some foods characteristic of three groups for values of the 5 major elements: Na, K, Ca, Mg and P. Chlorine is not cited because it varies much like sodium. The two most common foods, bread and milk, are each mentioned five times: it can be seen that their mineral constituent variations are not in parallel; in bread there is ten times more sodium but six times less calcium than in milk. Table 6.2 gives the approximate biological values.

II. MAJOR ELEMENTS

1. Sodium

This is the principal cation in the extra-cellular medium; per litre of water there is 14 times more in the extra-cellular than in the cellular medium (140 and 10 mEq, respectively).

Table 6.1 — Mineral value of foods (mg per 100 g edible portion)

	Rich		Average		Poor	
Sodium (Na=23)	Salted cooked meats	1000–3000	Fresh meat	60–70	Pasta (raw)	5
	Sauerkraut	600	Milk	50	Flour, rice	3
	Fish preserves	400–750	Saltwater fish	75–100	Fruits	3
	Matured cheeses	400–850	Eggs	130	Cabbage, radish	10–15
	Bread	500	Spinach, celery	100	Other vegetables	2–6
			Carrot, artichoke	50		
Potassium (K=39)	Ham	600	Fresh meat	300	Honey	5
	Lentils	1200	Pork, milk	150	Butter	15
	Stone fruits	600	Common vegetables	200–300		
	Potato	500	Fish	300		
			Bread	100		
			Fruits	150–300		
Calcium (Ca=40)	Comté cheese	1000	Milk	125	Apple, peach	7
	Roquefort cheese	700	Soft cheese	170	Fruit (others)	25–50
	Fish	300	Onion, cress	100–200	Meat	15
			Leek	60	Bread, pasta	20
					Ham	10
Magnesium (Mg=24)	Cocoa, soya	300–400	Maize, barley	125	Meat	35
	Almonds	250	Wholemeal bread	90	Fish	20–30
			White bread	60	Milk	12
			Vegetables	40–80		
Phosphorus (P=31)	Comté cheese, soya	600	Milk, bread	100	Pulpy fruits	20–30
	Stone fruits	450	Pasta (raw)	165	Butter	15
	Roquefort, lentils	400	Vegetables	80–12		
			Meat, fish	200		

Table 6.2 — The minerals in the body

	Content in the human body (g per 70 kg)	Needs (g per 24 h)
Sodium	100	1.0 (in NaCl)
Potassium	140	1.0[a]
Calcium	1000	0.4–1
Magnesium	30	0.3
Phosphorus	700	0.8
Iron	3	0.005–0.01

[a] In diet poor in sodium.

The contributions in the diet vary considerably according to the countries concerned (on average in France, 10 g/day of NaCl, which is 435 mEq); however, the concentration is well regulated in the body for contributions ranging from 1 to 10 g/day. In humans, excessive intake of sodium results in arterial hypertension.

Urinary excretion is usually the only method of elimination, except where the person has been subjected to intense physical exercise or is put in a hot atmosphere (cutaneous losses, sweat).

Natural plant foods are low in sodium, except for some species of vegetable (celery, spinach); fruits are always very low in it. It should be noted that vegetable preserves are salty; they contain 300–400 mg Na per 100 g.

Preserved cooked meat products are highly salted and are forbidden in salt-free diets. However, human beings, who have a taste for sodium, like them.

2. Potassium

There is much to distinguish potassium from sodium:

— it is essentially intracellular (more than 90% of the total);
— there is no deficiency in the diet; it is found in vegetables and in meat in comparable quantities;
— there is no real taste for it;
— there is no strict regulation of blood potassium.

Elimination is almost entirely urinary, as with sodium; diuretic salts eliminate both K and Na.

There are only a few natural foods which are low in potassium. There is less in preserved foods than in fresh foods.

3. Calcium and phosphorus

These two elements are linked because their common absorption is mutually helpful. The ideal Ca/P relationship is close to 1.7. Dairy products (milk, cheese, yoghurt) are very interesting from this point of view.

Calcium is above all a constituent of the skeletal framework (1 kg of Ca); it constitutes about 25% of dry bone. The plasma content is strictly regulated at 100 mg/l.

Plants are not very effective in calcium absorption: they contain little of it; sometimes they produce oxalic and phytic acids which make calcium insoluble; and fibre carries some proportion away in faeces.

Phosphorus, as well as being linked to calcium in the skeleton, is important in its metabolic role. Its absorption depends on vitamin D, but deficiency in phosphorus absorption does not seem to exist. Its distribution in foods is better than that of calcium. In the body, phosphorus is always present as phosphate in the bone, phosphoproteins, phospholipids and nucleic acids in the cell. It is also of importance in the phosphate cycle enzymes, the phosphatases and the protein kinases.

Urinary elimination is controlled through hormones and not faecal excretion.

4. Magnesium

Dietary change towards more refined food results in a decreased magnesium contribution (wholemeal bread 90 mg/100 g, white bread 60 mg/100 g).

The content in the human body is 25–30 g, of which half is in the bone, barely exchangeable. The tolerance levels are much wider than in the preceding cases. The Mg balance is established through kidney clearance.

III.   TRACE ELEMENTS

Iron content in the human body shows variations according to sex. Iron deficiency is very rare in men but is frequently found in women (menstrual losses, pregnancy). The total quantity of Fe varies from 3.5 g in a man to 2 g in a woman; 60% is retained in the haemoglobin. Absorption is always in the form of ferrous iron.

Copper shows variations according to age; deficiencies have only been found in infants fed over a long period with cow's milk. The level of need seems to lie between 1 and 3 mg/day. Copper is quite widely found, especially in animal foods, but in small proportion (the maximum is in calf's liver: 12–14 mg/100g).

In connection with *zinc*, the question of retardation in growth and sexual development arises — this occurs in 'developing countries' where there are few animal foods available. Meat contains an average of 5 mg/100 g and milk 0.4 mg/100 g. Vegetables are much poorer in it. The level of need has not been established; it is thought to lie around 10 mg/24 h.

Iodine is an essential trace element, which is found almost entirely in the thyroid gland and a little in blood plasma; the clinical symptom of deficiency is the appearance of a goitre, known as endemic goitre, due to an overactive thyroid gland. The level of need is evaluated at 0.3–0.4 mg/24 h; but foodstuffs are low in it, with irregular content. Marine fish contributes about this quantity (0.4 mg/100 g).

IV.   BIOLOGICAL ACTIVITY OF MINERAL ELEMENTS

The different bio-active metals in the metabolism of the living being are situated between sodium and zinc in the periodic table. The complexes formed between organic molecules and these metallic cations have a role to play in different biological activities. They may be classified into four types:

— The metallic cation, by virtue of its electrons from bonds in the outermost external orbits, may form a *'transport'* complex which easily frees the molecule in the presence of an acceptor. In such a complex — for example, haemoglobin — the central metallic cation does not change its valency as a result of its bonding with the substrate.

— The enzyme–metal substrate is a *transfer of charge complex.* In such a complex the transfer of charge may happen transitionally between the substrate and the metallic cation through delocalization of the mobile electrons inside the substrate. The transfer of charge may also take place between two substrate molecules through the intermediary of the orbits of the central metallic cation.

   The central metallic cation is also energized through the enzyme catalysis and the organic part which constitutes the enzyme proper 'chooses' the metallic cation and its substrate according to its stereochemistry. It should be noted that certain metallic elements are undissociable, whilst others are dissociable from the enzyme after catalysis and because of this may link with other enzymes.

   One of the points of interest of this type of complex is the possibility of isolating a reaction in the cell and so several enzyme reactions may take place simultaneously.

   In a certain number of physiological mechanisms, a coupling exists between some metallic cations belonging to the same chemical group. In the majority of cases, an antagonism is seen between the two elements: whilst one activates the reaction, the other inhibits. As an example, the Mg^{2+} ions activate the freeing of phosphate groups by transphosphorylases, whereas the Ca^{2+} ions inhibit the reaction and activate the opposite reaction.

— Metallic cations may form with the organic molecules *'sandwich' complexes* in which they keep them in parallel layers, giving the whole substance an organized structure.

   For example, the Mg^{2+} ions allow the transduction of luminous energy and transmissible electronic energy into the chlorophyll layers. This energy is then transformed into the chemical energy necessary for organic reactions. The metallic cations play the role of positive 'holes', following the example of the metallic cations present in the semi-conductors.

— In the *cation exchanger complexes,* since the metallic ions are the strongest, electroaffinity represents the energy freed when one electron is added to one atom to form a negative ion, thus displacing other ions. In this way, in the sodium pump, the K^+ cations, freed in the external solution, go to displace the Na^+ ions in the neural membrane.

7

Water

Water, which represents the most important constituent of living beings, imparts to living matter its fluidity which allows and facilitates exchanges and movement in the cell. It represents 50% of protoplasm and acts as a vehicle for salts, organic substances and gases in solution. The proportion of water in tissues is very variable: 22% in bones, 69% in the liver, 75% in muscles, 82% in the kidneys. The quantity of water in the tissues is often related to the intensity of the biological activity of the organ. In tissue building, it takes part in and is indispensable to osmotic phenomena and thermal exchange.

The water content of foods is also very variable: 10–20% in cereals, 60–75% in meat and muscle, 80–90% in fruit and fresh vegetables, 90–95% in edible mushrooms.

Since water does not bring any energy value to the foodstuff and since it does not aid the keeping process, it is often useful to reduce the water content as much as possible. In contrast with natural products, it is possible for manufactured goods to contain a varying water content in cases where there is no regulation of water content (e.g. maximal water content of butters and margarines: 16%). For this reason it is useful to control the water content of foods during any processing and when they are marketed.

I.   PROPERTIES OF WATER IN FOODS

1.   Fundamental properties of water

1.1   Structure

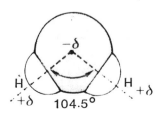

Because of its conformation the water molecule has a partially ionic character with separation of the charges. The molecule behaves like an 'electric dipole'. In an electric field, dipoles turn and partially 'neutralize' the applied field.

Thus, at ambient temperature the dielectric constant of water is 80, which means to say that the two opposite electric charges in water are attracted with a force 80 times weaker than in air.

Water has a high solvent power for ionized and polarized substances (ionic crystals):

— it attaches to all ions, forming hydrates;
— through hydrogen bonds it attaches to the hydrophilic macromolecules possessing the OH, NH_2 groups.
— substances not miscible with water may form hydrophobic bonds.

1.2 Distinction between free and bound water

One part of water has not got the same properties as the rest (free water) since it is bound to the macromolecules through Van der Waal's forces and hydrogen bonds.

According to the state of the water (free, hydrated or bound) the physical and chemical properties vary. Thus, bound water has lost its solvent power, and it cannot be frozen since the energies of water-molecule bonds are higher than those between the water molecules in ice.

1.3 Physical and chemical properties of water in the food industry

Throughout the cooking, sterilization, concentration, dehydration or freezing processes for foods, the properties relating to changes in state and transfers of heat and matter are involved: specific heat, latent heat of fusion and vaporisation, thermal conductivity, viscosity, etc.

When different chemical and biochemical materials are introduced into water, it is the solvent properties which are significant: dielectric constant, dipolar moment, surface tension, binding properties. There is a rise in the boiling point, a lowering in the freezing point and the surface tension, an increase in viscosity.

2. Availability of water in foods

2.1 Water activity

Biochemical constituents may partially immobilize water by stopping vaporization and lowering its chemical reactivity.

The state of the water in a food has as much importance as the water content. The 'availability' is defined by the a_w activity, which is itself defined by the partial lowering in the vapour pressure created by the food:

$$a_w = \frac{P_w}{P^o_w}$$

where P_w=partial pressure of water in the food, P_w^o=partial pressure of pure water at the same temperature.

In a container, there is equality between the activity of the foodstuff and the partial vapour pressure which it exerts.

In fact:

$$a_w = \frac{\text{equilibrium relative humidity (ERH) (in \%)}}{100}$$

Placed in the open air, the activity of the foodstuff equals the relative humidity of the air.

The majority of chemical compounds lower water activity rather more than the theoretical position would suggest. This is because of interactions with water and poor dissociation of electrolytes.

The activity of water depends slightly on temperature. However, when a dilute solution is frozen, the residual water activity of the liquid phase depends solely on the freezing temperature.

2.2   Water behaviour in foods

2.2.1   Isothermal adsorption
At equilibrium this is a curve showing:

— the quantity of water retained by a foodstuff as a function of humidity at a given temperature.
— the partial pressure of water vapour exercised by the water in the food.

2.2.1.1   Relationship between adsorption isotherms and water in foods — The adsorption (or sorption) isotherm may be divided into two parts:

— for $0<a_w<0.2$–0.3, the water is strongly retained at the surface of the solute in the form of a monomolecular layer of water fixed to some polar groups ($-NH_3^+$ and $-COO^-$ of proteins, OH of carbohydrates, water of crystallization in salts and certain sugars). The bound water represents about 3–10 g/100 for dry weight.
— For $a_w>0.2$–0.3, the water is weakly bound. However, though free, it is not easy for water to leave animal and plant tissues. It is present in capillaries and its retention is influenced by the pH, the ionic force, the nature of the salts and certain modifications.

2.2.1.2   Hysteresis cycle (or loop) phenomena — The sorption and desorption curves do not coincide (Fig. 7.1); in fact, in the course of the desorption, equilibrium is established, for the same water content, at a lower vapour pressure than in the course of adsorption. The hysteresis phenomenon is only seen with water activities higher than 0.2–0.3, which is to say, when water is weakly bound.

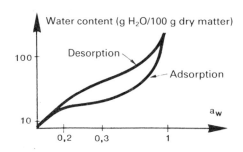

Fig. 7.1 — Water adsorption and desorption isotherms.

This phenomenon is explained by the fact, that since the diameter of the capillaries is narrower at the surface (neck) than inside (body), the water vapour pressure necessary to fill is higher than to empty. These partial pressures depend on the diameter of the orifice and on the surface tension.

2.2.1.3   Influence of temperature on isotherms: sorption heat — The variation in the partial pressure of the water vapour of pure water as a function of the temperature is given by the equation:

$$\frac{\mathrm{d}\,(\ln a_{\mathrm{w}})}{\mathrm{d}(1/T)} = -\frac{Q_{\mathrm{s}}}{R}$$

where R = perfect gas constant, T = absolute temperature, Q_{s} = the heat of adsorption.

It is thus possible to calculate the heat of adsorption for a given water content. We should note that the Q_{s} increases with dehydration and becomes very high for the monomolecular layer of bound water.

2.2.2   Importance of isotherms to food technology
The curves make possible:

— the forecasting of the water activity in complex mixtures.
— the forecasting of the behaviour of a foodstuff in the course of a technological process or storage in atmospheres with varying humidity.

Some examples may be given:

— Rehydration of a dehydrated product (Fig. 7.2): It is seen that for the same water content, the rehydrated product has a greater activity than the partially dehydrated product. This is notably the case with fruit and vegetables which are foods rich in sugars and salts.

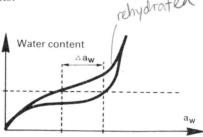

Fig. 7.2 — Rehydration of a dehydrated product.

— Forecasting the influence of temperature variations on water activity of a sample in airtight wrapping (constant humidity) (Fig. 7.3): At constant humidity and for activities in the order of 0.4–0.5 an increase in temperature increases the activity; at constant activity (constant hygrometry) an increase in temperature dehydrates the product and vice versa.

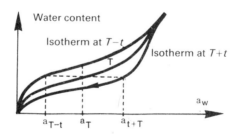

Fig. 7.3 — Influence of temperature variations on water.

— Forecasting the water absorbed by a dehydrated product if the wrapping is permeable to water vapour.
— Forecasting the stability of food items: Maximal stability is generally obtained when only the monomolecular level of water is present (bound water) which corresponds to an activity of 0.1–0.2 (freeze-dried foods).

2.2.3 *Influence of the composition and the physical state of the foodstuff on water binding*

Table 7.1 groups the values of water activity in some food products. It can be seen that the composition of the foods has a marked influence on these values. Thus at low water activity, proteins and starch retain more water than lipids and crystalline substances. Dehydrated fruits, rich in sugars, are especially hygroscopic above a certain level of activity ($a_w > 0.3$).

Table 7.1 — Water availability (a_w) in some food products

Fresh meat	0.99
Liver pâté, ripe cheeses	0.95
Frankfurter sausages	0.93
Paris ham	0.91
Fresh cream cakes	0.89
Smoked pork	0.87
Jams	0.86
Dry sausage (28–34% moisture)	0.84
Condensed milk (sweetened)	0.83
Frozen foods	0.81
Concentrated fruit juices	0.79
Fruit cake	0.78
Honey	0.74
Dried meats (15–16% moisture)	0.72
Sugar syrups	0.70
Biscuits	0.69
Cereals	0.66
Dried fruits, ice creams	0.65

At the same time, the physical state is one of the factors influencing water binding. At equal activity level (constant hygrometry), powdered sucrose binds more water than the crystal form. The transition between the two forms with the passage of time (crystallization of chocolate, honey, fruit spreads) frees water and some volatile soluble compounds.

Elsewhere, in the technological processes, modifications to a medium produce variations in the water content of foods. For example, preliminary heating of starches improves gelling through higher water absorption. The changes in pH and in ionic forces cause changes in the conformation of the protein chains or a swelling of the gels — or the minimum level of water retention at the isoelectric pH.

Certain additives modify the activity of water without changing the content — as a consequence of the 'mobilization' of a fraction of the latter. The addition of NaCl, sucrose, glycerol, and propylene glycol lowers the activity. These additives are especially used in foodstuffs with intermediate moisture content (15–35% with an a_w of 0.6–0.8) and those kept for a long time (biscuits, dates, fruit spreads, large sausages). Foods so treated have great stability, even without pasteurization or refrigeration; with adequate packaging they may be kept for several months. They have a soft structure and need no preparation before being eaten.

II.   WATER ACTIVITY AND MODIFICATION OF FOODS

In this section, the concept of biological activity of water will be examined to see how it is of the utmost importance in food since it enables the carrying out of a policy of food protection by controlling physical and chemical deterioration, enzyme activity and the growth of microbial populations.

1.   Chemical and enzyme alterations

1.1   *Oxidation reactions*
Fig. 7.4 shows four phases:

$a_w < 0.1–0.2$

Oxidation is very fast, reactions develop according to a general process which comprises:

- initiation by the formation of free radicals on the carbon adjacent to the double bonds of unsaturated fatty acids (or of each unsaturated aliphatic group, or aromatic);

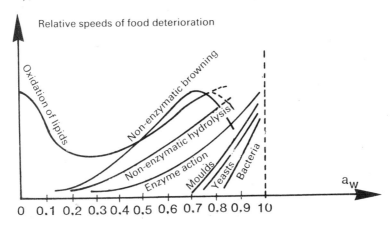

Fig. 7.4 — Speed of deterioration of foods as a function of water activity.

- binding of oxygen on these free radicals with formation of peroxides;
- formation of carbonyl compounds after degradation of the peroxides and scission of the carbon chain.

The consequence of this is the liberation of foul-smelling volatile compounds, the destruction of fat-soluble vitamins, the formation of complexes, the lowering of solubility and digestibility of proteins.

Maximal stability is obtained when the single layer of water molecules ($a_w = 0.2$) hinders the passage of oxygen to the lipids or enters into competition with the oxygen molecules to occupy the absorption sites.

$0.2 < a_w < 0.5$

The active peroxides are at a low concentration because a high proportion of them bind water. The antioxidants are mobile and active whilst the metallic catalysts are not very active because of hydration.

$a_w > 0.5$

The metallic catalysts diffuse freely towards the sites of oxidation and the catalyst has greater power than the antioxidant effect in the water. Consequently, the oxidation speeds up.

$a_w > 0.9$

At very high levels of activity, oxidation slows down; this is due to the effect of dilution (law of mass action).

1.2 Condensation reactions

The most important are the non-enzymatic browning reactions, also called Maillard reactions. The maximal speed of the reaction is attained at activities between 0.5 and 0.7, since the mobility of the reactants is optimal in this zone.

For $a_w > 0.6$–0.7 the speed decreases (effect of the law of mass action) because this corresponds to a tripling in water content. The water also restrains the reaction if $a_w > 0.75$, because it inhibits the reactions of internal dehydration affecting the Amadori compounds formed through the Maillard reactions.

1.3 Enzyme reactions

Often these reactions do not start if $a_w > 0.1$–0.2 and if they have a course parallel to the isotherms (as in the case of hydrolysis).

Enzyme activity follows water activity because of the greater mobility of the reactants at a high level of water content (as in the case of reactions in water phase).

There is an exception in the case of the lipases: they are active at very low or nil levels of water content and at very low temperature (frozen fish). In fact, the contact between the enzyme and the substrate may be made without water. Also, products destined for dehydration and freezing are blanched (destruction of enzymes such as oxidases and lipases).

2. Development of micro-organisms

For the majority of micro-organisms, optimum growth is achieved at $0.92 < a_w < 0.99$ (Fig. 7.4). The microbial stability is therefore very great in products which are dehydrated ($a_w = 0.2$–0.4) or at intermediate moisture content ($a_w = 0.6$–0.8) and in products where the water activity has been lessened by the addition of salt or sugar (as in cheese, large sausages, jams).

The minimal levels of water activity required differ according to the micro-organism: 0.91 for bacteria, 0.88 for yeasts, 0.80 for moulds. However, certain species may exhibit lower minimal values of a_w for growth; thus the halophilic bacteria, the xerophilic moulds and the osmophilic yeasts develop at a_w 0.75, 0.65 and 0.60, respectively.

Pathogenic or toxic bacteria do not multiply at water activity levels of less than 0.85–0.90. For moulds, the lower limit is 0.7–0.8, which can be dangerous if mycotoxins are produced.

8

Vitamins

I. GENERAL OBSERVATIONS

Vitamins are chemical substances which the organism is not capable of synthesizing. They are necessary for growth and the functioning of the organism and must therefore be obtained in regular and periodic fashion through the diet.

They belong to very varied chemical groups. They are classified artificially according to their solubility in water (water-soluble vitamins) or in lipids (fat-soluble vitamins). This distinction is a useful one, however, since it means that not too confused a picture is drawn of the foods where vitamins are to be found and that all aspects of their preservation are better understood. Water-soluble vitamins leach into water in the course of operations like soaking and cooking — which has very important practical consequences.

There is a need to draw a distinction between the vitamin, a chemically defined product, and the vitamin activity, which other provitamins or active derivatives may have as well as the vitamin itself.

Most often, vitamins have a co-factor role in enzyme and membrane systems. The absence of a vitamin stunts growth and leads to a specific deficiency disease. In practice, in man, straight deficiencies are exceptional, especially in developed countries. They are most often associated with a state of malnutrition, which plays a major role in the clinical picture. Finally, it must be pointed out that a high consumption of some drugs can lead to a neutralizing effect on a vitamin and lead to symptoms of avitaminosis.

Table 8.1 sums up the state of knowledge of the biological role, daily requirements and main food sources of vitamins.

Table 8.1 — Biological role of vitamins and daily requirements

Vitamins	Chemical name	Daily requirement	Biological role	Main sources
I. FAT-SOLUBLE VITAMINS				
Group A (Fig. 4.3)	Retinol or axerophtol	0.75–1.2 mg	• Derived from β-carotene (=provitamin A) • Photosensitive component of rhodopsin • Helps the formation of mucopolysaccharide-sulphates • Participates in the synthesis of the sex steroids • Plays a role at the level of the cellular membranes • 'Growth' vitamin • Its deficiency leads to a loss of twilight vision or to hemeralopia, a hyperkeratinization of the skin	• Animal livers (notably of fish), butter, milk, cheese, eggs • In the form of provitamins in the carotenoids of many vegetables: lettuce, spinach, carrots
Acetate: R=CO CH₃ Palmitate: R=CO (CH₂)₁₄ CH₃				
Group D (Fig. 4.3).	D₂ or ergocalciferol D₃ or cholecalciferol	2.5 µg	• Increases the intestinal absorption of calcium and phosphorous and the tubular reabsorption of calcium • Mobilizes the calcium at the expense of the old bone to help its deposition in the young bone. It behaves as a hypercalcaemia hormone • Deficiency states (due to diet and/or lack of exposure to sun) lead to rickets in the child and osteomalacia in the adult	• Liver, fatty fish, milk, butter
Vitamin D₂				

Vitamin D₃

- At high dosage, vitamin D results in serious signs of hypervitaminoses, hypercalcaemia, renal insufficiency, arterial hypertension

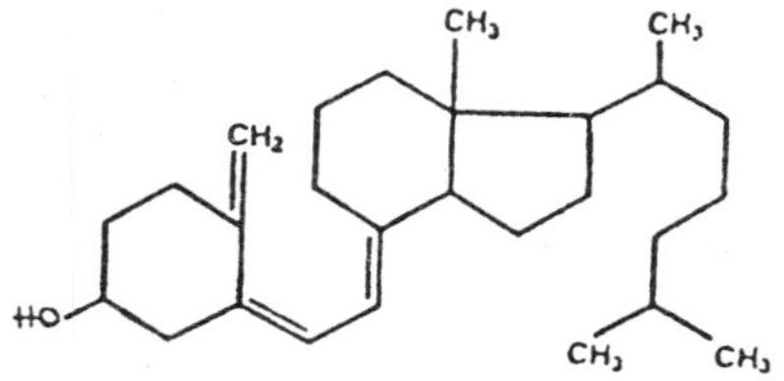

Vitamin E

α-tocopherol

5–15 mg (increase with richness of diet in lipids).

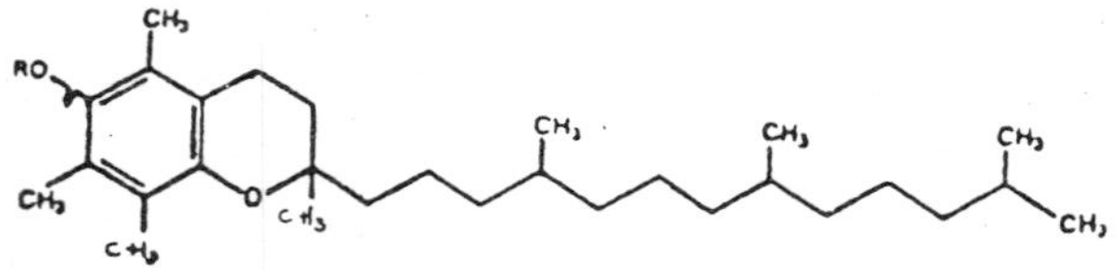

d₁-α-tocopherol: R=H;
d₁-α-tocopherol acetate: R=CO CH₃

- Powerful antioxidant which protects essential fatty acids, vitamins A and C, and cellular membranes
- Deficiency states do not seem to exist in man and the therapeutic effects in sterility treatments are debatable and probably nil
- No hypervitaminosis

- Cereal seed oils
- Green organic plant matter (green salad plants, cabbage, spinach)
- Liver, milk, butter, eggs, lard

Group K

K₁ or phylloquinone
K₂ or difarnesyl-naphthoquinone
K₃ or methylnaphtho-quinone (vit. from synthesis).

1 mg

- Necessary for the synthesis of II, VII, IX and X factors in the prothrombin complex which are involved in blood coagulation. Anti-haemorrhagic vitamin

- Liver, meat
- Spinach, green cabbage, strawberries

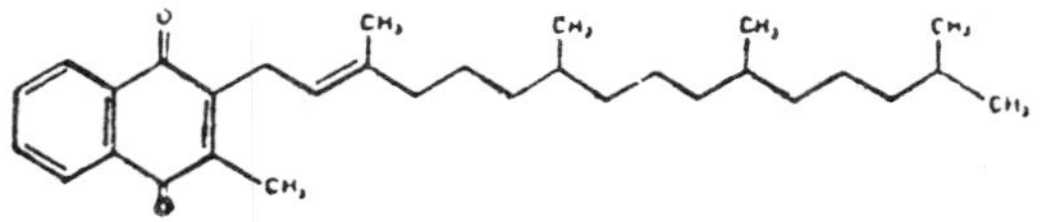

II. WATER-SOLUBLE VITAMINS

Group B.
Vitamin B₁ — Aneurin or thiamin hydrochloride   1.5 mg

Hydrochloride: X=Cl, HCl
Mononitrate: X=NO₃

- Coenzyme (thiamin pyrophosphate) of several decarboxylases
- Takes part in the assimilation and metabolism of carbohydrates.
- Deficiency leads to beri-beri, neuritis and polyneuritis

- Yeasts, cereal grains, leguminous plants, dried vegetables, dried fruit and oleaginous plants, meat, offal, egg yolk

Vitamin B₂ — Riboflavin or lactoflavin   1.5 mg

Riboflavine : R =OH.

Phosphate : R =O – P = O / ONa \ OH

- Factor in growth
- Enters into the make-up of coenzymes and hydrogen carriers
- Closely linked with protein metabolism
- Deficiency leads to dryness of the mucous membranes, conjunctivitis, one of the symptoms of beri-beri

- Yeasts, cereals, liver, milk, eggs, meat

Vitamin B₃ or vitamin PP — Nicotinamide or niacin   10–20 mg

Nicotinic acid   Nicotinamide

- Involved with the hydrogen carriers (NAD-NADP)
- May be supplemented by the association: vitamin B₂+vitamin B₆+tryptophan
- Its deficiency leads to pellagra, with associated diarrhoea, dementia and dermatitis

- Yeast, wheat, almonds, fish (especially salmon), liver, meat

Vitamin B$_5$	Pantothenic acid 10 mg CH$_2$OH–C(CH$_3$)$_2$–CHOH–CO–NH–CH$_2$–CH$_2$–COOH	• Enters into the make-up of coenzyme A • Very widespread in nature • No known deficiency	• Yeast, liver, eggs, meat, fish, cereals
Vitamin B$_6$	Pyridoxin or pyridoxal 1.5 mg	• Coenzyme of many enzymes, particularly of the transaminases • Involved in the elaboration of biogenic amines of the central nervous system • Is active in the saturation and desaturation of fatty acids • Enters into the synthesis of nicotinic acid • Its deficiency causes cutaneous lesions, glossitis, nausea, anaemia, nervous problems	• Yeasts, cereal germs • Meat, liver, offal • Egg yolk • Fish • Milk
Vitamin B$_8$	Biotin 150–300 µg	• Coenzyme in decarboxylation reactions and in transcarboxylation • Involved in the synthesis of fatty acids • Its deficiency leads to cutaneous trophic problems	• Liver, kidneys, egg yolk, chocolate, leguminous plants, mushrooms
Vitamin B$_9$	Folic acid 200–400 µg	• Permits the synthesis of serine, of nucleic acids with purine and pyrimidine bases • Is active in the metabolism of tyrosine, ascorbic acid, folic acid and B$_{12}$	• Green vegetables • Liver, kidneys • Meat, eggs

Vitamin B$_{12}$ — Cyanocobalamin — 2 μg

- Extrinsic factor for the antipernicious anaemia factor
- Is active in the metabolism of carbohydrates by the central nervous system
- Plays the role of coenzyme in a transformation reaction of coenzyme A
- Deficiency (as with folates) blocks DNA synthesis

- Yeast
- Meat, liver, kidneys
- Fatty fish

Vitamin C — L-ascorbic acid — 10–75 mg

- Carrier of H$^+$ ions (equilibrium ascorbic acid → dehydroascorbic acid)
- Indispensable to collagen synthesis
- Reduces iron to ferrous state and facilitates its absorption
- Participates in the biosynthesis of glucocorticoids
- Deficiency leads to scurvy with asthenia, and gum disease with bleeding (gingivitis)

- Fresh vegetables

II. STABILITY OF VITAMINS

For several reasons the food industry is placing more and more importance on the preservation of vitamins:

— nutrition experts are interested in the losses caused by food processing, in order to ascertain the real vitamin content of the processed food;
— technologists are evaluating the extent to which processes currently used in the food industry effect the preservation of these substances and are making changes where possible to improve them;
— those responsible for quality control have to be satisfied that the vitamin content of the product is as specified. In addition, changes in the vitamin content often indicate the overall product quality.

Vitamins belong to a great variety of chemical groups; each compound may react differently according to the conditions. The following are some examples of this:
— group A vitamins are most sensitive to oxygen and light, because of the polyenic structure of the side chain;
— the structure of vitamin B_1, a compound of pyrimidine and thiazole, is the reason for the thermal sensitivity of thiamin.
— niacin is virtually indestructible through food processing. Some may be lost through washing;
— the ene-diol nature of ascorbic acid is of value technologically, because of its reducing properties.

In the course of manufacture, storage and preparation of food products, vitamins are exposed to a series of physicochemical factors: temperature, humidity, pH, oxygen, light and enzymic activity. These factors give rise to a multitude of possible combinations, as each process is based on a multitude of different conditions.

It is to be borne in mind, however, that in most cases, excellent stability can be obtained in the dry food preparations.

9

Pigments

There are many other substances, in addition to those already mentioned in previous chapters, which are responsible for the colour of a certain number of foods. The three broad categories of the main natural pigments are:

— the porphyrin pigments, which include the chlorophylls, the blood pigments (for example myoglobin and haemoglobin, mentioned in Chapter 14);
— the carotenoids (among which β-carotene, the forerunner of vitamin A (Chapter 8), may be especially mentioned), lycopene, the xanthophylls;
— the flavonoids and their derivatives.

Others also deserve a mention: the tannins, the betalains, the quinones and the xanthones. In Chapter 17 we discuss artificial food colourings.

I. THE CHLOROPHYLLS

1. Structure

There is very little structural difference (Fig. 9.1) between the pigments chlorophyll a and chlorophyll b, which occur in the chloroplasts of higher plants. The two chlorophylls have a tetrapyrrole nucleus, rather like that of the haem (Fig. 14.2) but with one Mg^{2+} atom in the centre. The molecule is liposoluble because of the long phytyl hydrocarbon side chain (at C_{20}).

Chlorophyll a seems to be the main pigment responsible for photosynthesis since its absorption spectrum — which shows two peaks, at 430 and 680 nm — coincides quite well with the optimal efficiency curve for light in photosynthesis as a function of wavelength.

The chlorophylls are associated in chloroplasts with smaller particles, the grana, composed of lamellae and stroma. The chlorophyll molecules are embedded in the lamellae and are closely associated with lipids, proteins and lipoproteins.

2. Degradation

There are several possible routes:

H₂=CH   X

H₃C—   —CH=CH₂

—N   N—

Mg

—N   N—

H₃C—   —CH₃

CH₂   COOCH₃

COOC₂₀H₃₉

Fig. 9.1 — Structure of chlorophylls a and b. a: X=–CH₃ b: X=–CHO.

— Heat treatment or addition of H^+ ions will catalyse the removal of the magnesium, as can be seen in cooking in water or steam. It is possible to lessen the action of heat through the use of high-temperature short-time thermal treatments or by raising the pH of the medium.
— Chlorophyllase catalyses the cleavage of phytol. This fairly heat-resistant enzyme is found only in certain plants and is only activated during maturation.
— Various types of oxidation (enzymatic, photo-oxidation) may occur and colourless forms may be produced by the opening through oxidation of the tetrapyrrole nucleus. Certain volatile compounds speed up (ethylene) or slow down (carbon dioxide) the degradation of the chlorophyll.

It is important to note that the compounds obtained after the removal of magnesium (pheophytin) or following the phytol removal (chlorophyllide) may both be oxidized to yield pheophorbide, and then chlorins and brown-coloured purpurines.

These degradation reactions are summarized below:

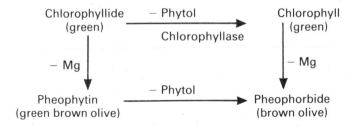

II. FLAVONOIDS AND THEIR DERIVATIVES

1. Structure

These substances have the following basic structure:

It is simply the extent of delocalization of the electrons of the central heterocyclic ring which is responsible for the different red or violet colours of the anthocyanins, the yellows of the flavones, or the colourlessness of certain flavonoids. From a certain level of delocalization, the flavylium cation starts to absorb — as illustrated below — within the visible spectrum, showing first yellow colouration, then orange, red and violet (maximum absorption levels are shown within square brackets).

Naringin
(Flavanone) [290 nm]

Pelargonidin
(Anthocyanidin) [520 nm]

Catechin
(Flavanol) [275 nm]

Arigenin
(Flavone) [269 and 336 nm]

Amongst the many pigments derived from this structure, several are worthy of note.

— *Anthocyanins.* In food biochemistry, only six of these colourings are of importance. In addition to the presence of an –OH group on the 3, 5 and 7 carbons, there are differences in the substitution of hydroxyl or methoxyl groups on the 3', 4' and 5' carbons of the B ring. These compounds, which, according to their structure, are red, blue or violet, usually occur in the form of anthocyanins, meaning linked to one or several sugars. The tint of these pigments changes either as a function of the pH or when the sugar group is removed by hydrolysis. Certain flavonoids, such as leucocyanidin, are colourless. In the oxidation process (heating in acid medium) these colourless compounds undergo transformation into anthocyanidins; the tint turns towards pink or red (this is what happens with certain varieties of apples, pears, cabbages and beans). For this reason we prefer to call them proanthocyanidins.

— *Flavonoids*, usually yellow, are characterized by the presence of a carbonyl group at position 4 and a hydroxyl group on position 3. In contrast to the anthocyanidins, the sugar group is usually linked to position 7. Quercitin and myricetin are found amongst the most common flavonoids.

— *Flavanones* show strong similarity in structure to flavonoids but have no −OH group in position 3. Some flavonoids, responsible for the bitter taste of some grapefruit, lemons and oranges, are placed in this category: naringin (naringinol linked to glucose and rhamnose), and hesperidin (Chapter 2, §XII.2).

2.   Importance in food technology

The electrophilic character of the basic structure of these pigments explains their great reactivity. Reactions which may give rise to colourless compounds are undesirable for the fruit and vegetable industry. With these products it is also important to control the pH, the temperature and the favourable or unfavourable conditions for oxidation during storage. The reaction of the red anthocyanins of cherries with the tin in preserving cans and the appearance of a mauve colouration, the removal of sulphur from fruit through heating or acidification, allowing the natural colour to regenerate are examples.

Flavonol glycosides are very common. They are to be found in over half the total number of higher plant species. They represent more than 30% of the dry extract in tea and contribute to its astringent quality.

However, the less commonly found flavonols are very interesting. For instance, treatment of naringin in the peel with an L-rhamnosidase yields prunine, which is less bitter. Naringenin, a non-bitter compound, may be obtained through the action of a β-D-glucosidase on this flavonoid (Fig. 9.2). α-L-rhamnosidase may also react with hesperidin to yield dehydrochalcone hesperidin glucoside, a sweet-tasting substance used as a sweetener.

III   OTHER COMPOUNDS

Along with these two broad categories of pigments, foods of plant origin contain numerous phenolic compounds which, through enzymic transformation, may give rise to coloured polymers, usually brown or black.

1.   Tannins

Tannins are a good example of this type of compound, since here two main groups may be distinguished: condensed tannins (also known at catechins), where the chemical structure is very close to that of the anthocyanidins, and hydrolysable tannins, including the gallotannins and ellagitannins, which stem from the esterification of the five alcohol functions of glucose by various polyphenolic acids (Chapter 12, §IV).

2.   Betalains

Betalains look rather like anthocyanins, hence their false naming as nitrogen anthocyanins. They all have the same basic structure and their colour results from the resonance between the different mesomeric structures (Fig. 9.3).

The best known betalains are those of red beetroot, from which two of the principal pigments, betanidin and vulgaxanthin, are illustrated in Fig. 9.3.

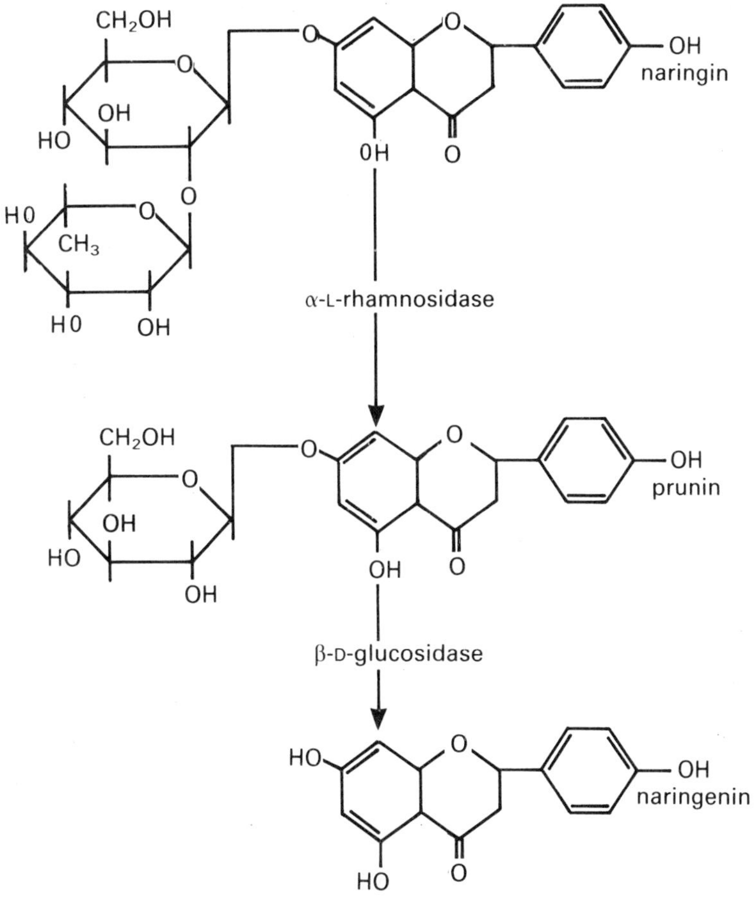

Fig. 9.2 — Debitterization of naringin.

3. Quinones and xanthones

These comprise a group of pigments commonly found in flowers, mushrooms, algae and bacteria. Among the 200 compounds identified, the naphthoquinones present most interest as colourings or purgatives.

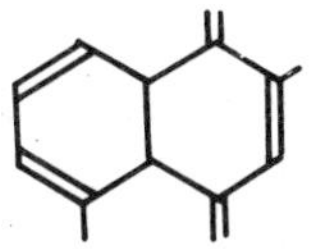

Naphthoquinone 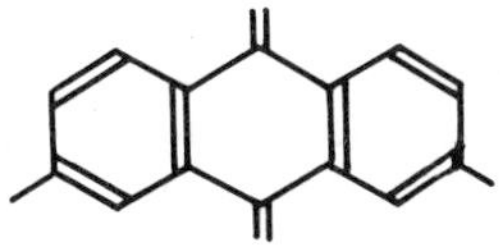   Anthraquinone

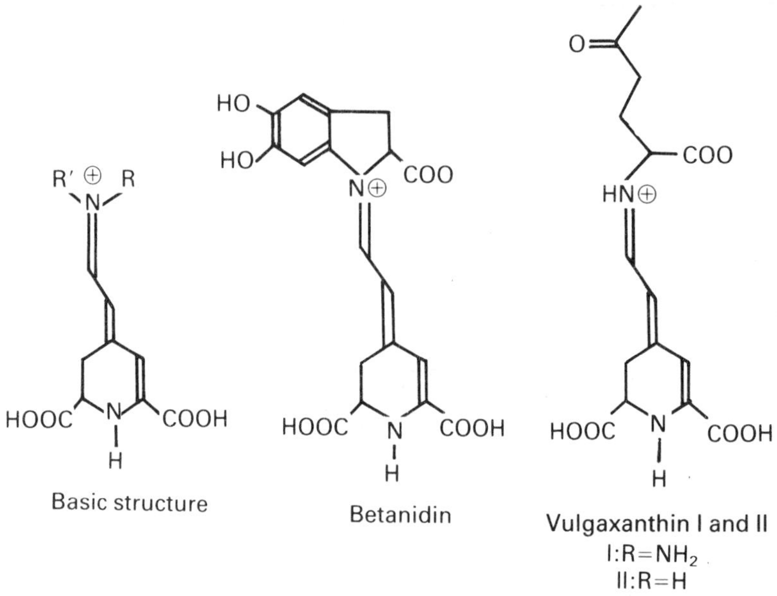

Fig. 9.3 — Structure of betalain derivatives.

Quinones may result from the enzymatic oxidation of polyphenols according to the general pattern:

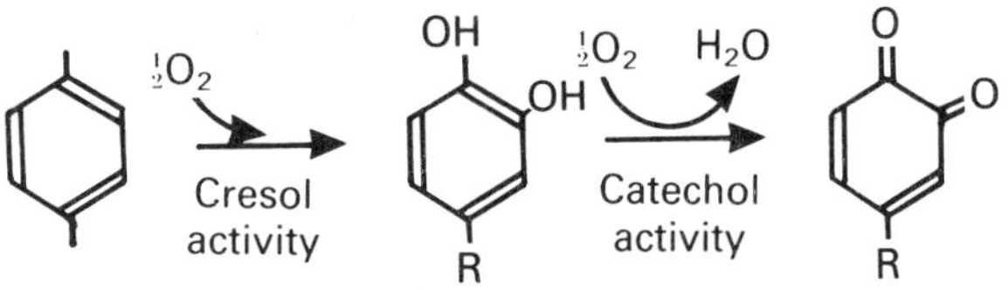

4.   Melanins

Pigments which are formed by enzymic browning are designated by the general term *melanins*. Although they are eventually brown/black in colour, intermediary tints may be observed: pink, red, blue/black. The formation of these polymers from quinones takes place without enzymic intervention.

Taken overall, these reactions give rise to colour problems in some fruits and vegetables. For instance, a bad colour may develop when plant tissues are diseased or damaged by thermal or mechanical trauma. On the other hand, in some instances a particular shade of browning may be deliberately sought in the ripening or drying processes for some plant products (dates, cocoa beans and tea).

Part II
Biochemistry of the principal foods

10

Cereals — bread

I. GENERAL OBSERVATIONS ON CEREALS

Cereals are a group of cultivated plants belonging, botanically, to the Gramineae family. Their grains are of major interest for human and animal feeding due to their abundance and composition. The food grains belong to about 10 plant species. The three most used in the present day are wheat, maize, and barley.

To these must be added those cereals which have become of secondary importance nowadays, in Europe: barley, rye, sorghum, mixed crop of wheat and rye, oats, buckwheat, millet, and triticale (hybrid of wheat and rye).

Table 10.1 shows the differences in composition between cereal grains, which are above all starchy, and some other grains rich in proteins and oil, which will be looked at later. These differences only partially explain the uses to which they are put; the quality of the proteins has much to do with their usage (Table 10.2).

Cereal flours contain, besides the starch, reserve proteins which are water-insoluble. In wheat, these proteins belong to two families, the gliadins and the glutenins, which are not found elsewhere. When they are present in the right proportion they make it possible to obtain a dough which is extensible (gliadin property) and elastic (glutenin property) which will make bread. Only two cereals lend themselves well to modern bread-making: soft wheat, in particular, and, to a very small degree, rye. Hybrids have been obtained from these two species. In addition, hard wheat is very suitable for making food pastas, which are being eaten more and more.

Other cereals have a variety of uses in food. One of the most universal is the preparation of alcoholic drinks, in two stages: hydrolysis of the starch by one or several amylase(s), and maltose or glucose fermentation using yeast. This is the procedure for making whisky and beer (barley), vodka (wheat), American bourbon (rye), Japanese sake (rice), etc. However, the most general usage of cereals is in cooking, either directly in the form of grain or flour, in starch form (cornflour from

Table 10.1 — Average composition of grains and seeds and micro-organisms used as food. (% of dry weight)[a]

	Proteins[b]	Lipids	Total carbohydrates[c]
Grains and seeds			
— amylaceous			
Wheat	12	2	80
Maize	12	6.5	79
Rice	9	2	82
— oleaginous and proteinaceous			
Peanut	28	50	15
Rape	30	40	20
Soya	38	21	25
Sunflower	35	45	5
— amylaceous and proteinaceous			
Broad bean	26	1.5	57
Haricot bean (white)	21	1.5	58
Lentil	26	1	56
Micro-organisms			
Spirulina	70	8	18
Yeast (lactic)	50	10	33

[a] Commercial products have a water content of 6–14%.
[b] Including the nucleic acids.
[c] The sum of the soluble carbohydrates (osides, oligosugars and starch) and the fibre; the fibre content is very variable.

Table 10.2 — Protein fractions of cereals (% of albumin proteins)

	Wheat	Rye	Barley	Oats	Rice	Maize	Sorghum
1. *Common water-soluble proteins*							
Albumins (water-soluble)	9	8	12	10	5	4	4
Globulins (soluble in salt solution)	6	10	12	55	10	3	9
2. *'Insoluble' reserve proteins (gluten)*							
Prolamines (soluble in ethanol 65–75%)	45	42	52	12	7	55	48
Glutenins (alkali- or acid-soluble)	40	40	24	23	78	38	37

maize), or as semolina, etc. In developed countries, increasing use is made of wheat and especially maize for animal feed.

II. CEREAL GRAINS — COMPOSITION

1. Food fibre

Before use, cereal kernels are often treated mechanically to remove the external layers which form the husk or seed coats. This part is in fact rich in dietary fibre, cellulose, silicon dioxide and lignin; it is hard to digest, if not inedible (rice hulls). Although this removal is helpful to the digestive process it lowers the vitamin and enzyme content of the flour,so that where the diet is largely composed of cereals a health problem may arise; for example the Vitamin B_1 deficiency in polished rice can be the cause of beri-beri.

Nowadays, dietary fibre is regarded as essential, as it absorbs water and provides roughage for the bowels, assisting intestinal transit. Changes in dietary trends involving a reduction in fibre intake had the effect of showing up certain characteristics typical of each constituent: cellulose (β-glucosan, predominant in bran), A and B hemicelluloses (xylans and mannosans), pectin (galacturonides), lignin (phenylpropenol polymer).

The fibre content of flours and grains varies a great deal, depending on their origin. In whole wheat and soya flours, values of close to 3% of dry matter may be permitted.

2. Composition of the wheat grain

In the case of wheat, the main parts of the grain have the characteristics outlined in Table 10.3. The aleurone layer, which surrounds the kernel , is rich in proteins and in minerals; it is usually eliminated with the bran in the course of sifting of the raw flour at the normal extraction level (in Europe, 75–80% of ground flours); in contrast, it is present in 'wholemeal' flours, which are thus enriched in the essential amino acids (Met/Cys, Val, Leu, Lys).

Table 10.3 — Principal parts of wheat grain (% of dry weight)

	Proportion	Proteins	Lipids	Minerals
Whole grain	—	12	2	2
Endosperm (flour)	80	10	1.2	0.6
Aleurone[a]	8	18	8.5	15
Seed coats[a]	8.5	6	1	3.5
Germ	3.5	25	10	4.5

[a] Forming bran.

Since the endosperm is heavier than the husk, there is a better flour yield when the specific weight of the wheat is high. Flours are also characterized by their ash content, which is lower the lower the extraction level: bread flour 0.55% or less, biscuit flour 0.45% or less.

Starch is always the main constituent of cereal flour (Chapter 3). In flour from natural wheat, with 12–13% water, there is about 75% starch. It is a reserve for the grain, comparable to fats in the animal. It is distributed in the albumen in separate granules, the diameter and shape of which vary with the species (see diagrams below); in wheat grain their dimension varies between 2 and 35 μm. Starch granules are visible under the microscope with low magnification ; they are characterized by the presence of a more or less pronounced 'equatorial groove'.

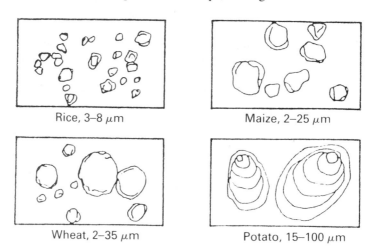

Rice, 3–8 μm   Maize, 2–25 μm

Wheat, 2–35 μm   Potato, 15–100 μm

Reserve proteins are found dispersed in the form of smaller grains (2–6 μm); these 'protein bodies' are subjected to a disordering process in some species, such as wheat. In the grain of mature wheat the reserve proteins adhere to the starch granules. Although these proteins are about 8 times less abundant in flour than starch is, they are the ones which display the most individual characteristics and they will be described here.

III.   RESERVE PROTEINS

The term 'gluten proteins' is also used to describe the reserve proteins in the case of cereals which give rise to the following phenomenon: when dough is kneaded under running water, a viscous and elastic mass is obtained, the 'gluten', which is starch-free. The notion of 'gluten' is somewhat artificial. This protein substance is formed by modification of the disulphide bond, the kneading supplying the necessary energy.

Table 10.2 shows the proportions of the two types of 'gluten' proteins. It can be seen that the flours from wheat, rye and to a lesser degree sorghum have in some respect similar composition, with approximately equal values for both types, around 40%. The two types are:

— *prolamines*: proteins soluble in fairly concentrated ethanol; the name changes with the species: wheat *gliadin*, barley *hordein*, rye *secalin*, etc.

— *glutenins*: proteins soluble in acid or dilute alkaline solutions, or in dissociating agents (urea, guanidine, sucrose esters).

The amino acid composition of wheat gliadin and glutenin (Table 10.4) shows, in comparison with globulin, a very high level of glutamine, a high proline content and a very low basic amino acid content (Lys, His, Arg). From this it may be concluded that the gluten proteins are little charged at neutral pH (pH close to 7) and that electrostatic reactions do not play an important role in bread-making. However, the formation of hydrogen bonds, especially in glutamine, is important, and these are associated with hydrophobic reactions; about 74% of the side chains in each of these proteins are capable of forming bonds and interactions as the dough is being prepared.

Table 10.4 — Amino acid composition of wheat proteins (molecules % molecules)

	Gliadin	Glutenin	Globulin
Glycine	3.1	7.5	9.5
Alanine	3.3	4.4	6.1
Valine	4.8	4.8	2.4
Leucine	7.0	6.5	9.0
Isoleucine	4.3	3.7	1.4
Phenylalanine	4.3	3.6	2.4
Proline	16.2	11.9	3.6
Tryptophan	0.4	1.3	—
Serine	6.1	7.0	11.1
Threonine	2.4	3.5	4.8
Tyrosine	1.8	2.5	1.6
Cysteine	3.3	2.6	13.4
Methionine	1.2	1.4	0.4
Aspartic acid	2.8	3.6	6.0
Glutamic acid[a]	34.5	28.9	5.1
Lysine	0.6	2.0	10.6
Histidine	1.9	1.9	1.8
Arginine	2.0	3.0	10.6

[a] Almost entirely in the form of glutamine.

The very low lysine and tryptophan contents in the gluten proteins should also be noted. In certain gliadins, like that in cornflour from maize, the contents tend towards zero. This has implications for public health, particularly in regions where maize is the basic dietary food (causing, for example, pellagra in Yugoslavia and in Mexico).

Some biochemical mutants of wheat and barley have been obtained in which there is a much higher glutenin/prolamine ratio, which produces an increase in the lysine content (of 3–4% for barley). But it should be noted that the mutants produce very little starch and yield less grain.

It can be seen that the lysine content has a negative correlation with the protein content of the grain, and the latter has a negative correlation with the grain yield.

IV. WHEAT GLIADINS

The wheat gliadins have great polymorphism, as can be seen in starch gel electrophoresis or by HPLC chromatography in the reverse phase, which reveal from 20 to nearly 40 constituents. In practice, these techniques are used mainly to identify varieties of wheat and barley. From the biochemical point of view, such variety of protein sequences does not exist; in fact there are only 4 gliadins in wheat, whose molecular mass varies from 30 000 to 40 000 Da and which show genetic polymorphism. These molecules appear to form single cations, but it is not known whether or not the lack of quaternary structure is due to the denaturing action of the ethanol which is used to dissolve them. On the other hand, the tertiary structure in 3 gliadins (α, β, and γ) is shown by the disulphide intramolecular bridges but not in the fourth gliadin (ω).

The sequences of the amino acids have been determined. The abundance of glutamine in the α- and β-gliadins appears mainly in the first two-thirds of the molecule; towards the end of the first half, the presence of a peptide formed by 18 consecutive Gln residues should be noted. It has been shown that a serious problem in the capacity to digest foods, which is called 'coeliac disease' and appears in susceptible people, is caused by peptides rich in Gln resulting from the proteolysis of gliadins.

Undenatured gliadin has been obtained by ultracentrifugation of the gluten. Experiments carried out with reconstituted flours have shown that gliadin contributes to the viscosity and extensibility of the dough.

V. GLUTENINS

The glutenins are very polymorphic because of their marked tendency to gather together, mainly through hydrogen bonds, hydrophobic interactions and disulphide bridges. The molecular mass of large aggregates is more than one million Da. After the rupture of the —S—S— bands by a reactive reducer, 'sub-units' are the end product. Their masses vary from 20 000 to 130 000 Da and three types are distinguished:

— A sub-units: small mass (20 000 to 60 000 Da), the richest in basic amino acids, insoluble in ethanol.
— B sub-units: of 60 000 to 130 000 Da, rich in Gln, Pro and Gly, without cysteine, insoluble in ethanol, with a great surface hydrophobicity allowing associations of great molecular mass.
— C sub-units: close to gliadins, soluble in ethanol, molecular mass about 40 000 Da.

These sub-units inter-associate through non-covalent bonds. It should be noted that B sub-unit types are not present in hard wheats, which are not suitable for bread-making. The large-sized complexes are the cause of the elasticity of gluten and are good for bread-making.

When glutenins are dissolved in 0.1 M acetic acid, the presence of a 'protein residue' may be seen. This comprises the same sub-units A, B and C, but there is a positive correlation between their abundance and the 'bakery potential' of a flour (see later). In the case of wheat, the proportion of protein residue depends on the variety; but it must also be stressed that the method of extraction has a bearing on the result.

VI.   BIOCHEMICAL POLYMORPHISM OF PLANT PROTEINS

Given the economic importance of plant proteins, the improvement in yield and in the nutritional value of cultivated plants must be a permanent objective. In order to achieve this end, the person making the selection modifies the protein composition in order to obtain properties required for quality. Thus it becomes necessary to know which genes control the proteins, their respective contents and the way in which they act on quality.

It is now appreciated that the biochemical polymorphism of proteins is much greater than was supposed a few years ago. To this must be added the fact that the electrophoresis technique underestimates the true variability by a factor of about 2.

However, even though this analytical tool is imperfect, it has permitted the resolution of the problem of identification of varieties of many species and the establishment of the relationship between various agronomic characteristics and multiple forms. The example taken is the case of barley proteins, which have been the subject of a great deal of work in view of their importance in malting and brewing. The three main groups of proteins from barley albumen, called hordeins, have been identified in zones D (100000–110000 Da), C (55000–85000 Da) and B (28000–50000 Da). The proteins have their structure genes localized in the loci hord-3 for the zone D proteins, hord-1 for the zone C proteins and hord-2 for the zone B proteins. These three loci are situated on the 5 chromosome of barley. The polymorphism of the proteins in each zone permits identification of barley ecotypes and varieties (Fig. 10.1).

Even when the genetic placement of the structure genes of all cereal proteins is known, the chronology of the biosynthesis of these molecules would remain to be explored. In general, it can be confirmed that the reserve proteins of cereals are synthesized after a certain period of latency after fertilization of the ovule, then follows a period of rapid accumulation until the grain becomes mature. It is likely to be the same with leguminous plants.

Within the context of this work it is not possible to explore the significance of this biochemical polymorphism. Let it simply be said that genetic heterogeneity certainly represents an advantage for selection.

VII.   BREAD

1.   Flour

Nowadays, bread is seldom made from anything other than wheat flour (the term 'wheaten bread' has fallen out of use). Until quite recently, rye, buckwheat and a

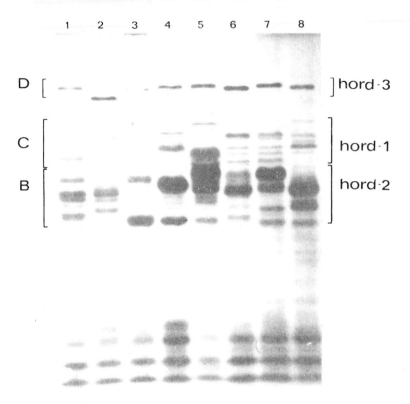

Fig. 10.1 — Electrophorogram of barley proteins in polyacrylamide gel (13% concentration) in the presence of sodium dodecyl sulphate. Varieties of barley: 1 — Himalaya; 2 — Lyallpur; 3 — Maris Canon; 4 — Chiro Chinco; 5 — Nepal; 6 — Intensive I; 7 — Black winter barley; 8 — Nackte Italia. (Document kindly provided by Messrs Montembault & Moll, Tepral Laboratory.)

mixed wheat and rye crop were used in Europe. Many varieties of wheat exist, and they fall into two types:

— soft wheat (*Triticum aestivum*), the flour from which is used in bread and biscuits; the most widely cultivated in Europe.
— hard wheat (*Triticum durum*), from which are made semolina, edible pastas, cous-cous; generally cultivated in hot countries (but also in France, where production is increasing). It is richer in proteins and its grain is harder and vitreous, breaking down into semolina rather than being crushed into flour.

The correct choice of variety is essential. Of the more than 80 soft wheat varieties cultivated, some varieties selected because of their high yield are not suited to bread-making.

The composition of wheat flour has already been given (Table 10.3). To this must be added the enzymes present: α- and β-amylases (Chapter 3) and lipase (rancidity factor) in appreciable quantities; and, in small proportions, proteases (endo- and exo-) activated by reducers of –S–S–, and a lipoxygenase which oxidizes non-conjugated double bonds, such as in linoleic acid.

2.   Preparation of the dough

Smooth and homogeneous dough is formed in the course of rapid kneading (20–25 minutes). Rough proportions are as follows: flour 100 kg, water 64 kg, salt 35 grams/litre, yeast 33 grams/litre.

The yeasts used are *Saccharomyces cerevisae* strains specialized for bread-making and cultivated on sugar molasses (brewer's yeast and grain yeasts are no longer used). Their fermenting activity is maximal at about 30°C; above 47°C yeasts die rapidly.

Flour made from broad beans may be incorporated (1%) in the flour at the mill in order to improve quality of the bread. It is a question of increasing the lipoxygenase, which plays the role of an oxidizing agent through the hydroperoxides which it produces. It is a way of improving 'weak' flours, that is to say, those which do not knead well, which do not yield a firm dough and which do not produce a sufficient volume of bread. Moreover, broad bean flour activates the whitening of the dough; it may also be the cause of a flavour defect through hexanal production.

Ascorbic acid is added with water to the dough mixture in order to improve the gluten content (0.002% of the flour).

Numerous other 'bread improvers' have been suggested. In the USA, the millers make up real 'mixes', flours enriched by various additives: soya lecithin, vitamins, etc.

The dough obtained is a complex mixture comprising several phases. Two of these phases are continuous: the network of hydrated gluten, which confers a strong cohesion, and a solution formed with the free water. Two others are discontinuous: the starch grains embedded in the gluten, and the inclusion of air during the course of kneading.

The role of proteins has already been described above. Generally, the most important role in the bread-making process is that of the glutenins because of their ability to form films and networks.

N.B. Traditional 'leavened' bread-making involved the addition of a rather stale piece of dough made days earlier. In this way, not only a strain of yeast was incorporated, but also a mixture of micro-organisms, including products of milk fermentation. The texture and taste (more acid) of the bread was somewhat different from the usual. This method is rarely used today.

3.   Bread fermentation

Fermentation of bread is carried out in two stages, in a medium which is not strictly anaerobic:

(1) The yeast ferments the free sugars in the flour (about 1%). During this time the β-amylase attacks the starch granules damaged in the milling process; maltose and limit dextrins are formed. The α-amylase cleaves the chains into dextrins, which give the β-amylase a new substrate. (In certain countries it is permissible

to add microbial amylases to speed up this phase of amylolysis; in France, only malt may be added. In sprouting wheat there is too much amylase, and so too much degradation, making for the formation of a sticky, crumbly and porous dough.)
(2) The yeast can then develop at the expense of the freed sugars in the fermentation proper. Carbon dioxide gas is produced as well as alcohol and the organic acids: acetic, lactic, propionic, pyruvic.

'Rising' is the name given to the initial fermentation in the vat, where alcohol predominates. After this comes 'proving' of the pieces of dough before they are put in the oven; here the role of the CO_2 is the most important: the volume of the bread triples during this period. The total duration of the fermentation process is about four hours on average, but it may vary according to the bread-making method employed, and especially the type of kneading and the amount of yeast added.

4. Cooking
This is done at about 250°C for 20–30 minutes in an oven with a water-saturated atmosphere.
The following transformations are produced:

— Brisk expansion in the volume of the bread occurs as a result of a swift speed-up in CO_2 production and a reduction in gas solubility; at the same time a film forms on the surface, the precursor of the crust. These two changes stop when the internal temperature rises to about 60°C, whilst the alcohol produced evaporates (so-called oven spring).
— The gluten proteins denature and coagulate from 70°C, they lose their affinity with water, which then moves towards the starch. This water plays an important part, together with CO_2, in the alveolate structure of the bread.
— Crust formation and concomitant distribution of water vapour in the crumb of the loaf occur when the temperature reaches 90–100°C. The temperature of the crumb remains at a little under 100°C.
— Dextrinization takes place, then caramelization from 110°C, and finally there is the appearance of roasted products on the surface. The temperature of the crust reaches 170°C to 230°C. The Maillard reaction between the NH_2 group of proteins and the CO group of a reducing monosaccharide play a part in the colour formation (Chapter 5 §IX).
— In the course of cooking, the starch modifies at about 70°C, going from the semi-crystalline state to the amorphous state; it becomes more hydrophilic. At first accelerated, the amylolysis stops when the β-amylase is rendered inactive (about 75°C). The α-amylase is more thermoresistant: its activity disappears at about 85°C. If there is too much enzyme activity, the excess of small molecules (dextrins and maltose) makes the crumb sticky and the crust too deeply coloured.

5. Cooling of bread
The hot bread is cooled slowly, so that its freshness lasts for 12–18 hours. It is therefore a fragile product. It grows stale even in a humid atmosphere; it is not simply

a drying-out process. Starch 'retrogradation' develops, which starts as soon as the temperature drops to 60°C, the colloid state is modified, with the freeing of hydrated water; the amylopectin 'folds' again, with associated chains, taking a new semi-crystalline state of progressively increasing rigidity. At the same time, the softening of the crust is the consequence of the migration of water away from the crumb.

The rigidity of stale bread may be partially overcome by reheating to about 60°C; in this way, weak bonds become dissociated and, in particular, there is a freeing of the aroma molecules adsorbed on the dried crumb.

Various additives have been recommended for slowing down the staling process; in particular surface active agents such as monoglycerides, which might form a complex with the amylose and stop its diffusion. The term 'softeners' has been used for these agents, which yield an excessively soft crumb. Carbohydrate hydrocolloids (dextrans, carboxymethylcellulose), lecithin, etc., have also been proposed for this purpose.

VIII.   EDIBLE PASTAS

The preparation of pastas is in principle very simple. In the past this was done in the home; nowadays it is done in large factories.

The commercially made pastas result from the drying out of a non-fermented piece of dough, less hydrated than that of bread, and made from fine semolinas of hard wheat: 20–25 litres of water to every 100 kg of semolina. (Addition of local soft wheat is forbidden in France, whereas some other countries allow its addition.) The pasta is then put through processes of lamination and drawing into strands, then dried. Its average composition is as follows: water 9%, proteins 13%, lipids 1.5%, carbohydrates 76%.

The density increases greatly after cooking, from 3 to 5 times.

Pastas are also made using eggs and are thus enriched in protein (32%) and poorer in carbohydrate (57%).

For a long while, food pastas were dried at a moderate temperature (about 60°C), whereas nowadays drying takes place at high temperature (90–100°C).

130

11

Proteins from leguminous plants and single-cell organisms

I. COMPOSITION

A summary of the composition of the grains of cereals and the seeds of leguminous plants was presented in Table 10.1. To this data, Table 11.1 should be added, which

Table 11.1 — Average composition of seeds and tubers (% of dry matter)

	Proteins	Lipids	Carbohydrates (total)	Anti-nutritional factors
Seeds				
Cotton	50	30	12	Gossypol
Soya	40	20	35	Antitrypsin, α-galactosides haemagglutinins
Sunflower	30	45	22	Polyphenols
Field bean	30	2	70	Vicin, antitrypsin
Peanut	25	50	16	
Rape	25	38	30	Erucic acid
Peas	25	2	70	Antitrypsins, phytic acid
Tubers				
Potato	9	0.4	82	Solanine
Yam	9	1	82	
Cassava	3.5	1	85	

Water content: seeds, 7–12%; tubers, 65–78%.

deals with various seeds and tubers of food interest, classified according to their protein content. The composition of legumes was given in Table 1.1(b), where their high water content was stressed (peas 75%, green beans 89%).

The big problem towards the end of the twentieth century concerns world production of proteins, of which there is an increasing shortage. Seeds rich in proteins, particularly those of leguminous plants, could reduce the level of malnutrition. However, there are cost problems, which are linked to the difficulty of cultivating a given plant in a certain country, for example soya in France; and thus the research to find substitutes.

The seeds of leguminous plants generally have a protein content in the region of 25–30% dry weight, but this content is a lot higher in some other plants, such as soya bean and cotton. The two other main categories of compounds, the lipids and carbohydrates vary much more widely between plant varieties, e.g.: the field bean and the pea are amylaceous (starchy); the sunflower and the groundnut are oleaginous (oily, fatty). Rape has a balanced composition, between the three main categories of compounds as well as in the composition of its essential amino acids, something which is rare in plants. It must be stressed that other seeds and tubers are not as useful in this respect, with methionine usually and lysine sometimes, being the limiting factor.

Table 11.1 also shows the presence of some harmful factors in seed and raw tubers. Removal is recommended, but there are sometimes technical complications (in the 'wet process') and increased cost. However, one should mention the successful extraction of protein concentrates from cotton flour (50–60% protein in the product), with the elimination of gossypol; this product is incorporated in wheat flour (about 10%) in certain counties, for bread- and biscuit-making, etc. The green parts of plants are not mentioned in the table; they contain 1–4% protein and 3–7% carbohydrate in the fresh product (at 80–90% water). This is a potential source of proteins not used as human food; the same may be said for the leaves of trees.

The lipids will be looked at later, the starches have already been covered. Here the proteins are our main interest; they are quite different from the proteins looked at in the preceding chapter, because in this case we are dealing mainly with globulins.

II. SOYA BEAN — CONSTITUENTS

Because its seeds are rich in protein and quite rich in lipids, this is the most cultivated plant in the world, and it is also the one which has been the subject of the most extensive scientific and technical research. It is a leguminous herbaceous annual, Asiatic in origin, whose growth on a commercial basis was extended to the USA and Brazil fifty years ago. It is probable that its cultivation in Europe will increase because of some adaptations to climatic and geological conditions.

Table 11.2 shows the average composition of soya beans and the products extracted from them. The industrial treatment scheme is presented in Fig. 11.1. Once the oil is taken out, the flour is like cattle-cake; it is much used in animal feed, but must undergo other treatments before being used as human food. There is a dual aim here: removal of toxic constituents (see later) and enrichment of the proteins, which is the more important.

Table 11.2 — Average composition of products from soya bean

Soya bean product	Water	Protein	Lipids	Carbo-hydrate	Ash	Fibre
Soya beans	6	38	19	32[a]	5	—
Whole flour	5	41	21	25	5.5	2.5
Flour with oil removed	5	53	1	34	5	3
'Concentrated' protein	5	70	0.5	16	5	3.5
Purified protein (isolate)	4	93	0.1	—	3	0.2

[a]Carbohydrates and fibres.

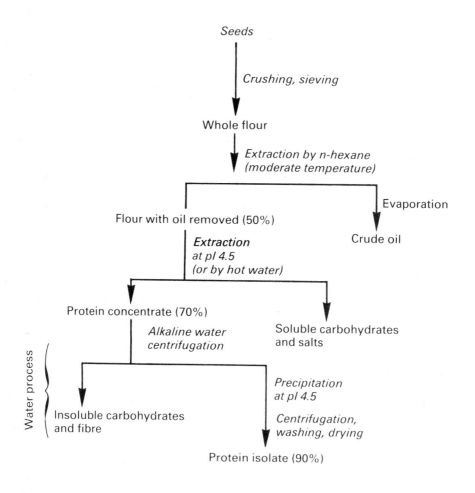

Fig. 1 — Scheme for industrial treatment of soya bean.

These treatments can be applied to other seeds (peas and field beans), where the solubility of the proteins as a function of the pH is known; the isoelectric point (pI) is usually on the acid side, and the solubilization, on the alkaline side. These procedures are designated by the term 'wet process'.

The product obtained by water extraction from the crushed beans, finally after swelling in water, is inappropriately called 'soya milk'. The milky solution is separated by filtering. Its sterilization (115–200°C for 15–20 minutes) improves the taste and the keeping-qualities. This product is mainly found in oriental countries. The only thing it has in common with milk is, of course, its appearance.

III.   CONSTITUENTS OF SOYA BEAN FLOUR

1.   Carbohydrates

Two categories are distinguished:

— insoluble polysaccharides: pectins, arabinogalactans, hemicellulose, cellulose (forming fibres with lignin).
— soluble oligosaccharides, comprising mainly sucrose and its α-galactoside derivatives, which are non-digestible sugars since we do not possess the α-galactosidase (1–6) enzyme. Stachyose, with four monosaccharide residues, is often dominant, at least in soya in which it forms 5% of the mass: then next raffinose (2%) and the other sugars. In actual fact, one part of these sugars is not soluble, and it is found in purified proteins.

Flatulence is the consequence of absorption of these sugars, and results from fermentation by man's intestinal microflora. It is for this reason that attempts are made to eliminate them from the oil-free flour. Ethanol (80% solution) treatment is efficient, but costly.

2.   Lipids

Soya oil is used mainly in margarine and in salad dressings; its richness in linolenic acid (6.5%), not very stable on heating, makes it unsuitable for cooking. The main fatty acids are linoleic acid (50%) and oleic acid (35%). This strongly unsaturated composition causes a problem in practice: the appearance of a rancid flavour during storage of soya.

3.   Proteins

Usually these are separated into four classes, corresponding to fractionation by ultra-centrifugation, and identified by the sedimentation coefficient: 2S, 7S, 11S, 15S. None corresponds to a pure substance; except the 11S fraction which contains predominantly one of the two soya globulins, glycinin, representing about 40% of the total protein. Fraction 7S (35%) contains the other globulin, conglycinin, in comparable amounts to the other biologically active substances: enzymes (β-amylase, lipoxygenase, cytochrome C) and haemagglutinin, having a specificity in relation to D-galactosamine-N-acetylate (this is a 'lectin').

The two minor fractions (each 10–15%) contain, for 2S, trypsin inhibitors of low molecular weight, and for 15S, heavy polymers of molar mass 500 000 and over.

IV. SOYA GLOBULINS

1.   Trypsin inhibitors (2S fraction)

These are small globulins which precipitate only imperfectly at pH 4.5; because of this, the protein concentrate only includes about one third of them. They are usually designated by the letters STI (Soya-bean Trypsin Inhibitor); they are found in quite high proportion (6–8% of the total proteins). They are strongly resistant to heat, to acids and to proteases.

The most abundant is Kunitz's inhibitor, molar mass of which is 21 700. It contains two –S–S– linkages in its structure. The other inhibitor, that of Bowman-Birk, has a molar mass of 7900, but it has seven –S–S– linkages; it represents only 0.4% of the proteins. Both of these form an inactive equimolecular complex with trypsin.

Some other anti-nutritional factors exist in soya, notably one with antichymotrypsin activity. All cause stunting in the growth of animals. They should be reduced or eliminated in the case of human food. Similar sorts of inhibitors to these are found in other leguminous plants but in smaller quantities (haricot bean, pea).

2.   Glycinin (11S fraction)

This is the most insoluble globulin of the soya bean, notably at low temperature (0°C) where it can be separated from the 7S conglycinin. It does not include monosaccharides.

The molecular mass indicated by ultracentrifugation, of about 350 000, is that of a polymer made up of 12 sub-units, of which 6 are basic (B) and 6 are acidic (A). In each of the A and B series, two groups, I and II, are distinguished. For A, the molecular masses vary from 31 000 to 38 000, and for B, from 18 000 to 20 000. We have 6 sub-units forming A and B by a disulphide linkage (A–S–S–B). The primary structure is known. Thermal denaturation starts at 70°C.

Dissociation of the sub-units is easily achieved, at low ionic strength, in the presence of dissociating agents (concentrated urea), reducing agents, or even simply in acid or alkaline medium, or again through heating. The structure is stabilized at high ionic strength. The same phenomenon is found in glycinin, leguminin or arachin of other leguminous plants. This fact is important in relation to the reserve proteins, which have the task of assuring growth of the embryo, to maintain a compact quaternary structure in the 'protein bodies'.

3.   Conglycinin (7S fraction)

This is the essential part of the 7S fraction, which is 30–35% of the total soya protein. It is a glycoprotein which contains about 5% of mannose and glucosamine. The molar mass of about 170 000 corresponds to 3 sub-units, acidic in character; α, α', and β. The characteristic of these compounds is that they do not contain cysteine; moreover, the β sub-unit does not have any methionine either. Thus the molecular associations are not made by disulphide linkage.

Dissociation in its sub-units is carried out in acid or alkaline medium. At an intermediate pH, of between 5 and 10, and at low ionic strength, conglycinin is in the dimeric state (6 sub-units); at higher ionic strength ($\mu \geqslant 0.5$), dissociation occurs.

Again, other leguminous plants have a 7S globulin similar to soya conglycinin (phaseolin of beans, vicillin of peas).

4. Observations

(1) From a technological point of view, there exists a 'conflict of interests' between the anti-nutritional compounds which can only be destroyed by vigorous heat treatment and the functional properties of proteins which require gentle treatment, or none at all, if they are not to be denatured.

(2) Soya bean proteins do not contain alcohol-soluble constituents (no 'prolamine') and so have no value in baking without some technological contrivance.

V.   FIELD BEANS

With a 30% protein content, this seed (a type of broad bean) is of interest in France, since its cultivation is easy in all areas (whereas the soya bean can only be cultivated in the south) with a good yield of 900 kg of protein to the hectare. It has a high lysine content (6% of the total proteins) but there is persistent deficiency in the sulphur amino acids.

The composition of field bean flour is similar to that of the soya bean as far as the proteins, legumin and vicillin are concerned. In particular, anti- enzymes are present (antitrypsin, antichymotrypsin) and also haemagglutinins. Among the α-galactosides, verbascose is the dominant compound, up to 3% of the dry flour, followed by stachyose (1%) and raffinose (0.2%).

The protein isolate is easily made, from the flour of decorticated seeds, by:

(1) extraction by 10 volumes of water at pH 7–9, agitation, centrifugation or filtration;
(2) precipitation of the liquid extract at pH 4.5 (water acidified with HCl), washing, drying.

It is possible to separate the legumin, which alone precipitates in the presence of calcium chloride (0.1 M): the vicillin stays in solution.

A nutritional aspect should be mentioned. The presence in the broad bean of glucosides (vicin and convicin), which pass into solution during the cooking process, are responsible for 'favism' — a haemolytic anaemia known especially in the Mediterranean basin, where broad beans are eaten raw.

VI.   LEAF PROTEIN

Lucerne (alfalfa) has been the most studied because of its high protein potential, about 2000 kg/ha. The fractionation (Table 11.3) is done in the following manner:

Table 11.3 — Composition of lucerne and lucerne proteins (% dried product)

	Water	Proteins	Lipids	NNE[a]	Cellulose	Minerals
Dehydrated lucerne	7	20	3.5	38.5	20	10
Concentrated green protein	10	45	9	18	1.8	16
White proteins	10	77	1	4.5	–	4.5

[a]Non-nitrogenous extracts (carbohydrate without the fibre).

(1) obtaining a green juice by grinding up fresh lucerne and filtering under pressure to separate the juice from the residue. The green juice retains 50% of the proteins; it is concentrated and drum-dried;
(2) precipitation of the proteins by heating of the green juice. Two types of proteins may be separated with progressive heat: first, the green proteins separate out; then a mixture is precipitated; finally the white proteins flocculate at about 80–85°C. These last contain neither cellulose nor chloroplasts; they are practically free from lipids.

Purer white proteins may be obtained, containing 90% protein, by initial soaking of the lucerne in water sulphited at pH 10 and 50°C, followed by centrifugal separation and thermal precipitation.

Acid precipitation, pH 4.0–4.5, has been tried with equal success.

These products are used as animal foods. It has been suggested that the white protein could be used for human consumption. These proteins are cheaper in price than the other plant proteins. They have quite a good lysine content, about 5% of the protein. The green products, which contain xanthophyll (in the lipid fraction), are very suitable for poultry.

VII. TEXTURIZATION OF PLANT PROTEINS

This section concerns mainly soya bean protein, but it may also apply to other proteins found in the non-textured form, that is, in soluble or non-chewable forms. The textured proteins may have certain physical properties close to those of meat and may be suitable as a meat replacement, at least partially (hamburgers, 'meat' balls, ravioli, 'cooked meats'). For texturized soya, the protein proportions in the meat part range from 50% to 80%, for moist products at 26% of dry matter.

The manufacturing processes are summarized in Table 11.4, with the quality obtained. The process of thermoplastic extrusion is the most used; it yields spongy chunks, made up of fibres lying in the direction of flow, which, after rehydration, have a chewable structure.

The procedure for obtaining surface films from heated soya milk is a traditional process in Japan. To make threads is more costly since it requires quite pure protein isolates: it can be applied to various proteins with a molar mass greater than 10 000.

Oxidizing agents have been suggested to help solubilize the raw material; they are however not to be recommended because of the lowering in nutritional value which results.

Table 11:4 — Texturization processes (soya bean)

State	Raw material	Technique	Structure
Fibrous pieces	Flour or protein concentrate, with carbohydrates, few lipids, concentrated solution (80%)	Thermo-plastic extrusion at high pressure and temperature (1500kPa, 175°C), plenty of cutting	Dry, spongy, fibres, all oriented in the same direction
Threads, fibres	Protein isolate (90 % of protein in dry matter) Solution with 20% protein content	Separation of the threads using 0.1 mm holes. Acid and salt bath.	Fibres compressed and heated
Films	Concentrated solution of proteins Soya milk	Coagulation on dryers with rollers Surface evaporation	Thin films

The physicochemical modifications which occur in these processes are not yet exactly known. Granules or protein bodies are broken up; the proteins are denatured because of the opening up of the spatial structure; finally, they align in parallel to the direction of the flow.

VIII.   PROTEINS FROM SINGLE-CELL ORGANISMS

1.   Single-cell micro-organisms

Many single-cell micro-organisms produce proteins in large quantities. Yeasts are particularly interesting. The following species have been studied or are still under examination:

(1) Yeasts
   — *Kluyveromyces fragilis* on deproteinized serum
   — *Candida tropicalis* on some alkanes (gas-oil)
   — *Candida lipolytica* on normal paraffins and on methanol
   — *Endomycopsis* and *Torula* for pre-treatment of agricultural byproducts which then allow the growth of yeasts
(0) — *Candida utilis* for protein enrichment of manioc after primary treatment with α-amylase
   — *Geotrichum album* on pulps and crushed barley residues
(2) Bacteria
   Pseudomonas g. on methanol
(3) Moulds
   — *Aspergillus, Rhizopus, Fusarium* on cereals and food production byproducts
(4) Algae
   — *Spirulina* in alkaline waters (Mexico)
   — *Chlorella* in sea-water (Japan), and various effluents (USA)
   — *Scenaedesmus.*

Note:
Multicellular algae: *Porphyra, Laminaria, Macrocystis pyrofera* (USA 'ocean farm'). Ciliates: *Tetrahymena pyriformis* on sugar effluents.

2. Media
Growth media of considerable quantity and little monetary value, or even having negative value because of the pollution of the natural setting, are used. In addition to sea and lake waters, which have to be complemented, the following media may be cited, which are unfortunately not all available in sufficient quantity and in controlled quality:

— molasses from sugarbeet processing, cane stems after sugar extraction (sucrose, raffinose, etc.).
— sulphite liquors and other residual liquids from the paper industry
— cellulose hydrolysates of wood, straw, cotton
— residues from starch refinery, 'corn steep liquor'
— whey from cheese-making
— low-priced plants such as Jerusalem artichoke, carob, certain cereals, maize.

To these must be added the petroleum oil alkanes, which are no longer cheap raw materials.

3. Petroleum oil proteins
Between 1955 and 1972 petroleum oil proteins were the object of important research and industrial installations were built. The oil crisis of the late 1970s put a stop to these developments. The price is no longer competitive with that of fish-meal.
    Roughly speaking, there are two micro-organisms involved and two culture methods.

— Micro-organism: Either a yeast, such as *Candida tropicalis*, or a bacterium of the *Pseudomonas* family is used. Yeast would be quite suitable for the production of animal food, but less so for human food because of the taste produced. In the latter case, the bacterium would be preferable. The final form is a dry powder containing the dead micro-organisms and 65% protein.
— Method: In the French method, yeasts are cultivated on a classic 'Petri dish' containing alkanes. In the English method, the paraffins (alkanes) are first separated at the refinery.

For preference, normal alkanes of between 10 and 20 carbon atoms are metabolized. The small molecules of less than 10 carbons are not suitable for protein production; above 20 carbons, the alkanes are solid at the optimal culture temperature (30–35°C).
    The culture is continuous, with forced aeration, since the medium is anaerobic, and with the injection of mineral salts bringing in nitrogen. The alkane is transformed into an acid, which then undergoes the usual β-oxidation. The 'yeast cream' is separated by centrifugation. Before being dried, the product is treated with

solvents, which remove the traces of gas-oil and the lipids (risk of going rancid during storage).

The culture conditions have been adapted to get a high production of protein and low nucleic acid content. The composition of amino acids is favourable, with an excess of lysine, but a slight deficit in the sulphur amino acids (Lys 7.8, Met 1.6, Cys 0.9). Table 11.5 summarizes the composition of French yeast.

Table 11.5 — Composition of industrial micro-organisms (% of dry matter)

	Proteins	Lipids[b]	Carbo-hydrates	Minerals	Other
Spirulina	70[a]	8	18	2	2 (colourings and vitamins)
Yeast BP	70	2	19.5	8.5	
Protibel	50	10	33	7	0.08 (vitamin C)

[a]Of which 4.5% nucleic acids.
[b]Highly unsaturated.

4. Spirulina

This is a green algae which is a traditional food in certain parts of the tropics and whose production has been developed industrially, notably in Mexico. The culture is made in very alkaline waters with addition of nutrients and carbon dioxide (for photosynthesis). The harvest is made by filtering, followed by break-up, then spray-drying.

The protein yield is high. There is no deficiency in the amino acid content. Spirulina is used for animal food; some satisfactory tests have been made on humans.

5. Lactic yeast

This is made in France (Protibel) by the culture of *Kluyveromyces* on whey, from the cheese-making process, deproteinized and filtered (the 'lactalbumen' is preserved). After washing, the cells are allowed to autolyse and then dried. The product is used in animal and human foodstuffs. The protein content is lower than in the products discussed above and the carbohydrate content is higher (Table 11.5). Lactic yeast is rich in vitamins.

A note on the potato: A resumé of the composition of this tuber is given in Table 11.1 and a diagram of its starch granules is on p. 122. It is the typical amylaceous food in areas of France; others exist, of comparable origin, in other countries, with starch contents between 80% and 85% (dry weight).

Potatoes have two biological peculiarities; alcoholic fermentation produces appreciable amounts of amyl alcohol (fusel oil), which gives a disagreeable flavour to the product obtained; and hydrolytic enzymes can be isolated from potatoes, in particular the Q enzyme, a transglycolase (transfer of 1-4 chain in position 6 in the starch).

Potatoes have a level of protein comparable to that of cereals but better in quality. Certain varieties contain up to 18% protein (of dry weight).

12

Fermented drinks

I. THE FERMENTATIONS

Alcoholic fermentation has long been the most general method of preservation of thirst-quenching drinks. It was the only method before modern times when thermal preservation treatments have become widespread. Ethanol is an efficient preserving agent as long as its concentration is adequate; moreover, it is not really toxic for man at moderate doses (less than 0.6 g/kg/day).

The ethanol concentration is usually expressed as a percentage of the volume. In France, the Gay/Lussac degree is used (°GL); to convert to weight at 20°C, this measurement has to be multiplied by about 0.81.

The sensitivity of micro-organisms to alcohol is very variable. Absolute sterility is only obtained at a concentration of 16°GL. This is too high for present-day drinks; but wine at 10°GL keeps well, especially in an airtight container, for a limited period. The presence of carbon dioxide (CO_2) aids the preservation at ambient temperature; thus beer at 3 or 5°GL keeps well, even if it has not been pasteurized.

Acidity, produced mainly by lactic fermentation, is little used in fermented drinks, except for drinking yoghurt and similar lactic products, always supposing it is considered that they belong to this category. From the biochemical angle, these two fermentations differ only in their final reaction, as shown in Fig. 12.1.

Alcoholic fermentation is generally produced by yeasts of the *Kluyveromyces* and *Saccharomyces* families, which are respectively spore-forming and non-spore-forming. It is produced at the expense of the hexoses and hexobioses, all of which are transformed into glucose-6-P to enter the cycle of anaerobic glycolysis. The fermentation is described by the following equation:

$$C_6H_{12}O_6 \rightarrow 2CH_3\text{--}CH_2OH + 2CO_2$$

The hexoses may come from the hexobioses, which are hydrolysed by many of the yeasts; but the latter cannot attack higher carbohydrates. To get alcohol from

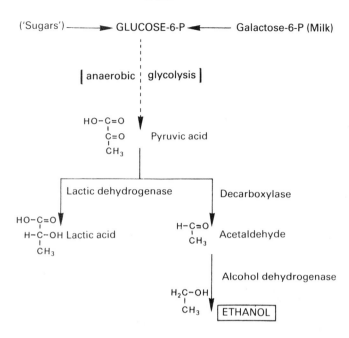

Fig. 12.1 — Fermentation scheme.

amylaceous substances, it is necessary first to hydrolyse, which is generally done by enzymes; amylases are often produced during the process of germination of cereal grains (Chapter 3).

II. WINE

1. Preparation

The term 'wine' is only applicable to the product of the alcoholic fermentation of the grape or of the must of the grape. The sugars involved are mainly glucose and fructose (in almost equal quantities in the ripe grape). There is 150–200 g/l of juice (it is calculated that 17 g/l of sugar is needed to get 1°GL); this yields 9–15°GL after total fermentation; that is, 73–120 g/l of ethanol. The addition of sucrose to the grape harvest is allowed for certain wines (chaptalization).

White grapes can only yield white wine (the term "blanc de blanc" is used).

Red grapes which have white juice yield a white wine if there is immediate pressing of the grape harvest with separation of the solids before fermentation begins.

Red grapes which have white or red juice yield either rosé or red wine if the fermentation is of the whole fruit without pressing of the juice or skins. The skins possess the red pigment or anthocyanins (Chapter 9), which goes into solution when the alcohol develops. For rosé wines, a limited time is allowed for this stage (10–15 hours of maceration).

The pressing process is a crushing of the grapes till the pips break up, without separation of the liquid. Less astringent wines are made by removing the fruit peduncles and shortening the fermentation process. It is permitted to heat the grapes to deepen the colour, or to heat the wine to ensure its preservation.

2. Composition
Three parts are distinguished :

(1) *Water* at a level of 830–900 g/l.
(2) *Volatile substances*, mainly ethanol, accompanied by minor alcohols: methanol, propanol, isobutanol, isoamyl alcohol. In France, the ethanol content varies from 9 to 14°GL (from 73 to 113 g/l); the methanol content depends on the nature of the vine, and varies from 0.03 to 0.2 g/l; the higher alcohols are more regular, with a content 0.25 to 0.60 g/l (a little more in red wines than in white wines). The methanol comes from the hydrolysis of pectins; the propanol, isobutanol and amyl alcohol come from the denaturation of certain of the grape amino acids.

   The constituents of the 'bouquet' (aroma, particular taste of each wine) are organic esters which fall partially into the category of volatile substances.
(3) *The dry extract*, or dry matter, is about 20–32 g/l for red wines and 14–15 g/l for white wines, in France. Two types of components are recognized:

   — the mineral substances, which come from the must, predominate: potassium (0.4–1.5 g/l), sulphates (0.03–3 g/l), phosphates (0.03–0.9 g/l) and chlorides (0.01–0.6 g/l). Also found in smaller quantities are: Na, Ca, Mg, Fe, and Mn, and bromides and iodides. It should be noted that some of the cations, especially potassium, are present as salts of organic acids. Tartaric and malic acids are the predominant acids in grapes.
   — the organic substances, which stem in part from the fermentation: glycerol (4–15 g/l) is the most abundant; then succinic and lactic acid. However, they may also come from the must, like the polyphenols and the tannins of the polyphenolic acids from the skins and seeds, various nitrogenous substances (amino acids, peptides), gums and pectins, colouring matters (red wine), etc. Moreover, wine contains vitamins, principally of the B_2 group, it is poor in vitamins C and B_1 and it is naturally free of fat-soluble vitamins (A, D).

Wine is an acid drink (pH 3.5); the organic acids which predominate are metabolized in the body.

$$OH$$
$$|$$

It should be noted that malic acid ($HOOC–CH–CH_2COOH$) may be converted, by decarboxylation, into lactic acid in the course of secondary fermentation.

Effervescent wines contain carbon dioxide gas dissolved in quantities varying between 2 and 6 g/l, which means being under a pressure of more than three times air pressure at normal temperature. In the champagne method, the formation of CO_2 is caused by a new fermentation; it is obtained by the addition of a certain quantity of sugar at the time of bottling; its development is slow — it takes two or more years for champagne to develop.

Note: Drinks comparable to wine are made from other fruits, e.g. cider from apples and perry from pears. Their composition varies a lot. Their alcoholic strength is not more than 6.5°GL. Malic is the most abundant of the organic acids. Pears contribute sorbitol. The mineral composition is often modified by the addition of cooking salt to control the clarification, which increases the quantities of chloride and sodium, which are low in the must, except in coastal regions.

III. BEER

This is a very ancient drink which is today brewed in most countries of the world. It is obtained from amylaceous musts, in three main stages.

1. Malting

(1) *The main aim of malting* is the development of enzymes, especially of the β-amylase group (Chapter 3).

   Both 'cytases', which break up the membranes, and proteases, which free the amino acids, are formed. These are assimilated by the embryo for later use in the development of the yeast.

(2) *The secondary aim* is the friability of the grain and making a contribution to the final flavour.

   Malt comes from sprouting barley; the amylases produced in the germination will later produce fermentable sugars (mainly maltose) — a phase unnecessary in wine production. Soaking for 2–4 days in water precedes the malting proper, and this is followed by placing in an oven. This last operation brings about dessication by a hot air blast and stops the germination process; this contributes to the colour and aroma of the beer. The rootlets are then taken out (germ removal) because they are harmful to the quality. The malting factory is nowadays separate from the brewery; it may supply a group of factories.

2. Brewing

The main aim of brewing is to hydrolyse the malt starch and, if the 'enzyme capacity' is sufficient, some non-malted amylaceous products which are less costly (maize, manioc, rice); it is not all hydrolysed since it is necessary to keep some of the dextrins to give the beer 'body'.

The bitter flavour of the beer is obtained during the brewing process by the addition of female hop cones.

The following operations are carried out:

(1) *Crushing* in a progressively tightening mill; the grinding is not homogeneous.
(2) *Brewing* in large vessels, formerly made of copper, nowadays made of stainless steel ('mask tuns'). The 'thickening' — the process of producing a suspension —

is done in water at 40–50°C, with control of the viscosity and with the pH regulated at around 5.5. The brewed product is liquefied by raising the temperature to around 70–75°C. This is an important phase; it seems that 'decoction' is better for the smoothness of the beer than 'infusion'. This last is simple heating in bulk, whereas decoction is heating in stages, with separate, short bursts of boiling of part of the liquid. Heating controls sugar production; if the temperature is raised, the quantity of dextrins is increased (control by iodine reaction).

(3) *Filtering* to remove the insoluble residues, which are used as animal feed.
(4) *Cooking and hop addition* (150–400 g of cones per hectolitre of first stock); prolonged boiling (1–2 hours) ensures sterility. The 'dregs' are separated in a second filtering and the juice cooled to 6°C.

3. Fermentation

It is brought about by selected yeasts, of the *Saccharomyces* type, which work in two stages:

(1) *Main fermentation* in the 'fermentation vats' at 7–10°C, for about a week with bottom fermentation, which is by far the most widely used. During the first day or two, the yeast bulks up, with first a white froth, then later a brown froth (because of the tannins). The 'easing' of the must is controlled by the saccharometer, which measures the density, and not the degree of alcohol.

With the *S. carlbergensis* species, a quick cooling helps to deposit the yeast.

Note: Top fermentation is little used; it is shorter (3–days) and at up to 20°C; the yeast stays on the surface.

(2) *Secondary fermentation:* the beer is decanted and kept in hermetically sealed tanks, where it will remain for 6–8 weeks at a temperature lowered to 0–1°C. It becomes richer in carbon dioxide gas; the maltotriose ferments; H_2S disappears. Here there is a risk of decomposition due to the formation of diacetyl (CH_3–CO––CO–CH_3), which has a low odour threshold: 0.2 ppm. Alcoholic fermentation takes place in all beers, even in the 'light' beers containing less than 3% alcohol, and alcohol-free beers, which in reality contain from 0.5°GL to 1°GL. The alcohol is reduced by reverse osmosis, which is actually an ultrafiltration through a fine porous membrane under high pressure.

The final Kieselguhr filtration does not yield a sterile beer; pasteurization at 65°C is recommended.

4. Composition

The dry extract of common beers is near to 40 g/l, that is, much more than in wines (22 g/l for reds, 15 g/l for whites); this is due to the high dextrin content, around 22 g/l, and to the reducing sugars, 9 g/l (as maltose).

The alcohol content varies widely according to the type of beer; on average 2.5°GL are found (i.e. 20 g ethanol) for ordinary beer sold by the glass and 5.5°GL

(44 g ethanol) for luxury beers. There is no beer with a degree of alcohol comparable to that of wine.

Beer contains water-soluble vitamins, especially those of the B group (6 g/l).

IV. CLOUDINESS IN BEER

There is, in beer, a type of decomposition which has no danger for health but has bad implications for the flavour of beer; it is necessary to produce a beer which, even after refrigeration, keeps its sparkle and colour in the glass.

Three factors have a bearing on the cloudiness : (1) proteins of high molecular mass, (2) tannins, (3) oxygen from the air. It is necessary to act on at least two of these factors to get a good result. Most often the oxygen is removed and the size of the proteins reduced.

The phenomena are of two types:

— oxidation, which affects the other two factors, and which leads to cloudiness under refrigeration, browning in colour, and a more acrid taste with a reduction in the aroma introduced by the hops. It is necessary to reduce to the minimum the introduction of air during decanting or storage, given the fact that CO_2 gives only limited protection against oxidation. It is possible also to use antioxidant additives, like ascorbic acid (synthetic vitamin C), which does not seem to modify either the physicochemical properties or the taste of the beer;
— formation of barely soluble or completely insoluble complexes through the combination of some proteins and some tannins; the end result is the formation of a persistent cloudiness.

The non-condensed tannins are present in the form of derivatives of a monosaccharide, mainly glucose, with 1 to 5 polyphenolic acid substituents.

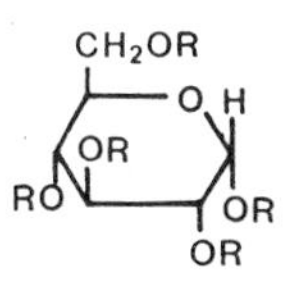

Glycosidic tannins 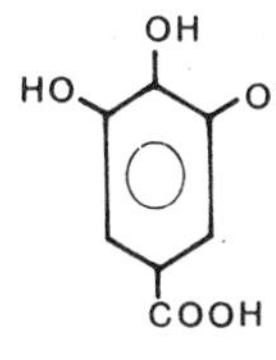   R: gallic acid 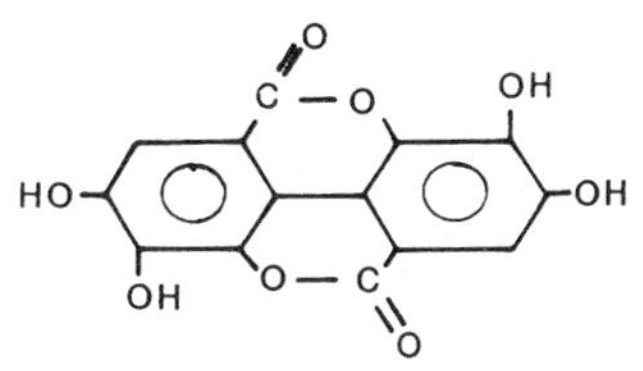   R: ellagic acid

They may unite with the peptide bonds of the proteins by hydrogen bonds, which become covalent bonds in time and through oxidation.

The limited hydrolysis of large proteins by some endopeptidases is one way of combatting this. In particular, papain, in the form of a concentrated solution, has been suggested, which avoids health problems posed by the use of traditional powder forms (irritation of skin and mucous membranes).

V. BITTER SUBSTANCES PRESENT IN HOPS

The female cones of hops, dried at 70°C, introduce resins which have three types of action on the beer:

— correction of taste (bitterness),
— antiseptic property, especially on Gram +ve bacteria,
— effect on the stability of the froth, by the formation of tenside active colloids after cooling.

Lupulin contains bitter resins and essential oils, more or less volatile (more or less taken out in the course of cooking). Only the soft resins have the above-mentioned properties; they are soluble in hexane and other organic solvents; they are made up of α and β fractions. The hard resins (fraction γ) are insipid and insoluble in hexane. The average ratio of the fractions is $\alpha:\beta:\gamma=7:10:4$.

(1) *The α fraction* bestows the most bitterness; it is made up of derivatives of phloroglucinol (1,3,5 trihydroxybenzene). Mainly humulone and cohumulone are found here — these are iso derivatives with side chains of 4 and 5 carbons.

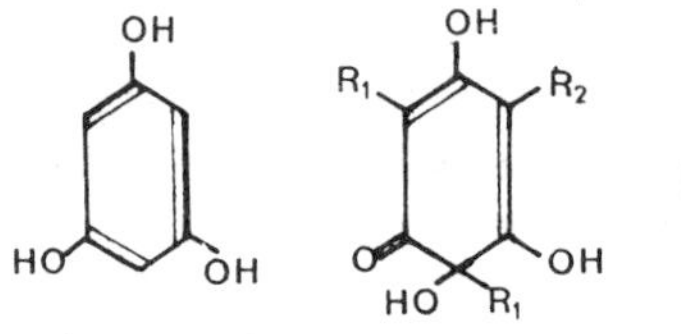

Phloroglucinol   Fundamental structure

Humulon

$R_1 : - CH_2 - CH = C \begin{smallmatrix} CH_3 \\ CH_3 \end{smallmatrix}$ (isopentenyl)

$R_2 : - CO - CH_2 - CH \begin{smallmatrix} CH_3 \\ CH_3 \end{smallmatrix}$ (isovaleroyl)

Cohumulon $R_2 : - CO - CH \begin{smallmatrix} CH_3 \\ CH_3 \end{smallmatrix}$ (isobutyroyl)

(R_1 as above)

These are weak acids (pH 4.6 to 4.7) which undergo various and complex transformations (hydrogenolysis, oxidation, isomerization) which result in both bitter and non-bitter residues.

(2) *The β fraction* has a more complex composition, with closely allied properties. Lupulone has the following structure:

In the presence of metals, these substances form non-crystalline complexes (Cu, Fe, etc.). Lead in solution precipitates the β fraction, but not the a fraction.

VI. ALCOHOL — BIOLOGICAL ASPECTS

Alcohol is a nutrient. It is oxidized in the liver to acetic acid and releases 7 calories/g, but this heat is not controlled by the thermoregulator mechanism and no forms for storing the energy exist, with the exception of a small part of ethanol which is transformed into lipids.

In moderate measure, ethanol is a factor in vascular protection; it seems that cardiovascular morbidity may be inversely proportional to the average consumption of alcohol, for people with comparable diets. However, the negative effects are much clearer when the alcohol intake is higher.

Table 12.1 — Levels of alcohol in human blood

	g/l	mmol/l
Legal limit	0.8	17.4
Excitement phase	1	21.7
Incoordination phase	2	43.4
Comatose phase	⩾3	⩾65

The levels of alcohol in the blood to remember (quantity of ethanol per litre of blood) are given in Table 12.1. The legal limit varies in different countries; it is relatively high in Britain and France. Drunkenness manifests itself at around 1 g/l; this leads to a loss of control of action and lengthening of reaction time. At above about 3 g/l, the person is in a state of deep coma with complete loss of sensitivity; if no aid is given there is a high risk of death.

It should be added that absorption of alcohol is rapid in humans. The contents of the digestive tract are in equilibrium with the blood between 45 minutes (alcohol consumed without eating) and 1 hour (alcohol with a meal). The level of alcohol in the blood, for the same weight and with an equal intake of alcohol, is higher for women than for men.

13

Milk and dairy products

I. GENERAL POINTS

(1) The term 'milk', unless otherwise stated, refers to *cow's milk*; this is what will be mainly studied here. In France, the milk of goats and ewes is also exploited commercially, but, in the main, used only for the preparation of cheeses. In some other countries, the milk of about a dozen different domestic mammals is still used (female buffalo, mare, yak, camel, etc.). But it must be stressed that in world terms the predominance of cow's milk is overwhelming.

. Table 13.1 shows the average composition of the milk of dairy cows. It can be seen that this liquid is a very watery (as a vegetable is), but has a remarkably balanced composition (in terms of weight), of carbohydrates, lipids and proteins (respectively 1.5: 1.0: 1.0), with as well an interesting selection of salts, vitamins and enzymes. The calorific power is about 650 calories per 1000 g of milk. Cow's milk is an excellent foodstuff for man.

Compared with cow's milk, differences in composition are seen in the milk of other species, as shown in Table 13.2. The values given for the one-stomached animals are only a tough guide, because there are important individual variations. Human milk is richer in carbohydrates, but much poorer in salts and vitamins than cow's milk; moreover, the proportion of casein is low.

(2) Milk is a *mixture* both from the physical and chemical points of view. Through the application of centrifugal force, the following are separated successively:

(a) The globular matter, in the form of cream, which is more or less yellow, separates from the white skimmed milk very easily (either several thousand 'g' or simple resting at moderate temperature suffices). Cream has the same structure as the whole milk; when it is agitated (churned), butter separates from the 'buttermilk'.

(b) Caseins separate through ultracentrifugation ($\geqslant 35\,000$ g) of skimmed milk in the form of a 'micellar' structure. At higher centrifugal power, the albumens and globulins are separated. Milk is thus a suspension of proteins in a lactoserum,

Table 13.1 — Composition of cow's milk

	Composition (g/l)		Physical state of components
Water	905		Free water (solvent) +bound water (3.7%)
Carbohydrates: lactose	49		Solution
Fats:	35		
True fats		34	Emulsion of fat globules
Lecithin (phospholipids)		0.5	(3–5 μm)
Non-saponifiable part (sterols, carotenes, tocopherols)		0.5	
Proteins:	34		
Casein		27	Micellar suspension calcium phosphocaseinate (0.08–0.12 μm)
'Soluble' proteins (globulins, albumins)		5.5	Solution (colloidal)
Non-protein nitrogenous substances		1.5	Solution (true)
Salts:	9		Solution or colloidal state
of citric acid (in acid)		2	
of phosphoric acid (P_2O_3)		2.6	
of hydrochloric acid (NaCl)		1.7	
Various constituents (vitamins, enzymes, gas in solution)	Traces		
Dry matter (total)	127		
Non-fat dry matter		92	

Table 13.2 — Composition of various types of milk (g/100 g)

	Dry extract (total)	Fat	Lactose	Salts	Nitrogenous substances (total)
(a) *Single stomach*					
Woman	11.7	3.5	6.5	0.2	1.5
Mare	10	1.5	5.9	0.4	2.2
(b) *Polygastric (ruminants)*					
Cow	12.5	3.5	4.7	0.8	3.5
Goat	13.6	4.3	4.5	0.8	4
Ewe	19.1	7.5	4.5	1.1	6
Buffalo	17.8	7.5	4.7	0.8	4.8

which retains the lactose and the salts. It should be noted that ultrafiltration leads to similar results.

(3) Normal milk is synthesized in healthy udders. Where there is a localized illness (*mastitis*), the liquid produced has an abnormal composition; it tends towards the composition of blood; such milk is of no use for anything. At the commencement of lactation, after calving, the udder secretes an abnormal milk, rich in immunoglobulins, called the *colostrum*, which can only be used to nourish the calf. In cows, the injection of the hormone BST (Bovine Somatotropin) increases milk production, whilst reducing the need for very careful rearing. If this procedure takes place quite late after insemination, it has no effect on the health of the animal or on the composition of the milk. Since this hormone is not very stable, it has no harmful effects on the consumer.

(4) *Milk minerals* form only a small part of the dry matter to be studied now, but they are of interest because of their calcium (1.25 g/l) and phosphorous (1 g/l) contents, which are much higher than in blood. This stems from the fact that a considerable amount of these two elements, about two-thirds, is found in colloidal form, having little influence on the osmotic pressure. Milk contains more calcium than lime-water. The yield of an average cow, 5000 litres of milk per year, produces 10–12 kg of phosphoric acid and 8–10 kg of calcium. Milk is one of the most important sources of calcium in human food.

Cow's milk contains potassium (1.5 g/l) and three times less sodium (0.5 g/l). In the milk from cows suffering mastitis, the sodium content increases.

(5) *The pH* of freshly milked cow's milk is situated a little below neutral, around 6.6–6.7. That of the milk of the human female is a little higher, around 7.2; this is mainly because of its low casein (phosphorylated protein) content.

A small change in the pH, on the acid side, has important effects on the equilibrium of the minerals (soluble and insoluble forms) and on the stability of the colloidal suspension of casein.

II.   LACTOSE AND OLIGOSACCHARIDES

(1) Nearly all the carbohydrates of cow's milk consists of *lactose*: β-D- galactopyranoside (1→4) D glucopyranoside α or β (Chapter 2, §IX). Only 1.0–1.6 g/l are free oligosugars or combined with proteins. In the colostrum of the cow, the content rises to more than 3 g/l. Human milk contains at least 10 g of oligosugars including, besides lactose, L-fucose, N-acetylglucosamine and neuraminic acid; these substances have varied biological activity, particularly a growth factor for *Lactobacillus bifidus*, a bacteria almost unique to the intestines of breast-fed infants; this is one of the reasons why the mother's milk is to be preferred to cow's milk.

(2) A *critical point of crystallization* of lactose exists, stemming from concentrated solutions. Above 94°C it is α-anhydrous lactose which forms (β-hydrated lactose is not known). Below 94°C, the α-hydrated lactose ($1H_2O$) crystallizes; this is the normal form of dry lactose; the α-anhydrous form comes from vacuum-drying using moderate heat.

In solution, mutarotation brings the β/α mixture to 1.63 (15–20°C). The physical properties of each anomer have been given in Chapter 2 and the poor solubility of lactose pointed out (170 g/l at 15°C). In other milks, such as human milk, the same equilibrium between the two forms α and β is seen.

(3) *Lactose α crystals*, formed naturally, are relatively large and very hard. In sugared condensed milk, they are responsible for the 'gritty' defect. For this reason, the formation of very small crystals (of less than 0.1 mm) is preferred, through culturing the mass with lactose crystals.

Rapid elimination of the water by drying may lead to the formation of vitreous lactoses, which correspond with a hyperconcentrated solution in the presence of damp air; the particles tend to stick together (formation of lumps). Industrial techniques are available to aid crystallization and to improve the solubility of milk powders or lactoserum.

(4) For practical purposes, the two physicochemical *degradation reactions of lactose* that are of interest are:

— heat decomposition; at about 100°C after lengthy heating, a complex occurs between the casein and the lactose; a browning appears at about 120°C; above 120°C the lactose decomposes into various substances, especially hydroxymethyl-furfural and formic acid. The consequence of this is the activation of growth of certain lactic bacteria;

— the Maillard reactions, between the reducing groups and the free nitrogen groups of the amino acids, in particular lysine, take place to give formation of compounds by addition and so reduce the nutritional value. These reactions are speeded up by heating; with them come several modifications, in particular the appearance of the brown colouring and the increase in reducing capacity. In powdered milk, at ambient temperature, the reactions are slow, but considerable. Methods to combat these are maintenance of a dry atmosphere, low temperatures, elimination of iron and copper from the material (catalysts for the reactions).

(5) *Lactic fermentation* is the most important biochemical modification of lactose. True lactic bacteria produce almost pure lactic acid, without gas, using the Meyerhof-Embden pathway:

$$C_{12}H_{22}O_{11}H_2O \rightarrow 2C_6H_{12}O_6 \rightarrow 4CH_3\text{--}CHOH\text{--}COOH$$

These bacteria are frequently found in milk. Alongside these, there exist bacteria which yield a heterogeneous fermentation, with production of about 50% CO_2 and other bound or volatile substances. In milk which is to be consumed, lactic acid is harmful; the milk 'turns' when the content reaches 0.5% at 20°C. In some products, notably cream, butter, cheese, and yoghurt, controlled lactic acidification is absolutely necessary, with the production of small quantities of flavour substances: diacetyl $CH_3\text{--}CO\text{--}CO\text{--}CH_3$, ethanal $CH_3\text{--}CHO$.

III. LIPIDS — CHEMICAL ASPECTS

1. Fatty matter

The appropriately named 'fatty matter', the neutral lipids, are composed of glycerides, making up the predominant fraction: 98% of the total lipids. It is solid at ambient temperature (it is a fat); it is almost entirely free, and is found finely dispersed in the fat globules.

— The *polar lipids* are nearly all phospholipids; they only make up 1% of the total; they are mainly in a bound form on the globular membrane.
— The *unsaponifiable lipids* are insoluble in water, but of very different nature and make up the balance. Mainly they include the carotenoids and sterols, which include vitamins A and D.

2.   Triglycerides

The triglycerides represent more than 98% of the neutral lipids, along with diglycerides (1.5%) and monoglycerides (0.3%). The radicals of the fatty acids (R) are extremely varied and numerous.

$$
\begin{array}{lll}
CH_2 - O - CO - R_1 & & CH_2OH \\
| & \xrightarrow{\text{lipase}} & | \qquad R_1 \text{-} COOH \\
CH - O - CO - R_2 + 3\,H_2O & & CHOH + R_2 \text{-} COOH \\
| \quad \text{(triglycerides)} & & | \qquad R_3 \text{-} COOH \\
CH_2 - O - CO - R_3 & & CH_2OH \text{ (glycerol)}
\end{array}
$$

Table 13.3 gives the composition of fatty acids in the fat of cow's milk, listing any present at more than 0.2%. Palmitic acid predominates, with oleic acid. The acids which are not there are those with odd numbers of carbon atoms, branched chain or with differing double bonds. It will be seen that, overall, two thirds of the fatty acids are saturated and the remainder are unsaturated.

One important characteristic of the milk of ruminants is the presence of the short-chain fatty acids (C_4 to C_{10}). The volatile water-soluble acids (essentially butyric and caproic), have here RMW indices (Reichert, Meissl and Wolny) between 20 and 30, but only 2 in human milk and about 1 in common fats and oils, with the exception of coconut fat and fat from the small palm (5–8). This fact can be used in analysis.

3.   Unsaturated fatty acids

The *cis* forms of unsaturated fatty acids are important because of their reactivity, their biological properties and their low melting point. Their proportion varies especially with the food taken. Grass is very helpful from this point of view: the linolenic acid which comes mainly from grass is largely hydrogenated in the rumen to give mainly oleic acid and also linoleic and vaccenic acids (*trans*). The iodine number, which is a measure of unsaturation, is high and constant in the milk of animals fed on grass all the year round, as in Normandy, where the butter is excellent. On the contrary it is low in the milk of animals which are in stalls and the butter obtained is firmer and breaks up easily.

4.   Linoleic acid

Linoleic acid is essential, especially for the young infant, as it is the precursor of the prostaglandins and the double bond at 6–7 cannot be formed in the human organism

Table 13.3 — Principal fatty acids in the fat from cow's milk

Category	Name of acid	Number of carbon atoms	Content (% of total fat)[a]	Physical state[b]
I. SATURATED ACIDS	$CH_3-(CH_2)_{n-2}-COOH$			
(a) Volatile — soluble	Butyric	C_4	3–4 (tr)[c]	Liquid (−8)
	Caproic	C_6	2–5 (tr)	Liquid (−3)
(b) Volatile — insoluble	Caprylic	C_8	1–1.5 (tr)	Liquid–solid (+16)
	Capric	C_{10}	2 (2)	Solid (+30)
	Lauric	C_{12}	3 (8)	Solid (+42)
(c) Non-volatile	Myristic	C_{14}	11 (10)	Solid (+54)
	Pentadecanoic	C_{15}	1.5	Solid (+58)
	Palmitic	C_{16}	25–30 (23)	Solid (+62)
	Stearic	C_{18}	12 (7)	Solid (+70)
	Arachidic	C_{20}	0.2	Solid (+75)
II. UNSATURATED ACIDS				
(a) Monoenes:	$CH_3-(CH_2)_z-CH=CH-(CH_2)_y-COOH$			
	Palmitoleic	C_{16}	2 (5)	Liquid (+0.5)
	Oleic	C_{18}	23 (35)	Liquid–solid (+16)
	Vaccenic (*trans*)	C_{18}	2–3	Solid (+43)
(b) Non-conjugated: polyunsaturated	$CH_2-CH=CH-CH_2-CH=CH-CH-CH_2...COOH$			
	Linoleic (dienes)	C_{18}	2 (8.5)	Liquid
	Linolenic (trienes)	C_{18}	0.5 (2)	Liquid
	Arachidonic (tetraenes)	C_{20}	0.3	Liquid
(c) Conjugated: polyunsaturated	$CH_2-CH=CH-CH=CH-CH-CH_2...COOH$			
	Diene	C_{18}	0.8	Liquid
	Triene and tetraene	C_{18}	tr	Liquid

[a]In the brackets, some averages (less significant) are given for human milk. [b]With the melting point shown in brackets in °C.
[c]tr: traces.

(Fig. 13.1). The linoleic acid content in cow's milk varies little, from 1.2% to 2.0%. It is much higher in human milk: 8–9%. This is another reason why mother's milk is better. Attempts have been made to increase the content with cows: the best solution seems to be to distribute 'protected' foods, containing an oil rich in linoleic acid (soya, sunflower, safflower, etc.) included in a protein mass lightly tanned with formalin. It is thus easy to get a proportion of 6%, considered to be satisfactory for the small baby. It should be noted that it is not possible at the moment to effect such an improvement by fractional crystallization of cow's milk, without additives.

5. Oxidation of the fat

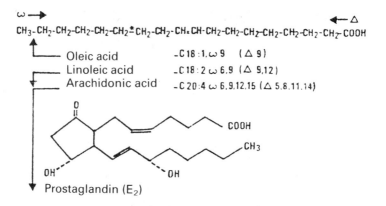

Fig. 13.1 — Polyunsaturated fatty acids. The prostaglandins.

Oxidation of the fat is a defect in the chemical system. The taste of an oxidized product is very unpleasant, both in milk and in butter; sometimes it is put down to the taste of the container, oily or metallic, and tallowy; but this should not be confused with rancidity, which is enzymatic in nature.

Autoxidation in the unsaturated fatty acids which keeps the double bond, involves the formation of a hydroperoxide.

$$-CH_2-CH-CH=CH- \rightarrow -CH_2-CO-CH=CH=$$
$$\qquad\quad |$$
$$\qquad\; O-OH$$

Ultimately carbonyl compounds are formed with α and β double bonds; these aldehydes or ketones have very strong smells and tastes. The speed of oxidation increases with the number of double bonds (Chapter 4, §IX).

The influence of the particular food on the ease with which oxidation occurs is the most marked; but it is complex. In winter milks, the most sensitive to oxidation, it is the level of reducing agents which must be too low (substances with a redox potential lower than that at which the bonding of activated oxygen to the double bonds of the fatty acids occurs).

In the case of butter, which is often more easily oxidized in summer, it is the higher proportion of the substrate, the unsaturated fatty acids, which comes into play. Copper and iron are the catalysts for the reaction. Sunlight, low pH, and salt (NaCl) are factors which favour oxidation. It should be noted that oxidized butters tend to lose their yellow colouring, as a consequence of the oxidation of the carotene.

IV.   LIPIDS: GLOBULAR STATE

1.   Fat globules

Fat globules are spherical, with varying dimensions between the species, ranging from 0.1 to 20 µm. In cow's milk, the average diameter is about 4–5 µm (like a little yeast cell). The fat is strongly dispersed; the fat globules of 1 litre of milk are made of a population of about 2 billion units and represent a surface of 80m², which is considerable.

These globules have a structure, with a membrane or protective film, but the lipid droplet in the centre contains no added material; it is therefore not a living cell. The membrane is complex, comprising two parts:

— *the internal layer,* which is perhaps a cellular membrane, with glycoproteins and phospholipids, which has little enzymatic activity and which is quite resistant. The Van der Waal's type forces suffice to explain the bond with the fatty part. Some metallic elements may be found in this layer (Cu, Fe) but also in the outer layer;

— *the external layer,* where the enzymes are found (alkaline phosphatase, xanthine oxidase, etc.) and various adsorbed substances. It is this layer which mainly undergoes variations during the course of various treatments. Heat and mechanical action reduce the thickness of the membrane.

When new surfaces are created between the globule and the plasma, a binding of a variety of proteins is seen; for example: with the dispersion of the fatty matter through homogenization under pressure, or the emulsion of an oil in skimmed milk. However, these new protective films are less efficient than the natural membranes; organic solvents (e.g. benzene, ether, acetone) may extract a large part of the fat substance, whilst in normal milk, the solvent takes out only very little.

2.   Separation of the fat globules

Separation of some fat globules is quite normal given the difference in density (fat 0.9 g/cm³; skimmed milk 1.035 g/cm³). However, the speed of the rise of the fat, in a resting milk, does not correspond with the calculation using the Stokes formula (V is proportional to the square of the radius, to the difference in density and to the acceleration, and inversely proportional to the viscosity). Spontaneous skimming occurs with clustering resulting in the agglomeration of globules, aided by a fairly low temperature, 7–8°C.

The adhering disappears when the milk is heated at about 65°C, as if an agglutinin had been destroyed.

V. BUTTER-MAKING

Where the fat content is quite high, brisk agitation results in the formation of a froth, which gradually firms up; then, if the agitation continues, the froth is destroyed and the fat separates in the form of globules of butter.

The incorporation of air plays a major role in classic butter-making. A discontinuous vapour phase is established in the cream through the adsorption of proteins which form a protective film at the air/liquid interface; it becomes stable when the air bubbles subdivide, forming small nuclei, around which the fat globules aggregate. The volume increases. Prolonged agitation compresses the fat globules, and a portion of the lipids (about 50%) is freed; butter globules form; the continuous fat phase surrounds the intact fat globules and a little water (butter contains a maximum of 16% water). An inversion of the phases is produced, from 'fat in water' to 'water in fat'. Fig. 13.2 shows schematically the industrial procedure for making cream and butter. The use of a lactic starter is seen, used to acidify the cream and flavour the butter.

Fractional crystallization yields butters with a specific melting point, since the triglyceride crystals are separated from the liquid phase. In this way, the milk industry offers several types of 'cooking butters' where the melting point lies between 27°C and 41°C.

Continuous processes for butter-making are very developed nowadays:

— the Fritz process or floating system, with faster beating (e.g. Contimab, Westphalia) a modern form of classic beating, producing a butter of good quality;
— processes with double centrifugation (80% of fatty substance) with special thermal treatment (e.g. Alfa, Meleshine); the texture is different from the one above; about 80% of the fat remains in the globular form; the cream must be very smooth. This process is used in countries in Northern and Eastern Europe;
— the 'Golden Flow' process, which involves the destabilization of the cream and removal of all gas from the butter oil. The butter is obtained by re-emulsification of the lactic starter and water. The advantages are that poor quality organoleptic creams may be treated in this way and storage of the dehydrated butter oil is easier. This process is not much used in France and Britain.

In France and Britain, pasteurized 'dairy' butter is mainly produced. 'Farm' butter goes off fairly quickly. 'Salt' butter, at 5–10% salt content, is not common.

It should be noted that the butter used in the food production industry may be protected from oxidation by the addition of permitted antioxidants (only for bulk units of weight above 1 kg). .

VI. NITROGENOUS SUBSTANCES — THE CASEINS

Table 13.4 shows that out of the 32–35 g/l of total nitrogenous material in cow's milk, only about 5% are non-protein substances, or NPN. The remaining is 95% made up of varied proteins. There is no appreciable quantity of peptides in the milk.

Once the proteins have been precipitated, for example by the addition of 12% trichloraceteic acid, the NPN substances stay in solution. Numerous substances of low molecular weight (less than 500) are present; the most abundant is urea (0.25 g/l)

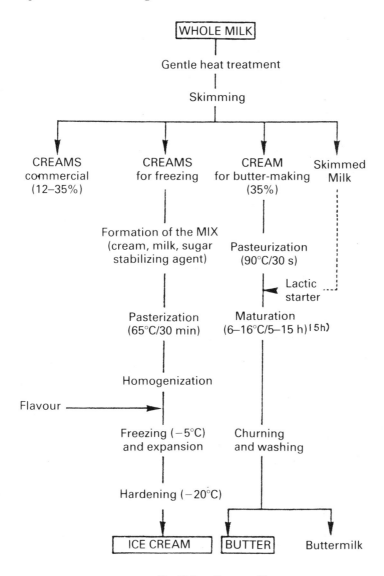

Fig. 13.2 — Cream and butter.

together with metabolic intermediates (orotic acid) and free amino acids. This fraction is of little importance.

The α_{s1}-, α_{s2}-, β- and κ-caseins are the molecules in the raw milk. With the γ-caseins, they make up 75% of the nitrogenous total. They are phosphorylated by an ester bond with serine or threonine, which accentuates their acid reaction. They have the essential characteristic of precipitating at pH 4.65 at ambient temperature, and not being rendered insoluble in heating at 100°C. Table 13.5 summarizes their properties. It can be seen that, for a biochemist, these are small proteins, with

Table 13.4 — Nitrogenous substances of milk

	Composition (%)		Average content (g/l)
100	34.0		
Proteins	95		32.3
Caseins	78	100	26.5
—α_{s1}-Casein		36	9.55
—α_{s2}-Casein		10	2.65
—β-Casein		34	9.0
—κ-Casein		13	3.45
—γ-Casein		7	1.85
Whey proteins[a]	17	100	5.8
—β-Lactoglobulin		50	2.9
—α-Lactalbumin		22	1.3
—Serum albumin		5	0.3
—Immunoglobulins		12	0.7
—Proteoses and peptones		10	0.6
Non-protein nitrogenous substances	5		1.7

[a]Also known as lactoserum proteins.

molecular weights close to 20 000 to 25 000. In the native state, they are found always closely associated with each other in relatively large and mineralized micelles.

The genetic variants are only distinguishable from each other by one or two amino acid residues, out of a total of about 200, except for two abnormal cases: α_{s1}-A casein, which has 13 missing residues, and α_{s2}-D casein. The variant α_{s1}-A is very rare; in each of the molecules of α_{s1}-A and β, there is one strongly predominant variant from the breeds of bovines which are exploited commercially, respectively α_{s1}-B and β-A, which may be present in certain breeds at up to 70% of the total casein content. The separation of the variants is possible through electrophoresis under certain conditions, except in the case of the so-called 'dumb' variants, where the substitution of amino acids without change in the charge occurs. Fig. 13.3 shows a classic electrophoretic examination of different caseins.

The primary structure of the principal caseins is known. An excess of acid groups at neutral pH exists; in electrophoretic examination at pH 8.6 or 9.0, α_{s1} casein is the most mobile, then come α_{s2}, β, κ and γ; it is however α_{s2} casein which ought to have migrated the furthest!

κ-*Casein* differs from the dominant caseins (α_{s1} and β) in various characteristics and properties:

(1) From the structural point of view, it is little phosphorylated, it contains two residues of cysteine and is partially glycosylated. The average monosaccharide content is about 5%; the *N*-acetylgalactosamine is linked to the peptide chain by

Table 13.5 — Main characteristics of major constituents of casein[a] from cow's milk

	α_{s1}-Casein	α_{s2}-Casein	β-Casein	κ-Casein	γ_1-Casein
Average proportion in %	36	10	34	13	3
Molecular mass	23 600	25 250	24 000	19 000 (peptide units)	21 000
Number of residues of amino acids	199	207	209	169	181
Phosphorus % (atoms/mole)	1.10 (8)	1.23–1.60 (10–13)	0.56 (5)	0.20 (1)	0.16 (1)
Carbohydrates (%)	0	0	0	5	0
Cysteine, residues/mole	0	2	0	2	0
Proline	17	10	35	20	34
Sensitivity to calcium[b]	++	+++	+	0	?
Sensitivity to chymosine[b]	+	−	+	+++	
Genetic variants	A,B,C,D	A,B,D	A_1,A_2,A_3,B,C,E	A,B	A_1,A_2,A_3,B
Hydrophobicity (kJ)	4.89	4.64	5.66	5.30	−
Acid groups (Asp+Glu+P×2)	48	49–55	31	18	16
Basic groups (Lys+Arg+His)	25	33	20	17	16

[a] Data for variants α_{s1}-B, α_{s2}-B, β-A_2, κ-B and γ-A_2.

[b] +: slow reaction imperceptible at moment of ordinary coagulation.

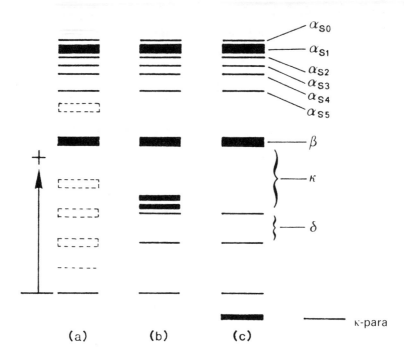

Fig. 13.3 — Electrophorogram of caseins in starch gel (pH 8.6; urea 8M). (a) Whole casein without reducing agent. (b) Whole casein with reducing agent (β-mercaptoethanol). (c) Whole casein after chymosin action.

threonine 133 (Fig. 13.4), then comes galactose and at the terminal position sialic acid; there may also be sialic acids in the branching. The electrophoretic pictures are only clear in the presence of mercaptoethanol, which stops the formation of —S—S— bridges; each A or B variant yields several bands; the slowest are not glycosylated but the peptide chains stay the same.

(2) κ-Casein has a stabilizing capacity, with regard to calcium for the other caseins; it allows the formation of micelles; it is soluble at all temperatures in the presence of calcium.

(3) The molecule contains a very labile Phe–Met bond; it provides the specific substrate for the rennin in the process of the primary reaction leading to milk coagulation.

It has not been possible to determine the secondary structure of any of the caseins. The random conformation leads one to think of a denatured protein; however, it is believed that the structure of caseins is more compact. The abundance of proline residues, their distribution and the absence of cysteine in the two large constituents α_{s1} and β mitigate against the establishment of classical secondary or tertiary structures. The high degree of hydrophobicity is linked with the high content of non-charged and non-polar side-chain groups: β-casein is notable in this respect. This observation has given rise to some ideas on micellar organization.

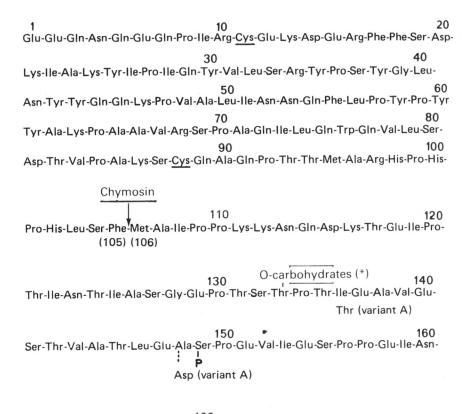

(*) Prosthetic grouping: Thr-O-(1)GalNac(3-1)Gal(6-2)NeuNac
(there are other groupings with several NeuNac).
The 11 and 88 cysteines are probably in the −SH form.

Fig. 13.4 — Primary structure of bovine κ_B-casein.

Phosphorylation, on Ser or Thr, seems to require the existence of the sequence code:

H ... Ser-X-Glu ... OH or H ... Ser-X-Ser (P) ... OH
(Thr)   (Thr)

with an acid group in the position n+2 : Glu, primary site, or Ser (P), secondary site. However, there are some exceptions. The phosphorylation is catalysed by a protein-kinase independent of the AMP cycle. Dephosphorylation is by a phosphatase or by heating at quite a high temperature.

The γ-caseins are the C-terminal fragments of the β-casein, formed by rupture between a lysine and another amino acid. It is perhaps the plasmin of milk which catalyses this reaction; but it is not known why it is limited to the β-casein and to three bonds in the casein chain (28–29, 105–106, 107–108). The remaining N-terminal fragments would seem to be the 'proteose-peptones'.

Note that the caseins of the milk of other ruminants are comparable with those of cow's milk, in spite of some variations in speed of electrophoretic migration. The few milk caseins of single-stomach animals so far studied, are, however, very different. Human caseins are almost entirely made up of β-casein with variants which are more or less phosphorylated.

VII.   WHEY PROTEINS

The whey or serum proteins (the 'soluble' proteins), are much less abundant than the caseins discussed above. Most often they remain isolated and do not take part in enzymatic coagulation; they have a higher nutritional value, especially in view of the sulphur amino acids and lysine present.

1.   β-Lactoglobulin

The composition indicated in Table 13.4 shows a predominance of β-lactoglobulin (about 3 g/l) which, in spite of its name, would be positioned with the albumin because of its low molecular mass (18 360), its great solubility, its electrophoretic mobility and its pure protein nature (although a glycolysated derivative has been found in low proportion). Of the four known genetic variants, only A and B are found in the milk of French bovine breeds. The substitution of aspartic acid by glycine has important effects on such a small molecule: the isoelectric pH rises from 5.23 (A) to 5.30 (B), water solubility at this pH also rises from 0.6 to 3.1 g/l and polymerization at pH 4–5 can only be seen clearly for the variant A. The supplementary Asp residue in the A variant must play a part in the active centre for polymerization. The spatial structure of this protein is very well known; there are two disulphide bridges and one free SH group (a total of 5 SH groups).

2.   α-Lactalbumin

The α-lactalbumin does not seem to be universal to all milks: it is characteristic of the milk of the artiodactylous (even-toed) species; it does not seem to be present in the milk of other species. In human milk, it is α-lactalbumin which predominates in the 'soluble' fraction. There are two properties of this protein which make it of scientific interest:

— The α-lactalbumin is the regulating factor in the raw milk enzymatic system, the lacto-synthetase. In its absence, the enzyme transfers the galactose onto the glucosamine: in its presence, the specificity changes and the transfer of the galactose onto glucose occurs.
— This protein is very similar to lysozyme: molecules mass in the region of 14 200, four disulphide bridges (8 Cys residues), great correspondence in the amino acid sequence. However, the replacement of the glutamic acid (active centre of

lysozyme) by histidine explains why α-lactalbumin has no hydrolytic activity. These two proteins are synthesized under the control of genes which stem from a common ancestral gene; a duplication seems to be the reason why reptiles became mammals, because it allows the synthesis of lactose and the secretion of milk.

3.   Immunoglobulins

Immunoglobulins (Ig) are present in all milks. In cow's milk they make up only one tenth of the soluble proteins (0.5–0.7 g/l); but their proportion increases considerably in the colostrum (12 g/l at the end of the first day and 80 g/l in the first hour). This increase is the result of the passage of the blood Ig, since there is no decrease in the biosynthesis of other constituents. However, not all milk Ig comes directly from the blood; one part is synthesized in the mammary gland.

Here there is a new difference between the milk of ruminants and that of single-stomach animals. In the milk of ruminants, it is the IgG class (molecular mass 160 000) which predominates strongly (as in blood); these are basic molecules, slow in electrophoresis, containing few carbohydrates (3%) and having the normal antibody function. In single-stomach animals, it is the IgA group which predominates (molecular mass 320 000); they contain 8% carbohydrate, they have the specificity as in the blood groups. The immunoglobulins are of importance because they ensure the transmission of the mother's immunity to the young animal. Work is in hand to modify their specificity in cow's milk, to improve the health of children.

It is likely that immunoglobulins from milk will be produced industrially. The main objective is to incorporate them into babies' milk in order to improve the capacity of the immune system in new-born babies who are bottle fed.

It should be noted that trials similar to those first mentioned have been carried out on two other minor proteins of cow's milk — lactoferrin and lactoperoxidase. These may protect the human organism against intestinal infections.

4.   Proteose-peptones

Proteose-peptones make up the minor protein fraction of whey. They remain soluble after heating to 95°C with acidification at pH 4.6. There are the following two main groups.

4.1   Compounds from enzyme proteolysis

To date, three small parts have been identified, coming from β-casein:

— β-CN-5P (or compound 5) is the longest fragment. N-terminal, molecular mass 14 300. This peptide seems to be responsible for the 'deflating' effect on bread volume induced by the whey used in baking.

— β-CN-1P (or compound 8-slow), molecular mass 9900; and β-CN-4P (or compound 8-fast), molecular mass 4000. These compounds may result in the precipitation of casein in drinks with a fermented milk base.

4.2   Hydrophobic fraction of the proteose-peptones (or 'compound 3' fraction)

This fraction is made up of thermostable glycoproteins which are markedly hydrophobic in character and strongly clustered together. After sodium dodecylsulphate dissociation the molecular mass ranges from 7000 to 30 000. The 'compound 3' fraction includes 17% carbohydrates, of which 3% is sialic acid.

It shows a common antigenic identity with the glycoproteins of the membranes of fat globules. It has an inhibiting effect on lipolysis in cow's milk.

At present, there is some controversy over the classification of this fraction in the proteose-peptones group.

VIII. CASEIN ASSOCIATION — MICELLES

(1) *In the absence of calcium* each of the caseins link together mainly through hydrophilic bonds between the abundant non-polar groups (α-casein: 53% of the side chains). The uneven distribution of the charges on the molecule explains the differences observed in the size of the polymers. κ-Casein has an abnormal behaviour, in that the usual parameters seem to have no bearing on the size, which is about 650 000.

In the same way as the caseins link together between themselves, there are three known binary and one ternary association.

These properties cannot be seen at high values of pH, above 10, which have a dissociating influence, nor in the presence of some reactive substances, such as urea, guanidine, etc.

(2) *In the presence of calcium* the difference pointed out concerning κ-casein (see section VI above) is seen. The α- and β-caseins precipitate whilst the κ-casein forms a solution. In a mixture, the κ-casein forms micelles in accordance with the molecular relationship $\kappa/\alpha_s + \beta = 1/10$. It is difficult to explain the stabilizing capacity of the κ-casein; tyrosine residues play a part in this important property.

'Perfect' micelles are only formed in the presence of several ions: Ca^{2+}, PO_4^{3-}, citrate, Mg^{2+}. They have a lax structure (water content higher than 70%). There is still debate as to whether they are homogeneous or heterogeneous in character. Many ideas have been elaborated, the most recent, that of D. G. Schmidt[†], is convincing: the micelle is composed of sub-micelles formed from a hydrophobic nucleus, surrounded by a polar layer which gathers together the parts which are rich in phosphoric groupings and hydrophilic groupings; κ-casein may be found here in concentrated form. It seems that arrested growth of micelles might be caused by the occupation of the external surface by the hydrophilic groupings (Fig. 13.5).

The natural micellar form is calcium phosphocaseinate. On average 1 litre of cow's milk contains: (27 g of casein+0.37 g of CaO)+1.7 g of calcium phosphate.

Perfect micelles are spherical and non-uniform in diameter. In cow's milk the average diameter is 100 nm and the maximum 300 nm. The relationship between the different caseins seems to be 3:3:1:1 for $\alpha_{s1}:\beta:\kappa:\alpha_{s2}$; but in small micelles the proportion of κ rises.

In milk, a small part of the whole casein, about 5–10%, is not found in the micelles and can be separated by ultracentrifugation (35 000 g, 90 min). It is possible to move the casein from one state to another by activating the calcium ions which displace the equilibrium towards the micellar form.

† D. G. Schmidt (1982). In *Developments in Dairy Chemistry 1. Proteins*. Ed. P. F. Fox. Applied Science Publishers Ltd, London.

IX. COAGULATION OF MILK

(1) *The lactic acidification of milk,* or addition of acid at pH 4.65, precipitates the whole demineralized casein. This method of coagulation or flocculation is not much used in French cheese-making but is widely used in eastern Mediterranean cheese-making. It produces a crumbly curd.

(2) *Coagulation using rennin,* or another coagulating protease, results in the more or less specific cleavage of the 105–106 (Phe–Met) bond in the κ-casein molecule (Fig. 13.4). A large peptide, acidic in character (65 amino acids) then separates; it is formed from about 1/4 of the hydroxyamino acids (Ser, Thr) and it is deficient in 6 amino acids (Cys, Phe, Tyr, Trp, His, Arg); this part of the molecule has a high solvation capacity, which explains both the 'colloid protector effect' of the κ-casein properties and the 'coagulation mechanism'. The protein part is 'κ-paracasein', hydrophobic and insoluble, with a basic character; after hydrolysis by the rennin, this is the only constituent which migrates, in electrophoresis at pH 8.6, to the cathode.

This enzymatic reaction occurs at various temperatures (from 0°C to 50°C); it is not the cause of the coagulation. The presence of ionized calcium is essential. The rennin does not coagulate a solution of whole casein, in a milk pH (6.7) obtained using the sodium ion; on the other hand, the measure of soluble nitrogen in 12% trichloracetic acid allows the reaction to proceed. The temperature coefficient has been calculated as close to 3.

Fig. 13.6 summarizes the three phases of enzymatic coagulation of milk. The secondary phase (formation of the curd) is a rearrangement which becomes extremely slow when the temperature is below 15°C, because its temperature coefficient is raised (as with that of a denaturation reaction); coagulation does not occur in milk with rennin added at 5–10°C. One important application of these kinetic studies is the continuous manufacture of curd for the cheese industry: rennin is put into cold milk, which is coagulated through heating in a heat exchanger.

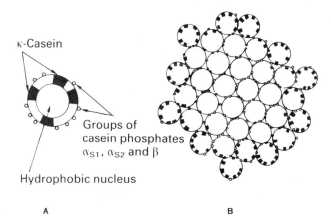

κ-Casein

Groups of
casein phosphates
α_{S1}, α_{S2} and β

Hydrophobic nucleus

A   B

Fig. 13.5 — Sub-micelles (A) and micelles (B) (Schmidt's theory).

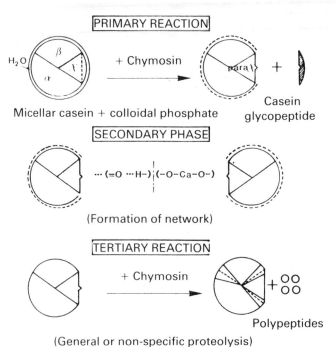

Fig. 13.6 — The three phases in the enzymatic coagulation of milk.

X. PRINCIPLES OF CHEESE-MAKING

(1) *Cheese* is a preserve of two insoluble constituents of milk: casein, which of necessity provides the framework, and the fatty material, which is present in variable proportion. The manufacturing process consists mainly of the following phases:

(a) coagulation (as above);
(b) curd separation: separation of curd and serum;
(c) moulding, to give the shape in a mould;
(d) salting, for the flavour and to influence enzyme activity;
(e) maturing, which generally produces the ripe cheese through the destruction of lactose, a rise in the pH, loss of water and above all proteolysis and lipolysis. The rind forms during this stage.

For certain types of cheese, this scheme is amended: e.g. with additions such as pressing for Saint Paulin, and cooking at 53–55°C for the Gruyère types, or with some steps omitted to give unsalted and unrefined cream cheeses.

Using genetic engineering techniques it is possible to prepare a curdling enzyme of pure chymosin. This comes from the cloning of the gene on certain micro-organisms (*Escherichia coli, Kluyveromyces, Aspergillus*). This process is author-ized in the USA and Britain.

The coagulation time is a very important factor. It depends on the temperature of the milk, its pH and its ionized calcium. The pH depends, in part, on the development of lactic ferments. Recently, an acidifying agent, glucono-deltalactone, has been brought into use as a technological aid.

(2) *The coagulating enzyme* most used is still rennin, extracted from the fourth stomach (abomasum) of the young unweaned calf. It contains chymosin (E.C.3.4.23.4) and a variable quantity, from 10% to 20%, of pepsin. These two enzymes are very similar, with molecular masses of 31 400 and 33 400 respectively, and both arising from an inactive zymogen by the action of protons. In practice, there is, however, an important difference, in the influence of pH on the activity: chymosin remains active at about pH 7.5, whereas pepsin no longer coagulates the milk at a pH above 6.7.

These enzymes are aspartate proteinases, very different from the digestive enzymes in the intestine (e.g. trypsin, chymotrypsin, which are serine proteases). Belonging to the same group are some replacement enzymes, which are not so large and are used a lot in countries where the abomasum is not readily available. In this category the enzymes from *Endothia parasitica*, *Mucor pusillus* and *Mucor miehei* are included. A rennin mixture with pig pepsin 50/50 is used a lot in the USA. These replacements require adaptations in the cheese-making techniques.

(3) *Salting* is most usually carried out by brine saturated with salt (NaCl). This may happen before moulding, when the curd is drained and milled. NaCl has several effects:

— protects against dangerous micro-organisms, all the more necessary when the cheese is moist; there is a reduction in water activity in relation to the concentration of the salt;
— it helps drainage of the serum and in this way complements the drainage process;
— it brings out the cheese flavour;
— it slows down the enzyme activity; if there is too much salt, the cheese remains hard;
— it produces a slight rise in the protein solubility;
— it assists in formation of the rind, especially in cheeses rubbed with salt.

The average concentration of salt in cheese is 1–2%; in some cases (blue cheeses and some goat cheeses) it may rise to 3–4%.

(4) *Disappearance of the lactose* is mainly the work of the lactic fermenting agents, the development of which is encouraged. Lactic acid and flavour substances form. Their roles are varied:

— influence on the aroma, especially in fresh and little-matured products;
— protection of the medium by the rapid lowering of pH to 5.0 and below;
— solubilization of minerals linked to casein and modification of the texture.

The acid formed is neutralized by the calcium remaining in the cheese or by the ammonia produced by the surface microflora, or else degraded in secondary fermentations. It is worth mentioning that among these secondary fermentations is the propionic fermentation which forms CO_2 gas, which produces the holes (the eyes) in cheeses such as Emmental and Comté.

(5) *The microflora* of cheese plays a large role in the maturing process, but it is complex and still evolving.

— The lactic microflora tend to reduce as the maturing process goes on. Lactobacilli persist for a long time in pressed cheeses and firm cheeses; their proteolytic and lipolytic enzymes are endocellular, but they pass into the medium after the death of millions of cells per gram.

— Enterococci are plentiful in cheeses made from raw or moderately heat-treated milk. Their proteases degrade the casein.

— Yeasts are found both inside and on the outside of cheeses. In general they are fast-acting because they have good tolerance of acid medium (pH less than 5) and salt medium (10% NaCl).

— Moulds are most often on the surface, except in blue cheeses where their growth is assisted by the pricking of the cheese body.

(6) *Enzyme reactions* are of prime importance in the process of turning the curd into cheese through the progressive digestion of casein. The result of this proteolysis is a smoother texture and the development of part of the aroma.

The proteases and the peptidases which take part in these reactions are very varied. The most important are:

— the coagulating enzyme which stays in the curd (tertiary reaction), the action of which stops at the level of large peptides;

— the proteases of the lactic bacteria (especially in hard cheeses);

— the proteases from types of fungi (soft cheeses with mould on the outside (*Penicillium caseicolum*) and blue cheeses with the mould inside (*Penicillium roqueforti*)).

The natural protease of milk plays a lesser role in the maturing process.

Table 13.6 shows some significant values for four types of cheese which are the most widespread in France and for fresh immature cheeses. It can be seen that the proportion of soluble nitrogen increases from 6% to 30% of total nitrogen in Camembert and the proportion of ammonia nitrogen rises to 24% of the soluble nitrogen. With a cheese which is cooked and hard, without moulds, such as Comté, there is less maturing; the corresponding values are 20% and 11%; and by contrast, the amino nitrogen develops in the opposite way.

Lipolysis is a much more limited process and does not affect the texture of the cheese; it does, however, play an important role in flavour formation. It is mainly the lipases of the moulds and the micrococci which are active : the milk lipase hardly seems to react in the pH zone of cheese.

Salt inhibits the enzymes, but lipases much less than proteases. In a highly salted cheese, lipolysis continues whereas proteolysis stops.

The many experiments which have been carried out to produce 'maturing with enzymes', using industrially produced enzymes, have not yielded quality cheeses.

XI.   DAIRY PRODUCTS (OTHER THAN BUTTER AND CHEESE)

1.   Milks for human consumption

Raw milk does not keep well; it soon goes off, particularly by the action of bacteria which degrade the lactose to produce acid. Low acidification is enough to make the milk coagulate at boiling point (a pH fall from 6.7 to 6.3). Moreover, raw milk may contain organisms pathogenic for humans. For this reason, heat treatment is necessary.

Table 13.6 — Data on cheese-making

	Fresh	Soft (Camembert)	Cheeses Blue (Auvergne)	Pressed (St. Paulin)	Cooked (Comté)
A. *Manufacture data*					
Starter culture (apart from lactic bacteria)	—	*Penicillium caseicolum*	*Penicillium roqueforti*	Red variety bacteria	Propionic bacteria
Coagulation					
—length of time	Long, at <20°C	1–2 h	1 h	30 min	15 min
—rennin used (ml/100 l)	2–5	15–22	20–30	25–35	30–35
Yield (kg/100 l)	20	14	12	11	9
B. *Cheese data*					
Length of maturation process	—	4 w	1.5 m	1–2 m	3–5 m
Dry matter (%)	13–20	45	50	47	62
Fatty substance (% of dry matter)	—	45	47	47	45
Soluble nitrogen (N_S % of total N)	6	30	25	20	20
Amino nitrogen (% of N_S)	6	10		15	30
Ammoniacal nitrogen (% of N_S)	0	24		5	11
Ca/P	0.5	0.5		1.4	1.6
pH	4.8	6.5	6.0	5.5	5.3

1.1 Pasteurized milks

Milk is heated to reduce the common flora and to destroy pathogenic organisms. There is no set combination in France regarding time/temperature, but the bacteriological quality and the sell-by dates are controlled. The normal pasteurization treatment is heating for 15–20 seconds at 72–75°C; this allows the destruction of the Koch bacillus (*Mycobacterium tuberculosis*) and inactivation of the phosphatase. Under these time/temperature conditions, there is no effect on the constituents of the milk, apart from a small loss in thiamin and vitamin C (7–10%). A 'high quality pasteurized milk', corresponding to grade A in the UK, has been recently defined in France, with strict conditions concerning the collection of the raw milk; it does not seem to be very popular, however.

1.2 Sterilized milk

The method of sterilization in sealed bottles, with heating for 20 minutes at 118–120°C, subjects the milk to quite important changes. The caseins are partially dephosphorylated and κ-casein has its sialic acid removed; the serum proteins are totally denatured. Protein–lactose interactions produce browning. The cooked taste appears. The mineral equilibrium Ca/P is displaced towards the insoluble form. The surface layer of the micelles is modified and their stability reduced. The sales of sterilized milk in glass bottles are now falling.

1.3   UHT milk

Diagrams of the effects of thermal treatments show that some changes brought about during sterilization are more drastic than the changes milk can undergo: one of the most perceptible being browning. The temperature coefficients are respectively 10 and about 2.5. It is therefore preferable to carry out the treatment at ultra-high temperature (UHT) during a very short period, to obtain sterilization with very little change. The conditions range from 5 to 1 seconds and from 140°C to 150°C, with instantaneous rise and fall in temperatures. The milk must be treated aseptically when it comes out of the sterilizer. This system involves the continuous flow of milk.

UHT milk is becoming more widespread; it is white, has a good taste and is only a little more changed than pasteurized milk; it can be kept for several months at ambient temperature. There is, however, the risk, rare with ordinary milk (more frequent with condensed milk) of thickening and gelling, in the absence of any microbial development, which is difficult to explain.

2.   Fermented milks — yoghurt

Three species of microbes are used in the production of yoghurt:

— lactobacilli which produce a lot of lactic acid at around 45°C (*L. bulgaricus*);
— lactic streptococci, giving a characteristic flavour (*S. thermophilus*);
— yeasts fermenting the lactose, producing carbon dioxide gas and a little alcohol (*Saccharomyces kefir*); they are only used in oriental products.

Yoghurt is greatly developed in Europe. It has to include at least 106 living bacteria per gram and contain at least 0.8% lactic acid (80°Dornic). The fresh milk may be enriched by powdered milk to a maximum of 5%; it must undergo high temperature pasteurization.

The qualities of yoghurt are varied. It may be coagulated in the final packaging. It may also be fermented in bulk, yielding a mass with creamy consistency, which can then be divided up. This is easier if the process is carried out under good conditions (preheating to at least 90°C and an acidity level greater than 70°Dornic).

There is developing use of 'Bifidus active' yoghurt, which includes a strain of the bifide (Y formed) lactic bacterium of human origin. According to the first manufacturer of this fermented milk, this is the *B longum* strain. This product has been much discussed.

3.   Milk desserts

These are creamy or gelled forms of non-acid milk. The required consistency is obtained either through rennin action or by the addition of a gelling substance (maximum 2%). Various gelling substances have been suggested: modified starch, gelatine, carrageenan, etc.

4. Evaporated and condensed milks

Ordinary 'condensed' milk, whole or skimmed, (known as evaporated milk) is obtained by thermal evaporation or by reverse osmosis. The degree of concentration varies; it is in general 2/1 or 3/1. It is sterilized in metallic cans in an autoclave. It is thus a sterile product. It can replace milk for the consumer; but it is little used in Britain and France. The great problem is to ensure the stability of the product.

Sweetened condensed milk is a 'sweet mixture' obtained through evaporation of sweetened whole milk. It is not sterilized. Dangers to beware of are of two kinds:

— bacteriological: the presence of yeasts producing gas, or staphylococci producing enterotoxins;
— physical: gritty texture; this is avoided by putting lactose crystals into the hot condensed milk.

Table 13.7 gives the composition of these products.

5. Dried milk (powder)

Table 13.7 — Composition of milk-derived products

	Water	Fat-free dry matter	Fats	Proteins	Minerals	Lactose	Various
Skimmed condensed milk	68.5	31	0.5	12	3	16	
Whole condensed milk	66	24	10	9	2	13	
Whole sweetened condensed milk	26	23	9	9	2	12	Sucrose: 41
Skimmed milk powder	5	92	1.5	34	8	50	
Whole milk powder	4	70	26	27	6	37	
Acid casein	8		2.8	87	2	0	
Powder from fresh milk	4		0	13	9	72	Lactic acid:2
Protein concentrate 75 obtained by ultrafiltration of milk serum)	4		6	75	3	9.5	Lactic acid:1

(*) ESD of milk.

Concentrated skimmed milk (dry extract 35–50%) is dried by one of two processes:

— on metal rollers heated internally to 140°C (Hatmaker process and variants). The intense heating yields a partly soluble product, which is usually reserved for cattle feed, especially if the treated milk has been neutralized with soda (badly kept milk). However, this product is used in certain food industries for human consumption (chocolate, sweets).
— by atomization in a current of hot air at 140°–150°C (fog process or Spray process). Water is evaporated instantaneously, the exit temperature is only about 90°C. The powder contains 4% water, it is white and little modified in composition apart from a reduction in some vitamins and enzymes. A problem is

presented by its affinity for water; the lactose is usually in the amorphous state, which is not a stable state. By encouraging crystallization after drying, the particulate structure of the powder is improved: in the solubility, absence of 'lumps', easy flow, etc. This 'instant powder' was developed a few years ago, by a light moistening of the raw powder and further drying. Nowadays the spray chamber procedure is modified.

Whole dried milk (not skimmed) is a fragile product, mostly because of lipid oxidation. The best method of preservation is *in vacuo* in a hermetically sealed container.

6. Caseins — caseinates
Three types of whole casein are made from skimmed milk:

— acid casein, by the addition to the milk of hydrochloric acid at pH 4.6;
— lactic casein, by lactic fermentation;
— rennin casein, as in the case of low-fat curd.

The first of these is the most used. The 'granule' is formed by cooking at about 50°C for two hours. Then the product is separated and ground; it is crushed in acidulated water and dried in warm air. A well-washed casein does not 'roast' during drying; the formation of brown-coloured granules, not very stable, is due to the presence of residual lactose (Maillard reaction).

Casein is little used as food, despite its excellent properties: it has a higher emulsifying capacity than many additives; it ensures a certain level of water retention in cooled products; and finally, it is an example of a protein which is not costly.

The recent introduction of caseinates, which render a food product soluble in a controlled way, has enlarged the market for casein. Sodium caseinates are mainly prepared by dissolving the mass of milk curd in soda, at pH 6.7. The dry extract of the solution can be as little as half that of skimmed milk (20–25%) because of the increase in viscosity.

Note that casein is also used in industries not concerned with food production: for glues, paints, etc.

7. Whey–protein concentrate
It is a major industrial problem to put to use this by-product from cheese-making. It represents more than 80% of the milk used. It is of interest because of its protein and lactose content; however there are great disadvantages: low dry matter content (6.5%), very salty (10% of the dry extract), low protein/glucose relationship (1/6) and also a very delicate product, because it is a good culture medium.

7.1
The classic way of using whey is by concentration and drying, for use in animal foodstuffs, especially for calves. Little of it is used for human consumption; it is, however, useful for making bread, biscuits, etc., because it improves both the quality of the dough (strength) and the organoleptic quality as far as taste and colouring are concerned (Maillard reaction).

7.2

The production of lactose, through crystallization of a concentrated solution followed by cooling, is a long-established process; lactose binds flavour well and does not sweeten much in foodstuffs (flan, ice cream, etc.); it is also used to improve confectionery and biscuit products (as well as the browning, the modification of the crystallization of sucrose and the emulsifying capacity should be noted). Chemical hydrolysis or enzymatic hydrolysis by a lactase is of interest because of the new outlets available, especially in confectionery, desserts, etc.

7.3

Separation of the proteins despite their reduced amount can be carried out in the following ways:

7.3.1   Thermocoagulation

This is the precipitation of the denatured proteins by heating, often in acid medium. For some time, 'butter-milk cheeses' have been made in this way, and, recently, a protein milk reincorporated in milk has been used in cheese-making (*Centri-Whey* process). The high pH, 6 or 7, yields proteins which are more easily dispersed and possess good structuring properties.

The addition of acid to the lactoserum increases the salt content. This content may be reduced by passage through an ion exchanger; but this complicates the operations.

7.3.2   Non-thermal precipitation

The use of cation or ammonia polyelectrolytes permits cold precipitation of proteins which are little or not at all denatured; but if the precipitating agent has to be eliminated, a complementary operation is necessary. The following have been suggested: carboxymethylcellulose, substituted to a greater or lesser degree, polyphosphates, polyacrylic acid, chitosan (polyglucosamine), etc. These processes do appear to be much used.

7.3.3   Ultrafiltration

This is a modern process which has been considerably developed in the last 15 years. Mainly protein concentrates are made, which still contain a little lactose and lipids. These products are used, in part, in human foods.

7.3.4   'Spherosil' process

This is a very recent process using chromatography with granules of porous silica onto which exchange groups have been bonded. Judging from the early experiments, this seems promising from the economic point of view.

14

Meat and blood products

I. MUSCLE PROTEINS

Meat is a striated muscle; generally, skeletal and heart muscles are grouped together. On average they make up 35% of the weight of an animal.

The average composition of the common red and white meats is given in Table 1.1, together with that of fish muscle. In lean meat, proteins always predominate; as a percentage of dry matter, they are about 65% for beef cattle and 85% for horse and fish. The lipids follow this dominant fraction. Although there is quite a large spectrum within which the lipid content of carcases may vary, the intramuscular lipids which we eat are not greater than 4–5% of the weight of fresh meat, except in the case of exceptional breeds of animals with intramuscular lipid content capable of reaching 9%. The proportion of phospholipids is relatively constant, at about $\frac{1}{5}$ of the lipids. Finally there are the carbohydrates and the minerals, each about 1%.

Research carried out on the properties and quality of meat is in general on the muscle proteins. Three types are distinguished, as indicated in Table 14.1.

From the anatomical point of view, the muscle fibre is the essential cohesive unit. It is a very long cell (up to some centimetres in length) with a diameter of 10–100 μm. It encloses about a hundred filaments each of 1 μm in diameter, parallel to the axis of the fibre; these are the myofibrillae. The surrounding cytoplasm is called sarcoplasm; it also contains nuclei and mitochondria; it is made up of more than 100 proteins which constitute the myogen and it also contains ATP and creatine. The external membrane of the fibre is the sarcolemma.

Fish muscle has a structure comparable to that of the muscle of warm-blooded animals. The stroma (soluble) proteins are abundant at about half the quantity and the muscular fibres are shorter. Rigor mortis (5 hours) and maturation (25–30 hours) are more rapid; the lowering of the pH is more limited (6.3–6.5) which lowers the microbiological stability of fish.

II. STROMA PROTEINS — COLLAGEN AND TENDERNESS OF MEAT

These are the least soluble proteins, typically fibrous, above all extracellular, linked by interactions to the mucoproteins and lipoproteins (scleroproteins, see Chapter 5, §VI).

Table 14.1 — Muscle proteins

Type	% Total muscle proteins	Main constituents[a]	Properties
Stroma proteins	15–20	Collagen (50) Elastin (10)	Insoluble, extracellular, conjunctive tissue.
Sarcoplasmic proteins (cytoplasm)	30–35	Myoglobin (5) Enzymes	Soluble, intracellular, biologically active.
Myofibrillar proteins	50–55	Myosin (50) Actin (20) Tropomyosin and troponins (15)	Slightly soluble, intracellular, with contractile properties.

[a]Percentage of total category is shown in brackets.

1.   Collagen

Collagen is very widespread in the animal kingdom; it is the main protein of the connective tissue and of the skeleton of vertebrates. In its state in animals, it has notable anatomical abilities; the fibrillae are resistant to traction. Collagen is associated with a second material, the polysaccharides; these form a hydrated network resistant to compression. The two together make up an abundant composite material.

The molecule is the 'tropocollagen', made up of three peptide chains, of which at least two are the same in all collagens. These are cylindrical chains, non-branched, of a thousand or so amino acids, in rods $280\,\mu$m in length and $1.4\,\mu$m in diameter, with a molecular mass close to $300\,000$. Their composition is very unusual. Nearly 70% of the total residues is made up of just three amino acids: Gly 35%, Ala 12%, Pro and Hypro 20%. It will be seen in the first two that there are no side chains or CH_3. The sequence bears a series of triplets where glycine occupies the same position; polar zones separate these sequences.

$$-Gly-Ala-Pro- -Gly-Pro-Ala- -Gly-Pro-Hypro- \text{, etc.}$$

The Pro and Hypro residues impose a helical conformation to the right, with a triplet in each spire, of which the frequency is 0.86 nm (progression of 0.29 per amino acid) without a hydrogen bond. The spatial structure is completed by the formation of a triple helix, this time with the establishment of numerous hydrogen bonds, and with the presence of glycine, not being bulky, inside the triple helix (Fig. 14.1).

Examination under an electron microscope, with negative colouration (using phosphotungstic acid — this fills the spaces which then become opaque) to reveal a

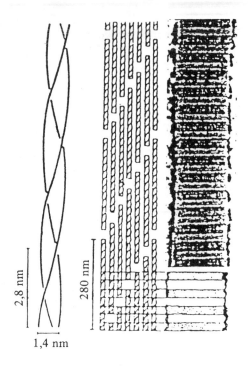

Fig 14.1 — Structure of collagen.

periodicity of 0.67 nm which seems to show a regular interval of 280 nm between each molecule. This interval permits interactions between side chains of amino acids positioned at every 67 nm in the peptide chain. Covalent bonds involve two Lys, ensuring the solidity of the fibrillae; the nature of these bonds is still under discussion. The desmosine residue, formed from four Lys joined together into a cyclic compound, is one possibility. Ester bridges and iso-peptide bonds are also possible.

The number of bonds existing between the chains making up the collagen is variable. The tenderness of a meat is not just due to the collagen content; it depends on the structure of this protein. The solubility of the collagen of a given muscle in a salt or acid solution diminishes with the age of the animal. It has been established that the bonds cross-linking the molecules are more labile in the young animal; they may be broken by pH variations or heating. In the older animal other cross-links are formed, which are more stable, and increase the toughness of the meat. This ageing phenomenon is normal; it is not possible to modify it without risk. Small peptides (telopeptides) liberated after the protease action, react on the links between the molecules; they are deficient in proline.

Thermal treatment of collagen in water produces gelatinization above 80°C. This solubilization is the consequence of the dissociation of the fibrillae with partial hydrolysis of the molecule. In a cooked meat, the tenderness depends solely on the denatured muscle fibres, and possibly, on the elastin.

Collagen is an unusual substance in proteins, because its denaturation solubilizes the molecule and because of its biochemical lability.

Several types of collagen are distinguished according to their origin and composition:

— type I, fibrous collagen (tendons, bone, skin, dentine): 2 chains α_1 +1 chain α_2, fibrillar structure;
— type II, predominates in cartilage and vertebral discs: 3 identical α chains, fibrillar structure;
— type III, predominates in the vascular system: 3 identical α chains, fibrillar structure;
— types IV and V, amorphous collagen of the membranes.

β and γ collagens are a dimer and trimer of the above.

Collagen is not a good protein from the nutritional point of view. On the one hand, its composition with regard to essential amino acids is not suitable (too much Pro, Gly, Ala) and, on the other hand, in the natural state it is resistant to trypsin and chymotrypsin digestion. It becomes more digestible in the denatured form. Peptides of hydroxyproline have been found in human blood after the ingestion of connective tissue.

2. Elastin

Elastin is the second constituent of the connective tissue, which characterizes the elastic tissues. It is not usually very abundant in the muscle; it is found mainly in the arterial cellular walls and in the yellow ligaments. Its structure is fibrous. It resists cooking in water, it swells but does not dissolve. It is also resistant to the majority of proteases: pepsin, trypsin, chymotrypsin; but it is partially hydrolysed by the elastase of the pancreas (and also by papain). Elastin is not attacked by acids and relatively concentrated bases.

The structure of elastin is complex: it has been possible to isolate two of its constituents, α-elastin of MM$\geqslant$70 000 and β-elastin of MM 5500. The peptide chains are interlinked as in collagen. The composition of amino acids shows a large quantity of glycine and alanine (30% of residues for each), and in addition valine and proline (each 12%): there is also a little hydroxyproline and hydroxylysine (1%).

III. SARCOPLASMIC PROTEINS — MYOGLOBIN, MEAT COLOUR

These are soluble proteins with pH close to 7.0 and weak ionic forces (<0.1). The number of species is considerable because of the presence of enzymes in the cytoplasm. The quantities are very low, apart from myoglobin.

Myoglobin is responsible for the red colour of meats where it makes up $\frac{9}{10}$ of the total pigments; in the $\frac{1}{10}$ remainder is haemoglobin, which is a tetramer resulting from the association of 4 units corresponding to myoglobin.

The concentration of myoglobin varies according to:

— animal species and muscle type;

— the age (meat of older animals is darker) and physical activity of the animal;
— the iron content in the diet (the veal from calves with a deficient diet is white).

Myoglobin is a porphyrin heteroprotein. It joins the prosthetic group 'haem' to the protein or globin, which is itself colourless.

Haem is made up of a nucleus of protoporphyrin linked to an iron atom Fe^{2+}; Fig. 14.2 illustrates this. It can be seen that the nucleus is made up of 4 pyrrole rings interlinked by 4 methene residues and with eight substituents, 4 methyl groups, 2 propionic acid groups and 2 vinyl groups. The molecule is totally conjugated in form $(-C=C-C=C-)$ which gives it important properties: the absorption spectrum of a coloured substance, high stability of the nucleus, a flat and rigid molecule. The main chemical property is the ability to form complexes with metals Fe, Mg, Zn, Cu, Co, etc., to give stable chelates, highly coloured, insoluble in water. Molecules of this type have a basic character.

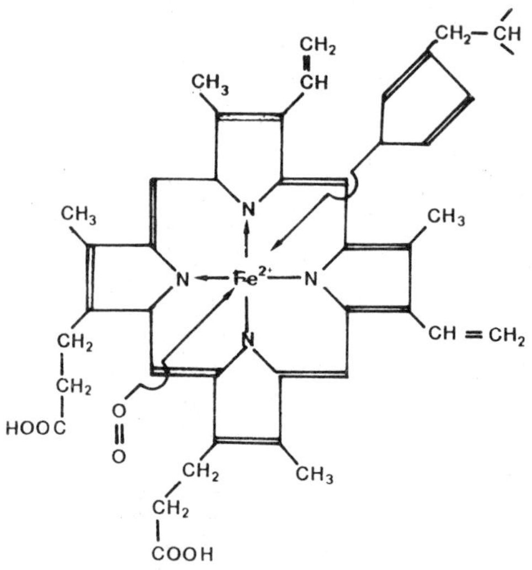

Fig 14.2 — Structure of oxymyoglobin.

The structure of globin is well-known, MM = 17 800; 153 residues of amino acids, of which 80% are in α-helical structure, in eight segments of 7 to 25 residues. The haem is fixed by its iron atom to histidine No. 93 in a fold. Together they make an ellipsoid of 4.3×2.5 nm; it is stabilized by hydrogen bonds, salt links and hydrophobic interactions.

The iron atom is coordinated with 6 atoms which each furnish the Fe^{2+} orbitals with a pair of electrons; 4 atoms are nitrogen of the porphyrin nuclei; 1 atom is the nitrogen of histidine 93; the 6th is the oxygen atom in the oxymyoglobin. This last is a reserve of oxygen for the muscle, this oxygen being carried by the haemoglobin of the blood, the affinity of which is lower than that of myoglobin; this function occurs only when the iron is divalent. It has been noticed that in diving animals (e.g. whale, seal) the myoglobin content of the muscle is high, about 8%, which allows them to go a long time without breathing. The native form is desoxymyoglobin in which the 6th coordination number remains vacant.

Fig. 14.3 shows an aspect of the spatial structure of the sperm whale myolobin, the first spatial structure to be determined. The letters outline the segments of the α-helix. The haem is seen in the upper part: the F8 bond corresponds with that of His 93. The hydrophilic amino acids meet at the surface of the molecule, forming salt links (Lys, Arg→Glu, Asp). Some side chain amino acids are positioned face-to-face inside; some Van der Waals bonds consolidate the fold. Finally, it should be noted that the two residues of propionic acid, attached to the tetrapyrrole nucleus, participate in the haemoglobin bond, because of the Lys and His in the globin.

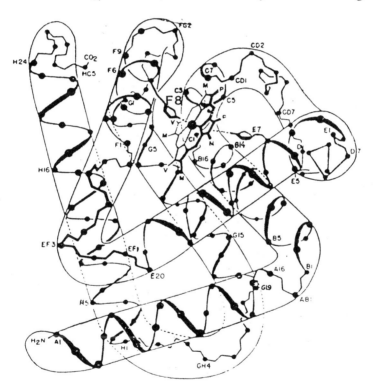

Fig. 14.3 — Spatial structure of sperm whale myoglobin.

Metmyoglobin is the oxidized form, in which the iron is Fe^{3+}; it is brown in colour. The preservation of the red colour requires conditions which favour the reduced form: e.g. the presence of glucose, or ascorbic acid.

Nitrosomyoglobin occurs in meat in the presence of nitrite (saltpetre or nitrite in curing salts); it has a red colour which is sought after, but it is not very stable.

Carboxymyoglobin occurs in the presence of carbon monoxide which bonds to the haem iron and thus impedes the transport of the oxygen; this gas is highly toxic, although it does not alter the red colour. Carboxymyoglobin is more stable than oxymyoglobin; however the introduction of a large amount of oxygen would displace the CO.

Heat or a low pH denatures the globin; ferro- or ferri-haemochromes form. The latter, oxidized, form has a brown colour; it appears in cooked meats.

IV. MYOFIBRILLAR PROTEINS — CONTRACTION

This dominant group of proteins includes 8–9 species which can be divided as follows:

— contractile proteins which form about 75% of the total, comprising two species: myosin (53%) and actin (22%);
— proteins which control contraction, making up the remainder: tropomyosin and troponins (each 8%), M proteins (4.5%), C proteins (2%), α- and β-actinins (2%).

1. Myosin

Myosin has a high molecular mass, 475 000, but six sub-units of it are recognized: two are heavy chains of 200 000 Da; four are light chains of 16 500–20 500 Da. The heavy chains have some parts with helical structure (about 55%) which make up the filament of the quaternary structure; the globular extremity, with which light chains are associated, forms the head of the molecule of myosin. A filament of myosin consists of molecules aligned in parallel with the head at intervals of 6 nm in relation to its neighbour. The filaments measure about 1500 nm.

Myosin has an ATPase activity which, in the presence of actin, is activated by Ca^{2+} and by Mg^{2+}.

2. Actin

Actin has a simple spatial structure. Its molecular mass is of 42 000 Da; there are no sub-units, but two forms: the globular form, or G-actin, which has the molecular mass already mentioned, and the fibrous form, or F-actin, which results from the polymerization of actin G in the presence of salts.

The sequence has been determined; amongst the 374 amino acids there are 5–SH groups, but no cystine. Linked with the molecule of G-actin there is a molecule of ATP and an ion, Ca^{2+} or Mg^{2+}. The spatial structure is once more fibrillar, with a double helix comprising 13 monomers per turn and per filament, and a length of about 1200 nm.

The regulating proteins are distributed periodically all along the actin. Their sequence is now known, as well as their method of bonding and the role of calcium in their displacement.

Actomyosin results from the association of many filaments of myosin and actin (Fig. 14.4).

3. Muscular contraction

Muscular contraction is the sliding in of thin filaments between thick filaments, without changing the length. The motive force stems from the bond between the

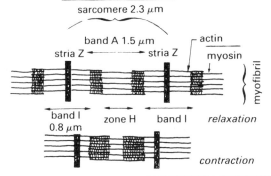

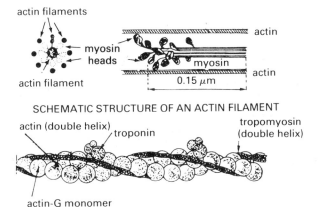

Fig. 14.4 — Myosin–actin relationship.

heads of myosin on a binding site in the actin, followed by modification of the structure of the heads. The command comes back to the nerve influx, which frees the Ca^{2+} ions; then, in the presence of Mg^{2+}, the ATPase activity take place, which produces the energy necessary for the contraction:

$$ATP+H_2O \rightarrow ADP+H_3PO_4+E$$

V.   *RIGOR MORTIS* AND CONDITIONING

1.   Rigor mortis

Rigor mortis, which sets in several hours after death (10–12 hours for beef cattle muscle at 20°C), results from the irreversible bond between the two constituents of muscle proteins, myosin and actin. The irreversibility comes from the decrease in ATP content. The speed at which this is produced becomes less than the speed of hydrolysis when the stopping of the blood circulation deprives the muscle of oxygen; the redox potential falls from +250 to −50 millivolts. The intercellular membranes no longer retain Ca^{2+}. As the concentration in the myofibrillae increases, there is exposure of the binding sites on the myosin. Finally the ATP hydrolysis frees a phosphoric acid residue and the pH falls from 7.2 to 5.5, which intensifies the actin–myosin link and promotes the passage from a gel to a more compact crystalline structure, with a fall in the capacity to retain water.

The transformations which occur in the muscle after slaughter may be summed up as follows, taking into account the modification of the myoglobin:

(1) Blood circulation ceases.
    (a) Lower oxygen content.
(2) Cellular respiration ceases.
    (b) Lower ATP content.
    (c) Fall in pH.
(3) Formation of actinomyosin (rigidity).
(4) Aggregation of the proteins (pI 5.5).
    (d) Fall in water retention.

If the temperature of the muscular tissue is lowered rapidly to about 0°C, before rigidity appears, a rapid and intense hardening can be seen. The sarcoplasmic 'calcium pump' frees a large amount of of Ca^{2+} in the myofibrillae, following a modification of the membrane lipoproteins, whilst the quantity of ATP is again raised. Then follows an interaction of the myosin and the actin, and muscular contraction. This phenomenon is seen in the fast-type fibres, since with the slow-type fibres the ATPase activity of the myosin is slowly inhibited at temperatures below 9°C.

Generally, meat is cooled slowly to allow rigidity to occur when the temperature is around 15°C. The quality of the meat is then at its best (weak contraction and high water retention capacity).

2. Conditioning

Conditioning stems from a limited proteolysis by the intracellular enzymes which bring *rigor mortis* to an end. Tenderness of the meat improves in the condititioning process along with other properties: flavour, succulence, etc. It has been shown that several enzymes are at work here: CASF (calcium activated sarcoplasmic factor), cathepsins B and D coming from lysosomes, etc.

The duration of conditioning depends on the temperature; you can reckon on 2 days at 20°C and 2 weeks at 0°C to get good results in the case of beef cattle. Small quantities of substances which improve the aroma are produced: e.g. diacetyl, acetone, hydrogen sulphide, ammonia, nucleotides.

3. Influence of temperature

3.1 At about 60°C

Denaturation of the two groups of the most abundant proteins occurs: myofibrillar and sarcoplasmic proteins. The reduction in solubility, accompanied in the case of the latter by coagulation, is a leading factor in the hardening of the meat. A brown colour is given by the ferrihaemochrome which comes from the denatured myoglobin. In any case, long cooking at 58°C–60°C allows the collagen to be attacked by endogenous proteases (cysteine proteinases), which results in tenderization. This tenderization process is more effective where the collagen content of the muscle is higher.

3.2 At about 65–70°C
Rapid heating leads to toughening due to denaturation of myofibrillar proteins and a thermal contraction of collagen.

3.3 Above 80°C
Reactions which mark the start of the degradation process occur; in addition, there is a diminution in the capacity of the myofibrillar proteins to retain water. The organoleptic qualities change, particularly the flavour, because hydrogen sulphide and other sulphurous compounds are produced.

Where heating occurs above 80°C in water with meat which is rich in collagen, the gelatinization of this protein has greater effect than the precipitation of myofibrillar proteins. The overall effect of this is positive, as, for instance, in the preparation of stews.

3.4 At about 95°C
The Maillard reactions, between the NH_2 groups and the reducing monosaccharides, speed up. They contribute to the browning of meats (see Chapter 5, §IX).

VI. CURED MEATS — SALAMI, SAUSAGE

1. Salt
The effects are as follows:

(1) Protective effect against undesirable micro-organisms, in particular the organisms involved in putrefaction. Salt has a selective effect: it favours the halophilic microflora which yield the qualities being sought after.
(2) The draining off of the liquid and helping the mixture to dry out; there is a lowering in water activity which accentuates effect (1).
(3) Partial solubilization of some muscular proteins, which helps the 'binding capacity'. At the end of the drying process the mixture is rendered insoluble and so a sticky mass is produced.
(4) Heightening effect on the taste. It should be noted that the salty taste is reduced in raw meat by the presence of proteins (formation of complexes). Cooking develops the salty taste (breaking up of complexes).

2. Additives
Nitrates and nitrites have a role from both the technological and hygienic points of view.

2.1

They allow the stabilization of colour after cooking and the maintenance of the colour of lean meat; without this the colour would tend towards a greeny brown. In reality, it is the nitrites which are efficient in contributing $-N{=}O$ to the myoglobin molecule. The nitrates must be reduced *in situ* to nitrites by the microflora, principally the lactobacteria; their action is slower. There is no point in adding nitrates and nitrites at the same time. These salts are always incorporated in common salt and never added separately to meat.

The use of nitrates and nitrites in the food industry is now subject to strict control. The lethal dose for man is of the order of one gram. At acid pH, they may also react with the secondary amine group of amino acids, peptides and proteins, whilst giving rise to nitroso compounds or nitrosamines. These nitrosamines are not all carcinogenic, though they may give rise to compounds which are. For example, nitrosoproline is non-carcinogenic, but may lead to nitrosodimethylamine, which is a known carcinogenic agent.

2.2

These two salts are inhibitors of toxic bacteria, particularly those involved in botulism; this is why they are considered to be 'preservation agents' from the legal point of view.

Sucrose is often added (cooked ham, mortadella). There is no justification for this apart from increase in the yield, and there is a disadvantage in that the acidification process is stimulated in the course of preservation at the pre-packaging stage.

2.3

The nitrite has an effect on the flavour.

3. Salami

3.1 *Manufacture*

As with raw ham, a most complex process is involved:

— preparation of the 'mixture', minced meat containing equal quantities of 'fat' and lean pork meat (more rarely mixed with lean beef or horse meat) to which is added some salt with added nitrate (about 3%), often lactic enzymes and some glutamate (flavouring agent). The initial pH is close to 6.3;
— forcing mixture into the gut casing;
— braising at 22–25°C for 1–3 days;
— maturation in the drier, at between 10°C and 15°C for a variable period. To yield a good quality product this should be done at a lower temperature over a long period. The final humidity level varies between 25% and 30%.
— cleaning, and covering with a coating which is generally flour-based.

3.2 *The bloom*

This appears on about the fifth day of drying out. The gut casing, once opaque and shiny, becomes matt and transparent and retracts with the filling. Along with salt crystals, colonies of various micro-organisms develop, mainly staphylococci (and micrococci), yeasts and moulds. The surface becomes first white and then coloured as the fruiting bodies of the moulds develop and take on the appearance of a greenish coating.

3.3 The sausage filling

The mixture starts off bright pink or red (lean beef is darker than pork meat). It then turns to a greyish brown colour (metymyoglobin), then turns back to red, a process speeded up by the amount of nitrites added (10th–12th hour). After that, because of dehydration, the colour darkens. The fat remains white.

The consistency improves. The mixture begins to have 'body'. A bonding is established between the small chunks because of physicochemical modifications due to the salt, especially the release of soluble proteins. Beef releases more soluble proteins than pork meat; for example, in a short period of maturation:

> Pork: 1 day=30% 15 days=75 (percentages of total proteins)
> Beef: 1 day=50% 15 days=80 (percentages of total proteins).

The pH falls from 6.3 to about 5.0 after 6–8 days. Then it climbs back gradually; at the end of a month, to about 5.2–5.4. This is an important development which reflects the changes occurring and the growth of the microflora. Braising and maturation at high temperature accelerates the fall in pH. The redox potential (E_h) is rapidly reduced; from the first few days anaerobiosis becomes increased; after that the micro-organisms disappear. A minimum E_h is to be seen, which might be the sign of the end of the maturation process. Finally, the oxygen diffuses and the E_h rises again slowly.

3.4 The flavour

This appears some days after the formation of the bloom. However, these two phenomena do not take place in parallel because of the activation of the bacteria in the sausage filling. Many substances are responsible for the flavour because of the varied biochemical transformations.

3.4.1 Lipids

There is a rapid increase in fatty acids, which may reach 10% of the total lipid. Alongside acids of 6–20 carbon atoms, some smaller molecules appear which probably arise from the metabolism of some proteins (deaminated amino acids). The classical indices show a slight fall in unsaturation and a slight rise in the degree of oxidation.

3.4.2 Carbohydrates

A hetero-fermentation produces acids such as lactic, pyruvic and acetic, some gases (CO_2), some ethanol and diacetyl, which is an indicative agent of flavour (there are about 1.5 ppm on the 8th day). In general, the maximum level of acidity appears on the 10th day; after that, oxidation leads to a fall in acidity, and little is left at the end of the maturation process.

3.4.3 *Proteins*

The metabolism is complex, since the proteolytic enzymes, whether from the tissue or microbial, are very varied. Above all, it is the bacterial enzymes which participate here, mainly those from the micrococci and the lactobacillae. The final aroma of the salami is largely determined by the nature of substances of low molecular mass formed at the expense of the soluble proteins and some nucleotides. The release of non-protein nitrogen starts off rapidly during the drying process in the first three days. After that the increase is small. The most characteristic substances are as follows:

— ammonia(NH_3), carnosine (β-alanyl-1-histidine) and hydrogen sulphide (H_2S);
— amino acids in increasing number in the non-protein part: Ala, Gly, Leu, Ser, Thr, Val;
— acids resulting from the decarboxylation of Tyr (tyramine), His (histamine), , Ornithine (putrescine);
— inosine monophosphate resulting from the deamination of the adenine and hypoxanthine, from the corresponding purine bases.

The inosinates are 'flavour enhancers', which means to say they intensify the taste. Glutamate, which is added to the mixture, has the same effect, but it is in large part decarboxylated in the course of maturation, yielding γ-amino- butyric acid (which makes it of much less interest).

VII.   FOOD GELATINE

Gelatine can be put to numerous uses in food and no legal limits are imposed. It is used in the making of various gels (jellied milk, yoghurt, etc.), in soups and sauces, fruit juices, salted products, in preserves (coating, cooked dishes, fish), in the dessert production industry, confectionery, etc. Moreover, there are many non-food uses.

The properties of gelatine are:

— thickening capacity and gelling capacity at higher concentration;
— water fixation, syneresis delay, avoidance of both exudation and the crystalliza-tion of sugar;
— capacity to protect suspensions of insoluble substances, provision of a protective film for sugared almonds;
— capacity to form a mousse for aerated products.

It has been seen in section II of this chapter that gelatine comes from the breakdown of collagen on heating. From the many tissues and organs which contain collagen, mainly bones and hides (from tanning and salting processes) are used in industry for making gelatine.

Because of their high mineral content, the treatment of bones is the more complex process; it involves the following operations:

— removal of fat by organic solvents of low boiling point in an extractor (both the solvent and the fat are recovered);

— mechanical polishing which removes the meat, followed by a coarse grinding;
— separation of the 'ossein' by acid treatment with hydrochloric acid; the calcium phosphate goes into solution and is then recovered.
— purification in lime: the ossein is immersed for a lengthy period (10 weeks) in a suspension of calcium hydroxide in water. The pH is brought back to 6.0 and in this way the fatty residue, mucopolysaccharides and elastin are separated.

Lime treatment is the only one used for hides, except for pigs hide, which is put in an acid bath.

The transformation into gelatine is carried out by cooking in a container, with hot water circulation. The denatured proteins and coagulants (albumens) are removed by filtration. Vacuum condensation at 45% and rapid sterilization at 120°C, followed by rapid cooling yields a gel which is finally dried.

VIII. BLOOD

1. Composition

Slaughtered animals yield, on average, blood in the proportion of 4% of their weight; this represents large quantities which, however, are not always used to the full, particularly in the case of poultry blood. The average composition of blood is given in Table 14.2; to this should be added small proportions of mineral salts (0.8–0.9), lipids (very variable) and (0.1%) carbohydrates.

Table 14.2 — Composition of blood (%)

	Total dry extract	Total proteins	Albumin[a]	Globulin[a]	Fibrinogen[a]	Haemoglobin[a]
Whole blood	20	17.5	3.0 (17)	2.3 (13)	0.3 (2)	11 (53)
Plasma	10	8.0	4.3 (54)	3.4 (42)	0.4 (5)	—
Serum	9	7.5	4.2 (56)	3.3 (44)	—	—

[a]Percentage of total protein of each category is shown in brackets.

Serum is the liquid which separates on the spontaneous coagulation of blood. Most often plasma is prepared, which has a similar composition, but which also contains fibrinogen, if it has not been first defibrinated. The plasma fraction is separated from the red blood corpuscles by centrifugation, otherwise the red corpuscles haemolyse sooner or later. Blood is a good protein food, despite the low content of certain essential amino acids: Met and Ile. In Europe it is most often found in black puddings, which are sold cooked.

Fig. 14.5 shows the electrophoretic distribution of the main constituents.

2. Serum albumin

The serum albumin is, by far, the most abundant protein in plasma. This is a strange molecule, with its unique and long chain (single polypeptide) of about 580 residues

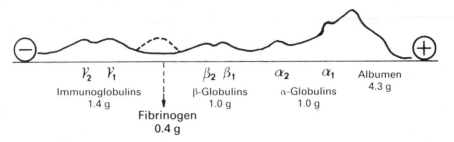

Fig. 14.5 — Electrophoresis at pH 8.6 of human blood plasma, with % quantities (densito-
metric in a standard electrophoresis).

end to end, made into a multiple loop by 17 intramolecular disulphide bridges, which
gives a total of 35 cysteine units with one free SH in the bovine molecules. The
primary structure has been established for several species, revealing great similarity
between them. Fig. 14.6 shows the N-terminal part of three types of serum albumin.
This is an interesting section because the histidine in position 3 forms part of the
ligand coordinate for copper and other metals.

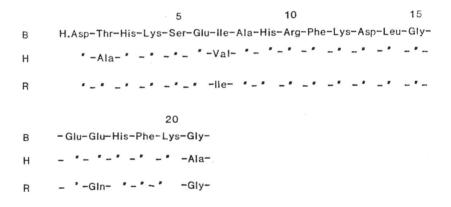

Fig. 14.6 — Start of the peptide chain of bovine (B), human (H) and rat (R) serum albumin.

The high solubility of serum albumin in water and its low viscosity are explained
by its acid character. The isoelectric point is close to 4.7. In the neutral zone it is in the
form of anions. It has marked influence on the oncotic pressure, which ensures the
return of water to the blood at the veinous extremity of the capillaries. There is a
clear tendency towards polymerization, which is the reason for apparent heterogeneity on examination.

The free SH group links with different substances, in particular with metals,
yielding mercaptides which crystallize easily. This molecule is a carrier of numerous

compounds in the organism: divalent metals, fatty acids, uric acid, acetylcholine, colours (fixation of bilirubin, a toxic derivative of haemoglobin), medicines (e.g. penicillin, quinine).

3.   α and β Globulins

The α- and β-globulins form a highly complex group of glycoproteins. From simple electrophoresis (Fig. 14.5) they are designated by Greek letters; but the γ-globulins form a category which is worth distinguishing. These proteins separate from albumins because of their ease in precipitation by ammonium sulphate at 50% saturation (it requires 90% to precipitate albumins).

a-Seromucoid acid, or orosomucoid, is a small glycoprotein, MM=44000, containing 40% carbohydrates. The peptide part has a molecular mass of 26000. The prosthetic grouping binds to the asparagine of the peptide chain by a N-glucosidic bond engaging with glucosamine.

The absence of glucose from this molecule should be noted. The high monosaccharide content explains the particular properties:

— substance not capable of denaturation by heat, no coagulation;
— soluble in the usual reagents for proteins (20% trichloracetic acid, 18% perchloric acid), but precipitated by 2N HCl.
— strong acidic character, pH=2.7, the only positively charged protein and migrates in electrophoresis at pH 4.5.

The α_1-antitrypsin is an inhibitor of proteases, the content of which in the blood depends on the physiological state. It is a molecule of 54000 Da, containing 12% sugars, and differs from the inhibitors which have been seen in soya bean (Chapter 11).

Two glycoproteins which ensure the transportation of metals have been found in blood:

— ceruloplasmin, of the α_2 group, which binds with copper; MM=150000 Da.
— transferrin, or siderophilin, of the β group, which binds with iron, MM=80000 Da, contains 6% carbohydrates.

4.   Immunoglobulins

The immunoglobulins (γ-globulins) are glycoproteins of higher molecular mass (see Chapter 13). Their function is to act as antibodies, that is to say, substances which react specifically with an antigen which has penetrated into the organism. In this way they ensure protection against infections, by combining with the antigen and forming inactive complexes, and also protection against the introduction of foreign proteins. They are found in blood and also in external secretions: milk, tears, saliva, intestinal secretions.

The immunoglobulins are extremely varied; however, they have some common structural characteristics, being formed from 4 peptide chains of which 2 are light (L) and 2 are heavy (H), interlinked by disulphide bonds (Fig. 14.7). Some of them are polymers of this structure, with linked 'pieces' at the C-terminal extremities of the H chains.

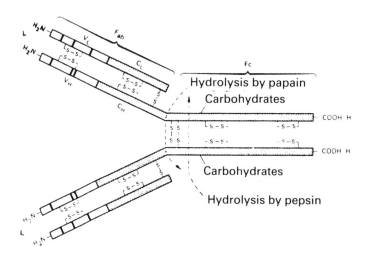

Fig. 14.7 — Schematic representation of an immunoglobulin.

The main properties of immunoglobulins are summarized in Table 14.3: the three categories A, G and M are the most important. The site of the combination with the antigen is in the variable zone of the 109 amino acids, on the N-terminal side. For a great number of Ig the sequences are known. They reveal a richness in hydroxylated amino acids, Ser+Thr 20%, and in tryptophan, Trp=3%. The basic amino acids are low — Lys+Arg+His=15% (in serum albumin=23%).

Two types of light chains exist, κ and λ, which are found in all the Ig classes; though there are several types of H chains, where each is characteristic of a particular class (see Table 14.3).

5.   Fibrinogen

Fibrinogen may be reattached to globulins because it is a soluble protein in the presence of salts and insoluble in pure water; but it does have a fibrillar structure and

Table 14.3 — Principal characteristics of immunoglobulins

	Content in serum (g/l)	Sedimentation constant	Content of carbohydrates (%)	MM	Heavy chain class	Biological characteristics
IgG	12	7S	3	160 000	γ with sub-classes	Designated under the name of γ-globulins in everyday usage; binds complement; acts against infections (bacteria, parasites) and neutralizes toxins.
IgA	3	7S	8	160 000	α with sub-classes	Tendency to form oligomers; 'Secretory' (form dimer) in mucous secretions (local defence).
IgM	1	19S	12	1 000 000	μ	Formerly 'macroglobulin'; aggregates of five molecules comparable to IgG, combined by the extremities of the heavy chains; active in primary immunization against bacteria; isohaemagglutinins.
IgD	0.1	7S	12	180 000	δ	Small number of antibodies whose role is not clear.
IgE	0.001	8S	11	200 000	ε	Corresponds to 'reagins', responsible for anaphylactic reactions; circulating antibodies localized on the skin or various organs; high level in people sensitive to an allergen; combination with the allergen provokes the allergic reaction (release of histamine from the basophiles and the mastocytes.

is easily transformed into fibrin in the course of coagulation. There are about 4 g per litre of blood.

It is a glycoprotein of MM 340 000, containing 2.5% carbohydrates (Gal, Man, GlcNac, NeuNac) with a pI of 5.5 and made up of three times two identical α, β and γ chains. It is possible that this quaternary structure, which is consolidated by numerous disulphide bonds, might be a dimer. About 30% of the molecule is found in the α-helix form. It denatures easily; it forms a gel in plasma at about 56°C, but it also can be precipitated by agitation (separation of the blood by beating). The binding properties of fibrinogen are put to good use in the cooked meats industry. Thrombin is the coagulating enzyme for fibrinogen in blood. This comes from the inactive form prothrombin through a complex mechanism in which calcium is involved. Some other non-specific proteases have the same action: trypsin, papain, reptile proteases. In the first stage, soluble fibrin forms by cleavage of 4 Arg–Gly bonds on the N-terminal side on the α and β chains. After that, the monomer, separated from the 'fibrinogen' immediately forms aggregates which are voluminous and fibrous in structure and are in fact insoluble fibrin. An amide bond, created between Glu and Lys, stabilizes its structure. Calcium intervenes again at this stage.

It can be seen that the coagulation reaction is similar to the action of chymosin on κ-casein in milk coagulation. Long sequences are homologous in the κ-casein and in the γ chain of fibrinogen.

6.   Haemoglobin

Haemoglobin is very abundant in blood (about 110 g/l). It results from the association of 4 units corresponding with those in myoglobin, which has been studied in section III of this chapter. It possesses 4 haems and 4 hexacoordinated iron atoms; the 4 globin molecules form 96%; the molecular mass is 68 000. Normal haemoglobin contains two pairs of chains in two by two combination always with two of the first;

— HbA in adults: $\alpha_2\beta_2$ (α is a chain of 141 amino acids and β has 146)
— HbA$_2$ in a minority of adults: $\alpha_2\delta_2$ (δ has 10 amino acids different from β)
— HbF, foetal: $\alpha_2\gamma_2$ (γ has 39 amino acids different from β).

More than 400 structural mutants are known, which are most often differentiated just by the substitution of a single amino acid. Some of these mutations involve diseases (Chapter 5, §III).

15

Eggs

I. HENS' EGGS — THE SHELL

The eggs produced by different animal species, especially birds, have a characteristic composition which does not vary much. That of the hen's egg is summarized in Table 15.1. There are three main constituents — an external mineral constituent, the shell, and two organic constituents: the vitellus, or egg yolk, and the albumen, or egg white, which completely covers the egg yolk as it moves around. In addition there are membranes.

Table 15.1 — Composition of hen's egg

	Whole egg	Vitellus (yolk)	Albumen (white)	Shell
Weight per unit (g):	60	18	36	6
Composition: (g/100 g):				
• water	66	48	87	—
• proteins	12	16	10.5	2
• lipids	11	34	—	—
• carbohydrates	0.5	0.4	0.6	—
• minerals	11	1.1	0.7	98

The two membranes of the shell are separated on one side (the larger) by an air sac. The shell is permeable to gas. The volume of the air sac increases in the course of storage, partly through exchange of gases and partly through water vapour loss. The height of this air sac is the official criterion of freshness: it is expressed in millimetres. It does not, however, reveal the state of the egg. If eggs are kept in a damp atmosphere the air sac will not develop much, though there may be bacteriological risks. The name 'air chamber' takes no account of the presence there of carbon dioxide gas which comes from the bicarbonates in the egg; the CO_2 is liberated more or less rapidly according to the temperature.

The shell is formed basically from calcium carbonate (96%) with a little phosphate and magnesium. These minerals are present in a fibrillar network of keratin (2%). The hardness of the shell is related to the nature of the network and the magnesium content. The chalazae are twisted albumen filaments attached to the egg yolk, which join it to the membrane.

On the outside of the shell there is a protein cuticle, not very soluble in water; however, it can be removed by brushing; in this case there is an increased chance that bacteria will penetrate, which is harmful for preservation.

The composition of the hen's egg has been most studied; it is very complex, especially in its proteins. However, there are considerably fewer proteins in eggs than in blood. The proteins from a whole hen's egg have long been considered to be the classic example of a foodstuff. The composition of essential amino acids serve as a basis for the calculation of the chemical indices of other proteins. This composition is remarkably stable, depending very little on the breed and the feed intake.

II. EGG YOLK

This is a dispersion of particles in a continuous aqueous phase or plasma. This system contains egg lipids. Triglycerides represent 70% of the total lipid content; palmitic and stearic acids represent 30% of the fatty acids of the triglycerides and 50% of the fatty acids of the lecithins. In addition, oleic and linoleic acids are found in greater quantity in the fatty acids of the triglycerides than in those of the phospholipids.

The two parts of the egg yolk have the following properties:

— the *particles* can be separated by centrifugation; they are spherical-shaped bodies with a diameter of 25–50 µm on average; they are not very strong and tend to break up in the course of handling. The particles make up 25% of the dry matter of the yolk and contain about 60% proteins, the remainder being lipids. The particles are essentially phosvitin and lipovitellin (Table 15.2).
— the *continuous phase* contains 75% of the dry matter of the yolk in the form of lipovitellenin, of weak intensity (LDL 65%) and globular proteins, livetins, coming from the blood plasma.

1. Phosvitin

This is a strongly phosphorylated phosphoprotein, 10% of the total protein, and is remarkably rich in serine which represents about 30% of the amino acid residues. The bonding of the two, constituents takes place, as with casein, in the form of the mono-orthophosphoric ester of serine; more than 90% of serine is esterified, which means that the peptide chain alone must represent a molecular mass of about 27 000. The sequence of the amino acids has been difficult to establish because of the

Table 15.2 — Composition of the yolk of a hen's egg

	% of total dry matter	Molecular mass (Da)	Lipid content (% of substance)	Protein content (% of total proteins)	Phosphorus (as % of proteins)	Localization
Phosvitin	4	36 000	0	10	10	Particles
Lipovitellin, HDL	16	400 000	20	36	$\begin{cases}\alpha=0.5\\\beta=0.25\end{cases}$	Particles
Lipovitel-lenins, LDL	68	$3–10\times10^6$	88	24	0.1	Continuous phase
Livetins	10	α: 80 000 β: 45 000 γ:150 000	0	30	—	Continuous phase

repetition of the patterns –(Ser–P)x; there is no cysteine and very little Tyr, Trp and Met. Phosvitin contains 80% of the yolk's protein phosphorous although it makes up just 10% of the proteins. This is a phosphorous reserve for the embryo, but it is also a source of iron since this protein fixes that metal with ease.

2.   Lipovitellin

It is of the HDL type, that is to say, high density lipoprotein. Two types of lipovitellin are distinguished, which differ from one another essentially in their phosphorous content, but they are little phosphorylated and they have an average lipid content (20%). The molecular mass of 400 000 is probably that of a dimer which is the stable form at pH <7.0. Two-thirds of the lipids are phospholipids and the remaining one-third are neutral lipids, cholesterol and triglycerides. The bond between the lipids and the protein is probably of hydrophobic nature; however it is quite firm in conditions where some other lipoproteins breakup. Vitelline is a well-balanced protein from the point of view of its composition. It is quite rich in cysteine. In the side chains, Asp and Glu predominate.

3.   Lipovitellenin

This is of the LDL, i.e. low density lipoprotein type. It contains a large quantity of lipids (86–88%). Their distribution is not the same as for lipovitellin. Two-thirds of the lipids are neutral, with 4% cholesterol. The remaining one-third are phospholipids.

There exist at least two varieties, which differ in their degree of polymerization, with molecular masses in the order of 3–10 million Da.

Vitellenin has a composition in amino acids close to that of vitellin, but contains only a little cysteine. However, it is bound to carbohydrates through the N-glucosamine–asparagine bond. Also, the prosthetic group contributes hexoses and neuraminic acid.

As with other lipoproteins, LDLs involves a nucleus of non-polar or hydrophobic lipids (triglycerides and esterified cholesterol) and a single-layered envelope made up of apoproteins and polar lipids (free cholesterol and phospholipids). It is this single-layered envelope which ensures the stability of the particle in the aqueous phase (Fig. 15.1).

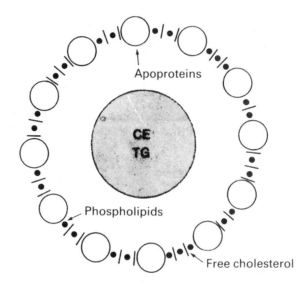

Fig. 5.1 — General structure of lipoproteins. (CE=esterified cholesterol; TG=triglyceride.)

4.   Livetins
They correspond to well-known plasma proteins:

- α-livetin is identical to serum albumin; MM=80 000; proportion: 2.
- β-livetin is identical to α_2-glycoprotein; MM=45 000; proportion: 5.
- γ-livetin is identical to γ-globulin; MM=150 000; proportion: 3.

5.   Ovovitellin
This is the name given to the group of the egg yolk proteins, as obtained from the residue insoluble in ether (used to extract the fat) which can be dissolved in a 10% NaCl solution and precipitated again by the addition of water. This substance possesses remarkable qualities, which can be compared with those of casein in milk:

— it contains 0.9% phosphorus and 0.95% sulphur
— it is coagulated by chymosin
— it is dephosphorylated by heating
— it yields peptides rich in phosphorus by protease hydrolysis (pepsin, trypsin).

6. Heat treatments

These treatments modify the properties of egg yolk. In the course of heating, the yolk thickens, then becomes dry. There is liberation of hydrogen sulphide which comes especially from the egg white. In the case of prolonged cooking of the egg, H_2S reacts with the iron in the yolk and a black precipitate forms (black Chinese eggs).

Dehydration by spray-drying or by freeze-drying denatures the proteins with a more or less precise loss in their functional properties. Concentrated and sweetened egg white is used in the patisserie and confectionery industries (reducing sugars = 60%, sucrose = 40%), as is salted egg yolk (10%) and sugar (10%). These can be stored at ambient temperature and rehydrated for use.

Freezing greatly increases viscosity following defrosting of the egg yolk. This is due to an irreversible aggregation of lipoproteins of low density. The addition of protective agents is recommended, for example 5% of glycerol, salt or ordinary sugar. Rapid defrosting preserves the functional properties of the egg yolk quite well.

III. EGG WHITE

1. Structure

Immediately after the egg has been laid, the albumen has a gel-like structure; but this gradually liquifies, especially during the first 48 hours. This is not the result of a hydrolysis of the proteins, but of evolution of the ovomucin–lysozyme complex; rise in pH aids the dissociation whilst the concentration of divalent ions slows it down. The pH of fresh white of egg is close to 7.4. It rises to pH 9 in about 3 days, then changes little. This rise often has harmful consequences. The storage of eggs in a carbon dioxide atmosphere (4% of CO_2) and at 10°C limits the rise in pH and the liquefaction of the white; nowadays it is also possible to preserve the quality of the eggs by putting them into storage at −1°C and 90% relative humidity.

There are some transfers of small molecules between the two parts of the egg, principally:

(1) from the white to the yolk, diffusion of water and the passage of bivalent ions.
(2) from the yolk to the white, the passage of free amino acids and iron.

Egg white contains, in dry matter, about 85% proteins; the relative values as a percentage of the total proteins differ little from the values as a percentage of dry matter (Table 15.3).

2. Ovalbumin

This is, by far, the main protein in egg white, about 60% of the protein total, similar to serum albumin in blood plasma, with which it may be compared. It has been found in the blood of laying hens (but not in cocks or in non-laying hens). It is, however, not a pure protein. It is weakly phosphorylated, 0.13% of P, and contains 8 residues of carbohydrates per molecule of 46 000 Da. It should be noted that ovalbumin contains some mannose and glucosamine in a single unit, but no neuraminic acid.

Table 15.3 — Proteins in the white of hen's egg

Type of protein[a]	% of total dry matter	Molecular mass (Da)	Carbo- hydrates (% of dry matter)	Iso- electric point	Properties
Ovalbumin	58	46 000	3.5	4.6	Gelling agent
Conalbumin (ovotransferrin)	14	82 000	2	6.5	Combines with metals, inhibits bacteria
Ovomucoid	11	28 000	23	4.0	Inhibits trypsin
Ovoglobulins	4+4	36 000– 45 000	—	5.6	Foaming properties
Lysozyme	3.5	14 300	0	10.5	Lysis of bacteria
Ovomucin	2	—	25	—	Viscosity factor
Ovinhibitor	1	45 000	6	5.1	Inhibits several proteases
Flavoprotein	0.8	34 000	14	4.0	Binds vitamin B_2

[a] In addition to these, several minor proteins are present, including avidin which fixes biotin.

Its amino acid composition is remarkably balanced. Only one acid is present at more than 10% (Glu 14%) and none at less than 1.3%.

It has been a difficult task to determine the spatial structure of the ovalbumin molecule, mainly because of the negative reactions with reactive agents for the terminal groups (dinitrophenyl derivatives for N^-, carboxylase for C-terminal). The C-terminal group is proline and the N-terminal group N-acetylated glycine. There are 6 residues of Cys and one disulphide bond, at the point of laying; the number of cross-links increase on storage. S-Ovalbumin forms, which is more thermostable than the native protein; the latter denatures at about 76–80°C.

Ovalbumin has gelling and foaming properties which are put to use. These properties depend on the state of the protein. They are reduced as the level of the S-ovalbumin increases.

Proteolysis of ovalbumin by subtilisin provides a notable example of limited proteolysis. The enzyme is theoretically capable of cleaving several bonds but here they must have some protection. In the first place, a cleavage of -Ala- Ser- takes place, without the splitting of the molecule into two parts (because of the –S–S– bond) then a dipeptide and a pentapeptide are detached in succession. After that plakalbumen-2 is formed which crystallizes in the form of a plaque.

3. Conalbumin

Conalbumin is also called 'ovotransferrin'. Its molecular mass is nearly double that of ovalbumin, 87 000 Da. However, it is not a dimer. It resembles siderophilin closely (β group glycoprotein of blood serum) in its composition of amino acids and also its ability to combine with divalent cations, notably Fe, Cu, Mn and Zn. It may be distinguished, however, in its carbohydrate part, which contains no neuraminic acid; it is made up of equal parts of mannose and glucosamine.

This protein has an inhibitory action on certain bacteria.

Conalbumin is more easily denatured by heat than ovalbumin. It coagulates at about 63°C. This is approximately the coagulation temperature of egg white since ovalbumin gels at the point where the conalbumin becomes insoluble.

4. Ovomucoid

Ovomucoid is a glycoprotein rich in glucosamine, about 14%. It also contains 7% mannose, a little galactose and some neuraminic acid. The bonding of these monosaccharides with the peptide chain occurs on the asparagine, as in the two previous cases. This protein is small compared with the previous two. The molecular mass of 28 000 is only 23 000 in the part containing nitrogen; it contains only 13% nitrogen, but has 2% sulphur, which is of a higher value. It is separated easily from the other proteins of egg white by reason of its solubility in trichloracetic acid, as with the orosomucoid of blood serum. It can be denatured by heat, though it is considerably more resistant than ovalbumin and conalbumin. In the course of denaturation, a new disulphide bridge is formed. Note that this protein is devoid of tryptophan.

Ovomucoid possesses biological activity which was unique at the time of its discovery, that is, an antitrypsin factor. Many others have since been found. The coagulated 'hard' white of egg is rapidly digested in the intestine, because it has been denatured. By contrast, raw egg white is resistant to the digestive process for a time. It should be noted that rapid drying of the egg may not render the ovomucoid inactive.

5. Ovomucin

Ovomucin is also a glycoprotein, but its structure is less well-known than the structure of ovomucoid. It contains more neuraminic acid than ovomucoid. This component explains the elastic and fibrous form of the molecule, which is responsible for the viscosity of the albumen. Neuraminic acid is totally dissociated at neutral pH and its negative charges are responsible for these properties. The role of the association of ovomucin and lysozyme in the structure of the thick form of the albumen has been pointed out at the beginning of this section. The protein is insoluble in pure water, but it becomes soluble in the presence of salt at pH 7.0. It is, as in the case above, quite thermoresistant but it is sensitive to surface denaturation. It contributes to the stabilization of cold mousses.

Ovomucin is an inhibitor of viral haemagglutination (agglutination of red corpuscles).

Note: Amongst the other proteins of egg white, notably *lysozyme* is to be found. This is used by the pharmaceutical industry (precipitation by sodium chloride at about pH 10) to make cow's milk 'more like mother's milk'. Quite recently this enzyme has also been used to stop the butyric fermentation in the production of processed cheeses which are subjected to a cooking process.

IV   NEW EGG PRODUCTS

It has been mentioned above (§II, 6) that the food industry uses both salted and sugared egg white and egg yolk. There are other more recent products:

(1) hard-boiled egg 'fingers', obtained by separating the yolk from the white in a special machine, which allows production of 'rolls' which are yellow in the middle and white outside. These are usually cut into slices 3–5 mm in thickness;
(2) pre-cooked omelettes, each weighing 100–150 g;
(3) frozen omelette granules ($-18°C$).

Usually all the individual components are pasteurized: $65°C/2.5$ minutes for the yolks, and $55°C/2.5$ minutes for the whites with salt added. It is also possible to pasteurize whole eggs under the same conditions used for the yolks.

V.   FUNCTIONAL PROPERTIES OF EGG PRODUCTS

In addition to their high nutritional value, eggs have, in their functional properties, another important attraction for the food industry. We shall consider these functional properties in the following order:

— coagulating capacity of the whole egg
— anti-crystallizing and foaming capacities of the egg white
— emulsifying capacity of the egg yolk.

1.   Coagulating capacity of whole eggs

The egg proteins of the white and the yolk are the basis of this coagulation. The mechanism of coagulation comprises a rupture of intramolecular bonds which causes an unfolding of the protein molecules with formation of new intermolecular bonds. There is a change in secondary structure with the passage from the α form to the β (pleated) form.

Proteins coagulate as the result of the action of different physical agents (heat, mechanical action) and chemical agents (inorganic ions, heavy metals).

Where heat is concerned, it can be noted that conalbumin and ovalbumin, in the egg white, are the most sensitive to heat and that the starting coagulation temperature of the white (57°C) is less than that of the yolk (65°C).

Coagulation is also a function of the relationship between time and temperature; for example, when baked custard is being prepared, overheating leads to coagulation with syneresis. The salt concentration is equally important; in fact, a dialysed white of egg will not coagulate.

This 'coagulating' property is much in demand, especially in food industries where cooking processes are involved, like bakery and the cooked meats industry (quenelles, poultry-based sausage).

2.   Anti-crystallizing and foaming capacity of white

The anti-crystallizing capacity of the egg white is specifically in demand in confectionery making. The addition of 3% egg white is enough to limit the formation of sucrose crystals which spoil the texture of the product. The basis of the capacity to form foams is still not very well understood. However, several hypotheses have been put forward suggesting that it is the ovomucin and the lysozyme which play the major roles. Lysozyme is considered to be responsible for the formation of a foam in the process of beating, whilst ovomucin might control the stability. Ovomucin is partially denatured by the mechanical action of the beating and forms a protective film round the air bubbles, thus ensuring the stability of the foam.

The globulins, in lowering the suface tension, help the formation of the foam, and proteins which can be coagulated by heating stop the foam from collapsing during the cooking process.

The foaming capacity is used essentially in biscuit-making, to make meringues and 'boudoir' biscuits.

3.   Emulsifying capacity of egg yolk

In order to get a stable emulsion, it is essential that it should contain a surface-active agent (e.g. yolk) which lowers the tension between the two phases, or a thickening agent which increases the viscosity of the continuous phase.

The surface-active capacity of the yolk is due to the presence within it of phospholipids (lecithins in particular) which are present in lipoprotein complexes and with cholesterol.

In addition, the viscosity of the yolk confers stability on emulsions. The addition of salt, sugar and spices reduces the quantity of extra-cellular water and so increases the emulsifying capacity.

The emulsifying capacity of the yolk is much used in the food industry for making mayonnaise, emulsified sauces and ice creams.

16

Oils and fats

I. GENERAL OBSERVATIONS

The distinction is still made today, on the basis of their physical state at 20°C, between *fats*, which are solids, and *oils*, which are liquids, although it is of virtually no practical significance. The term 'fat' tends to be generally used; but in Britain, with no other qualification, this is commonly used only for lard (pork fat) or tallow (beef fat).

An 'edible' fat or 'food' substance is a mixture of animal and/or vegetable fats. The term 'butter' is reserved for the fatty substance from milk which has been obtained by the butter-making process (Chapter 13). The term 'cocoa- fat' should be used and not 'cocoa-butter'. The term 'margarine' designates the industrial fat which is a copy of butter from the structural point of view, but not at all from the point of view of fatty acid composition.

The composition of fatty acids was given in Chapter 4 (Table 4.1). The fats used as foods are essentially made from triglycerides. From their water content, three types may be distinguished, as indicated in Table 16.1. Oils do not contain water;

Table 16.1 — Average composition of edible fats

	Butter and margarine	Vegetable and animal oils	Animal fats
Lipids	82	99.9	91–99
Proteins	0.8	0	1
Carbohydrates	0.8	0	0
Mineral salts	0.2	tr	tr
Water	16	0	0.1–8

tr: traces.

water is found at up to 8% in certain animal fats, and double that — 16% — is found in butter and margarine.

From this outline it will be seen that the composition in fatty acids varies widely according to the origin of the oils or fats used and according to the modification processes to which they are subjected.

II. MODIFICATION TREATMENTS

Three treatments are legally allowed and the fat industry puts all three to use: hydrogenation, interesterification and fractionation. These treatments give specific properties to fats and helps their interchangeability in applications for the food industry generally.

Hydrogenation and interesterification entail chemical modifications. Fractionation is a physical process; it is used to separate, more or less completely, the fluid and solid parts at a given temperature (§III, 3).

1. Hydrogenation

Hydrogenation means saturation by means of hydrogen of all or part of the double bonds of the unsaturated fatty acids.

In the case of *selective hydrogenation*, the content of polyunsaturated fatty acids of vegetable oils will be reduced and their stability to oxidation will be improved. This process is applicable to oils which are particularly sensitive to oxidation and to heat and which contain — as with the oils of rape and soya bean — a relatively high percentage of linolenic acid. This treatment results in some isomerization of the unsaturated fatty acids and for this reason aids the formation of *trans* isomers and positional isomers. The choice of good experimental conditions (catalyst, temperature, pressure) limits the formation of the isomers which appear in italics in the following scheme:

Linolenic acid → { Linoleic acid / *Iso-linoleic acids* } → { Oleic acid / *Iso-oleic acid*→Stearic acid / *Elaidic acid* }

Non-selective hydrogenation has as its aim the preparation of solid fats for use in, for example, margarine. This type of hydrogenation aims to saturate a high proportion, or even all, the double bonds of the unsaturated fatty acids. This type of reaction also forms isomers, of the *trans* variety, which also contribute to raising the melting point (Chapter 4, §III, 2).

From the practical point of view, hydrogenation is carried out generally as a discontinuous process, introducing pure hydrogen in the presence of a catalyst (a copper or nickel salt) into the fatty substance at between 150°C and 200°C. Parameters, such as the temperature, pressure and speed of the hydrogen injection and the nature and concencentration of the catalyst, vary according to the type of hydrogenation.

Whilst hydrogenation stabilizes the fat against oxidation and modifies its behaviour in the crystallization process, it always lowers the nutritional value as a result of the transformation of all or part of the linoleic acid and the carotenoid pigments which might possibly be present.

2.   Interesterification

Interesterification has the aim of modifying the glyceride structure of the fatty substances through intra- and inter-molecular rearrangement of the fatty acids on the glycerol (see Fig. 4.3).

This molecular rearrangement may involve either a single fat or a mixture of two fats. Numerous combinations of interesterification are possible.

The redistribution of the fatty acid chains on the 3 hydroxyl groups of the glycerol takes place according to a statistical law, so that it is possible to forecast the composition of the various triglycerides in the total mixture at equilibrium. This is the result obtained in *random interesterification.*

Using this technique of non-directed interesterification, it is possible to prepare a margarine from sunflower oil and palm oil which is totally hydrogenated and which has the advantage of containing no fatty acids of the *trans* variety.

In *directed interesterification*, which is less common, conditions are selected so as to assist the change of the state of the triacylglycerol in the liquid phase to the solid phase, for example by lowering the temperature. In this way the equilibrium is changed in the liquid phase and, gradually, the desired mixture is obtained. This process makes it possible to obtain from lard emulsifiable fats which are used in the preparation of ice creams and fancy pastries.

Interesterification which takes place in the presence of catalysts such as sodium methylate or ethylate at a temperature of between 100° and 160°C may — following changes in the position of the fatty acids on the glycerol — modify the digestibility of the triglyceride.

III.   OILS
1.   Fish oils

These are often described as 'fats' and are not consumed in the unmodified state. They are used in margarines, which are thus rich in long chain fatty acids of high molecular weight. Table 4.1 shows that whale oil contains 8% clupanodonic acid as $C_{22:5}$. It is found again, more or less hydrogenated, in margarine.

2.   Vegetable oils

These are much used in food, especially in countries where milk production is low. They can be classified as follows, on the basis of their composition:

(1) Oils rich in saturated acids and in oleic acid, e.g.:
 — groundnut oil, 19% and 60%, respectively
 — olive oil, 14% and 81%, respectively

(2) Oils rich in polyunsaturated acids, e.g.:
   — safflower oil, 75% (10% saturated)
   — sunflower oil, 64% (14% saturated)
   — soya bean oil, 58% (14% saturated)
(3) Intermediate oils, e.g.:
   — oil of the new rapeseed (saturated 7%, oleic 60%, polyunsaturated 33%).

The composition is important with respect to the thermal stability of the oil. Oils which contain more than 2% linolenic acid cannot be used for frying, as these oxidize readily, yielding suspect products (irritants and carcinogens). They may only be used in dressings (rapeseed, soya bean, safflower) or in light cooking at less than 150°C (sunflower, maize).

In Europe, groundnut oil and olive oil are frequently used for frying.

3. Refining of vegetable oils

As far as processing is concerned, it matters little whether the oil comes from a seed or a kernel, apart from the first stage (Fig. 16.1). The procedure is as follows:

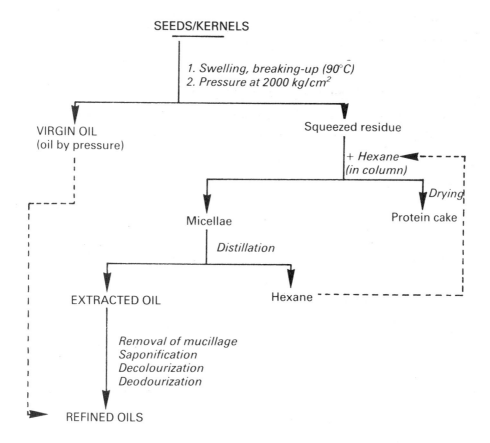

Fig. 16.1 — Scheme for refining rapeseed oil.

(1) Swelling and explosion of the seeds in 'heating chambers' at 80–90°C in a humid atmosphere: the proteins are coagulated and the flow of the oil facilitated.

(2) At relatively high pressure, about 2000 kg/cm^2, the virgin oil flows and separates from the residues in presses which these days run continuously. The proportion of oil obtained varies according to the raw material; 93% is extracted from maize and 80% from rape.

(3) Extraction from the residue of outer skins, etc., using hexane C_6H_{14} in a counter-flow extraction column. The oil goes into solution in the form of 'micellae', and in a nearby dryer the residues of the seeds are freed from solvent and used for meal destined for cattle feed.

(4) Filtration and distillation will separate the extracted oil from the hexane, which is then recycled.

(5) The refining process is applied both to oils obtained by pressing (virgin oil) and oils obtained by extraction; the following pattern is applied more or less completely:

    (a) Removal of mucilage, or degumming, which takes out the lecithins and the gums in the form of deposits. Water treatment is applied at 70–80°C for this and with the use of phosphoric acid for 30 minutes followed by centrifugation.

    (b) Neutralization using sodium hydroxide. The raw oils contain free fatty acids; the original acidity can vary from 4 to 8%; these can lead to rapid deterioration. Soaps are insoluble in oil.

    (c) Decolourization using a special type of earth, bentonite or Fuller's earth, which removes the pigments.

    (d) Deodourization by steam treatment at reduced pressure and high tempera-ture; in this way are removed volatile substances, the aldehydes and ketones, which are responsible for the seed taste. In this operation it is necessary to avoid oxidation of the unsaturated fatty acids by oxygen (Chapter 4, §IX). Nitrogen gas is therefore used to break the vacuum.

This outline is not always applied in this manner; sometimes certain operations are omitted. This depends on the nature of the raw material and also on its quality. For example, maize kernels undergo stages 2 and 5; there is no point in recovering the 7% of residual oil. Virgin olive oil is not refined, but undergoes a simple clarification by decanting and filtration.

The fractional crystallization of the fat, also called Winterization, is carried out to separate the solid fraction, more saturated than the mixture, from the more unsaturated liquid fraction. To achieve this, the oil is cooled to a well-defined temperature and the product filtered or centrifuged. This is the case with sunflower oil.

IV.　MARGARINES AND COOKING FATS

Invented in 1869 by Mège-Mouriès, margarine was prepared initially with animal fats in an emulsion with water and milk or cream. Later, vegetable fats, copra, palm and palm kernel took a larger and larger part in the formulation of the lipid phase of margarine. Currently, the lipid phase comes from varied raw materials, ranging from hydrogenated fish and whale oils to vegetable oils which are hydrogenated to some extent.

According to their use, different types of margarine are prepared: margarines for domestic use, for the food industry, so-called 'low calorie' margarines (also referred to as spreads), cooking fats or 'shortenings'. The composition of these changes according to the regulations in force and to the variations in raw material suppliers.

1.   Manufacture of margarines

The fats are heated to about 40°C and mixed in the desired proportions. The emulsion is obtained by energetic agitation of the lipid phase with an aqueous phase which is generally milk fermented by lactic bacteria as a 'starter'.

The functional properties of plasticity and spreadability require the presence of a certain proportion of lipid in the solid state. The texture is improved by the stage of solidification — creaming following the formation of small and uniform triglyceride crystals.

At the present time, refrigerated cooling tubes with internal scraped surface blades are used which enable the continuous operation of the successive phases of mixing, emulsification, cooling, crystallization and creaming.

2   Composition of the different types of margarines and cooking fats

The composition of margarines varies according to the origin of the fats and the use to which they will be put. Emulsifying agents and stabilizers are always added in every case; mono- or di-glycerides and lecithin are the most used. According to regulations in force, it is always necessary to put in other additives with these production aids, such as anti-microbial agents (sodium chloride), anti-oxidants, fat-soluble colourants, vitamins A and D. Antioxidants are not permitted in British margarine. The aroma depends largely on the 'starter' used.

Margarines for domestic use must be sufficiently firm at 20°C, easy to spread and have organoleptic qualities close to those of butter. They are most often prepared using triglycerides rich in unsaturated fatty acids. In the UK, France, etc., the maximal water content is 16%. Margarine contributes 740 kcal per 100g. Many varieties can be distinguished according to the polyunsaturated fatty acid content, which gives them differing degrees of hardness; less than 10% (hard), 10–20 % (semi-hard), 20–30 % (soft), more than 30% (extra soft).

'Dietetic' margarines also called *'spreads'*. In relation to butter they show the following characteristics: they are easy to spread straight from the refrigerator and, at equal weight, contribute fewer calories (400 kcal/100g). Their fat content is between that of a fat cheese (50% fat in dry matter) and butter (80%).

These products may be made from raw dairy materials: butterfat, caseinates, secondary use of buttermilks or ultrafiltered whey. They may also contain raw plant oils: soya bean oil, sunflower oil, rapeseed oil and other oils, used as they are or hydrogenated, so as to contribute the polyunsaturated fatty acids which are not present or exist as such in the butterfat or only in very small quantity.

Different types of 'low-fat butters' exist, and the average nutritional contribution for 100 g of the product is 7–8 g of proteins, 41 g of lipids, 1 g of carbohydrates and 2000 IU of vitamin A.

From the technological point of view, these products containing 50% water are able to be stabilized by the use of an emulsifier such as disodium phosphate or gelatine.

Margarines for the food industry are, according to their use, either stable at high temperature (fats for frying) or have good plasticity at a wide range of temperatures (biscuit-making and pastry-making).

These products must not contain free fatty acids and they must be resistant to oxidation.

Industrially, cooking fats or 'shortenings' have been greatly developed. These fats do not contain water, being characterized by the solid/liquid relationship of the triglycerides. This relationship determines the consistency and capacity to retain air during the making of a dough for pastry-making. It is the retention of air and water which plays a very important role during the making of cakes which rise; the emulsifiers also tend to improve this. In the making of flaky pastry it is necessary for the fat to participate and to be able to resist the work of the roller; to do this, the proportion of solid triglycerides may reach 30%.

17

Additives

I. DEFINITIONS

The term 'foodstuff' means'all materials which, through the digestive system, are helpful to the maintenance and development of the organism. Most often this concerns natural products of complex composition (Chapter 1).

The term 'additive' means any substance which is not a normal constituent of the foodstuffs and the purposeful addition of which is aimed at one of the three following areas:

(1) technological
(2) organoleptic
(3) nutritional.

Apart from some particular cases, their use is limited to a maximal concentration of 1%.

The term 'manufacturing aid' is applied to technological additives which have only a passing effect; they do not remain in the foodstuff other than as trace materials.

Within the EC, additives are classified with a conventional number which has to be displayed on the labels of foodstuffs. The following classification is still being used:

1. Colouring matter
2. Preservatives
3. Antioxidants
4. Emulsifiers, stabilizers, thickeners, gelling agents
5. Anti-caking agents
6. Texturizing agents, improvers, bleaching agents
7. Flavourings

8. Flavour enhancers
9. Processing aids.

It should be noted that very few substances belong to categories 5, 8 and 9. These will probably be modified in the future.

Numerous additives have been studied or quoted in earlier chapters; in view of this, little new data of importance will be given here. It should be stressed though that the appropriate authorities must be satisfied about the 'toxicological evidence' of any new additive before authorizing its use.

II.   TECHNOLOGICAL ADDITIVES

1.   Preservation

The aim of preservation additives is to maintain the initial quality of the item for as long as possible, or at least to the highest possible quality. To achieve this it is, of course, necessary to inhibit or slow down the varying mechanisms of deterioration which may modify the quality in three ways: food quality, nutritional quality and hygienic quality.

Biological deterioration is often eliminated or slowed down by physical means: heat treatment (pasteurization, sterilization and preservation processes) or refrigeration, which are not discussed here. The same goes for the reduction in water activity (a_w, Chapter 7) and for vacuum or inert-gas packaging (to avoid oxidation).

Preservation additives may be classified as follows.

1.1   Minerals

Sodium chloride is a flavouring agent, but it is also a primary preservation agent, it is especially helpful with its depressant effect on a_w which makes it a good agent; however, it is not considered to be an additive (see Chapter 13, §VII and Chapter 14, §III).

Nitrates and nitrites are used in cooked cured meats and salted products (Chapter 14, §III).

Sulphites and sulphur dioxide are widely used in wine-making, either to sterilize the material or to control fermentation. The SO_2 at more than 50 ppm is toxic to bacteria whilst having little influence on yeasts. It is also used to improve the preservation of fruits and certain vegetables. Apart from its bactericidal action it has a protective effect against browning. The SO_2 present in foods is made up free SO_2 and SO_2 linked to different compounds: carbohydrates, amino acids, nucleic acids, polyphenols. However, only the free SO_2 has antioxidant properties. In order to obtain the desired result, it is therefore necessary to use relatively large quantities of this additive and control the physicochemical conditions (pH, temperature, oxygen concentration) which have an influence on the equilibrium between the free and bound forms.

It is only recently that carbon dioxide has been recognized as an inhibitor of micro-organisms; it strongly inhibits aerobic bacteria responsible for deterioration, such as *Pseudomonas*, and allows lactic bacteria to grow; it is active against moulds but not against yeasts. Cold conditions aid the CO_2 effect with improved solubility. Refrigerated animal products (meats, fish, eggs, etc.) require this type of process.

Hydrogen peroxide, H_2O_2, is active against anaerobic bacteria which have no catalase, but it can only be used for surface treatment under aseptic conditions.

1.2 Organic compounds

Saturated straight-chain carboxylic acids, and their salts, are widely used, especially acetic acid (CH_3–COOH) a component of vinegar; but they have little effect at the low doses at which additives are normally used. Propionic acid, the next higher homologue of acetic acid (CH_3–CH_2–COOH), is particularly active against moulds. It is used in the baking industry and is advocated for the preservation of plant products (fruits, vegetables). Formic acid (H–COOH) is also used as a surface decontamination agent for meats. Monoglycerides, notably monolaurin

$$CH_2\text{–}O\text{–}CO\text{–}(CH_2)_{10}\text{–}CH_3$$
$$CH\text{–}OH$$
$$CH_2OH$$

are also used.

The unsaturation of carboxylic acids increases their antimicrobial activity. Sorbic acid (CH_3–CH=CH–CH=CH–COOH) is the most used: it inhibits, first of all, moulds; it has minimal effect on yeasts and bacteria; however, it clearly inhibits the growth of *Clostridium botulinum*. In animals this acid can be metabolized.

Benzoic acid (C_6H_5–COOH) and its derivatives are active against bacteria and yeasts, especially at pH⩽4, since it is the non-ionized form which acts. Benzoic acid is not very water-soluble; whereas the methyl or propyl esters of parahydroxybenzoic acid have good solubility; in addition, they are sensitive to pH and may be used in a neutral setting. These substances are used in low dosage (0.1%) for foods consumed in small quantities (caviar, fruit juices, etc.).

One reason for the preservation effect of the lactic fermentation, e.g. cream puffs, dairy products (Chapter 13), cooked meats, etc., is the production of lactic acid (CH_3–CHOH–COOH) in the foodstuff itself.

There is very limited use of ethylene and propylene oxides for the disinfection of seeds and relatively dry products which might be sensitive to heat treatment (dried fruits, spices, cocoa, dried yeast, etc.).

Antioxidants originating from phenol (Fig. 17.1) are also of interest in view of their efficacy against micro-organisms.

Some phenolic compounds, whose structure is linked to that of α-tocopherol are found in some plants, in particular in sage and rosemary. On the market are condiments based on rosemary extracts, said to protect the pigmentation of carotenoids, to stop browning and to stabilize the flavour. These extracts, which are either completely incorporated or used crushed on the surface of a product, at 0.002%, have shown an antioxidant activity identical to, or better than that for BHA and BHT (see Fig. 17.1).

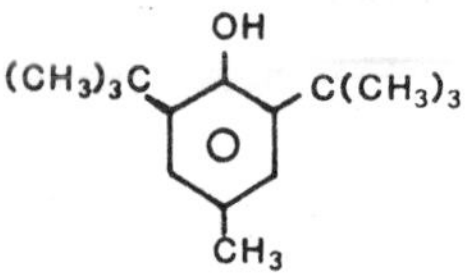

2,6-ditert-butyl-4-hydroxytoluene or BHT

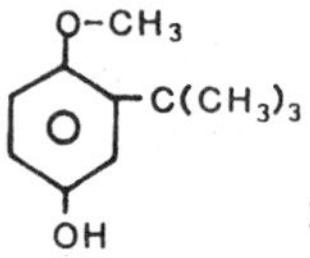

2-tert-butyl-4-hydroxyanisole (or 3-) or BHA

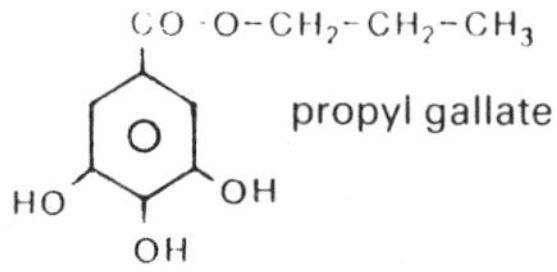

propyl gallate (or octyle or dodecyl)

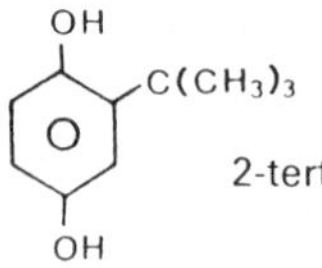

2-tert-butyl-hydroquinone (or TBHQ)

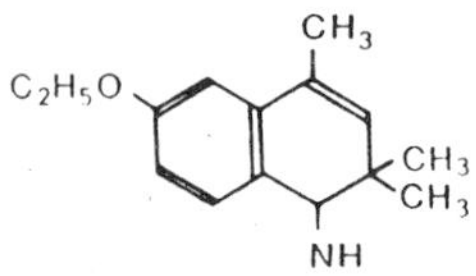

Ethoxyquin (or Santoquin)

Fig. 17.1 — Synthetic antioxidants.

1.3 Antibiotics

Although these are very effective, they are little used in the food industry because of the risk of undesirable effects on the consumer and of the possibility of the appearance of resistant strains.

Some years ago, derivatives of tetracyline (chlor- and oxy-) were used in the USA to prolong the storage-life of poultry. Pimaricin is used to protect the rinds or crusts or the surface of smoked meat products.

Nisin is used in the cheese-making industry in order to produce firm cheeses by avoiding swelling due to butyric acid. Nisin is one of the types of antibiotics produced by food fermentation organisms, which do not pose the problems presented by medical antibiotics.

2. Antioxidants

We are only concerned here with autoxidation, which is produced spontaneously under moderate conditions; this was explained briefly in Chapter 4, §IX.

Prevention of oxidation involves two methods:

(a) suppression of factors favourable to oxidation by reducing:
  (1) O_2 pressure

    (2) temperature

    (3) concentration of catalysts (metals, enzymes)

    (4) action of light.

(b) addition of a 'reverse catalyst' which prevents the chain reaction from propagating, i.e. an antioxidant:

    (1) natural products: tocopherol, ascorbic acid (Chapter 8)

    (2) synthetic products: these are nearly all derived from phenol (see Fig. 17.1).

These substances are fat-soluble; propyl gallate is also water-soluble, but not the others.

Some acid substances are 'synergistic'. They regenerate the antioxidant after use — examples are lactic, citric, tartaric and orthophosphoric acids and their salts. Moreover, they prevent catalytic reversion (acceleration of auto-oxidation).

From the point of view of toxicology in animals, the synthetic products have been thoroughly examined. The results so far have varied according to the species — effects on lung, liver, thyroid, blood-clotting, carcinogenic action. The results cannot be extrapolated to man, but it seems advisable to reduce their usage in human foodstuffs.

3. Available water

The microbiological stability of foodstuffs is directly linked to water activity: a_w (or A_w). This is considered in Chapter 7, and the relationship is described between this value and deterioration in foodstuffs, through chemical means (oxidation) as well as through the activity of bacteria, yeasts and moulds.

4. Staling

It was seen in Chapter 3 that stale bread (hardening without drying out) is due to starch retrogradation, with passage from the amorphous state obtained during cooking, to a type of crystalline state. Anti-staling agents slow down or stop this process, in bread and in some types of fancy pastries. Some examples are given in Chapter 10, §VII.

III. FLAVOUR ADDITIVES

1. Flavour enhancers

Flavour substances react with certain cells (chemireceptors) distributed in the olfactory site for volatile molecules (at the top of the nasal fossae) and the gustatory site for dissolved molecules (on the buccal mucous, such as the tongue). Regulatory and decision-making systems are found in the brain. The aroma plays a major role in our relationship with the foodstuff, remembering that it corresponds with an equilibrium of substances.

A flavour-enhancing substance confers, as a rule a new aroma.

Aromas may be classified as follows:

— 'sweet' aromas, resembling the aromas from fruits and citrus fruits, and other products, which include honey, vanilla, coffee, caramel, etc. They are the most widely used;
— 'salty' aromas, whether plant (bulbs, fruits, spices) or animal (meat, fish, milk);
— 'various' aromas, notably alcohols and bitter products.

According to their origin, the following may be distinguished:

(1) Natural extracts; essential oils and essences from which the terpenes have been removed, oleo resins, concentrated juices;
(2) Products of reaction from heat, enzymatic or microbiologial (fermentation) process;
(3) Synthetic products; these are extremely numerous (more than 10 000) and their structure is in general simple and they are comparable to materials isolated from natural products.

The 'flavour enhancers' or flavouring agents have already been mentioned (glutamate Chapter 14, §VI). It is not known how they act.

2.   Intense sweeteners

The principal sweeteners are listed together in Table 17.1. These are substances which are, in principle, non-toxic. The sweet derivatives of urea are not mentioned because their toxic or bitter qualities rule them out. Due to the enormous market involved, the number of sweeteners has risen remarkably to several hundred.

Natural protein sweeteners have recently been the subject of study; this goes against the long-held view that it was only small molecules which were sweeteners. However the sweetening capacity disappears as denaturation takes place, especially in acid medium.

Aspartame and thaumatin seem to offer the best chances for the future. Aspartame is an example of the random chance effect, resulting, as it does, from research on the synthesis of hormones. The amino acids which constitute it are not sweet, and the non- methylated dipeptide is actually bitter.

Recently another dipeptide, alitame, seems to have taken the lead. It is an amide of the dipeptide L-aspartyl-D-alanine. Its sweetening capacity is about 2000 times that of sucrose, that is, 12 times that of aspartame. Its solubility in water is excellent and its stability at raised temperatures and where there are variations in pH is greater than that of aspartame. Alitame has the advantage over aspartame in that it does not include phenylalanine, and therefore it does not have the same restrictions in use due to phenylketonuria.

3.   Colouring agents

These are the additives which are, in one sense, the easiest to do without. They are used mainly to regularize the colour of a foodstuff or a drink and, secondarily, to give an attractive appearance. The list of permitted colouring agents is given in Table 17.2. It can be seen that there are only about ten colouring agents which are normally allowed. Temporary authorization is given for about ten more.

Table 17.1 — Sugar substitutes

Origin	Name	Source	Sweetening capacity[a]	Observation	Usage
I. Natural (a) Sugar-based	Glycyrrhizin	*Glycyrrhiza glabra*	50	Toxicity at high dosage;	Not permitted in UK
	(ammoniated) Stevioside	*Stevia rebaudiana*	300	improver for beers Anti-androgen	Not permitted in UK
	Dihydrochalcone (neohesperidin)	*Citrus aurantum* (orange)	2000	Prolonged sugar taste; after tastes	—
	Osladin	*Polypodium vulgare*	3000		—
	Phyllodulcin	*Hydrangea macrophylla*	400	(?) Toxicity	—
(b) Protein-based	Thaumatin I and II	*Thaumatococcus danielli* MM 20000	1600	Good	Permitted in UK
	Monellin	*Dioscoreophyllum cumensii* MM 11500	2500	Unstable in acid medium	Not permitted in UK
	Miraculin (glycoprotein)	MM 42000		Modifies acid tastes to sugary taste	Not permitted in UK
II. Synthetic	Saccharin (Na)	[chemical structure]	300	Bitter after-taste; (?) toxicity	Permitted in UK
	Sodium cyclamate	[chemical structure] $NH-SO_3Na$	40	(?) Toxicity	Not permitted in UK
	Aspartame (L-aspartyl-L-phenylalanine methylester)	[chemical structure] $CH_2-CH-NH-CO-CH-NH_2$; $COOCH_3$; CH_2-COOH	160	Good	Permitted in UK, warning on phenylketonuria
	Acetosulpham (acesulpham K)	[chemical structure]	150	Good	Permitted in UK

[a] sucrose = 1.

Table 17.2 — Permitted colours in foods in Britain

	EC number
Natural colours	
Carotenoids	E 160
α, β, γ,carotene	E 160 a
annatto, bixin	E 160 b
capsanthin	E 160 c
Lycopene	E 160 d
β-appo-8′-carotenal	E 160 e
ethyl ester β-apo-8-carotenoic acid	E 160 f
Lutein and related compounds including canthaxanthin	E 161 a–g
Beetroot red, betanin	E 162
Anthocyanins	E 163
Natural substances with a secondary colouring effect	
paprika	
turmeric	
saffron	
sandalwood	
Curcumin	E 100
Riboflavin, lactoflavin, riboflavin-5′-phosphate	E 101
Chlorophyll	E 140
Copper complexes of chlorophyll and chlorophyllins	E 141
Caramel	E 150
Cochineal or carminic acid	E 120
Synthetic colours	
Tartrazine	E 102
Quinoline yellow	E 104
Sunset yellow FCF or orange yellow S	E 110
Carmoisine or azorubine	E 122
Amaranth	E 123
Ponceau 4R	E 124
Erythrosine BS	E 127
Red 2G	—
Patent blue V	E 131
Indigo carmine or indigotine	E 132
Brilliant blue FCF	—
Green S or acid brilliant green BS or lissamine green	E 142
Brown FK	—
Chocolate brown HT	—
Black PN or brilliant black BN	E 151
Carbon black or vegetable carbon	E 153
Mineral colouring agents	
Titanium dioxide	E 171
Iron oxides and hydroxides	E 172
Colouring matters for certain purposes only	
Aluminium	E 173
Silver	E 174
Gold	E 175
Pigment rubine	E 180
Methyl violet	—

See the Statutory Instruments, SI 1973 No. 1340, 1975 No. 1488, 1976 No. 2086, 1978 No. 1787, 1987 No. 1987.

4. Texturizing agents

4.1 Gelling and thickening agents

These, based on sugar, have been described in Chapter 3, together with the mechanism which comes into play in gelling. Casein and gelatine were reviewed in Chapters 13 and 14.

4.2 Emulsifying agents

The emulsifying agents used in the food production industry are amphophilic substances; their structure involves both hydrophilic and hydrophobic (or lipophilic) functions, whereby they are able to stabilize a system which is naturally unstable: oil/water.

— Monoglycerides are the most widely used. They are obtained by interesterification between a common triglyceride fat (bacon, lard, oils) and glycerol at about 200°C. The mixture of glycerides obtained, at least 60% monoesters, may be purified by vacuum distillation (200°C and 0.1 mm of Hg). With oils it is best to carry out hydrogenation of the double bonds.
— Monoglycerides esterified by an organic acid (lactic acid, citric acid, acetic acid, etc.) are more effective than the first-mentioned. The DATEM products, obtained from diacetylated tartaric acid, are used in bakery products.
— Sucroesters and sucroglycerides are of interest because of their ease of dispersibility in water and their weak taste, but they are used less than the preceding substances. Sucroesters are obtained by direct esterification of sucrose with methyl esters of fatty acids. Sucroglycerides are obtained by interesterification of sucrose and triglycerides in a solvent medium (propylene glycol).
— Various esters of fatty acids, formed from compounds with one or more OH groups, dimerized lactic acid (stearyllactylates), sorbose, sorbitans can be used. The monostearate of sorbitan is dispersible in water (SPAN-60). After reaction with several molecules of ethylene oxide, water-soluble derivatives are obtained (TWEEN-80: monoleate of sorbitan polyoxyethylene).

$$
\begin{array}{l}
\rule[0.5ex]{3em}{0.4pt}\; CH_2 \\
\big| \\
CH - (OCH_2 - CH_2)_w - OH \\
\big| \\
O CH - (OCH_2 - CH_2)_x - OH \\
\big| \\
\rule[0.5ex]{3em}{0.4pt}\; CH \\
\big| \\
CH - (OCH_2 - CH_2)_y - OH \\
\big| \\
CH_2 - (OCH_2 - CH_2)_z - OOC - C_{17}H_{33}
\end{array}
$$

— <u>Phospholipids</u>: these were reviewed in Chapter 4. Lecithin from egg yolk is much less used. Usually the origin is soya bean oil, which contains 2–3%. In general, the commercial products contain only 50% phospholipids; they can be purified. Their usage is very varied: bakery, chocolate-making, margarine production, animal foods, etc.

Lecithin Y is an artificial product not allowed in France. It contains phosphatidic acids (40%). It is more consistent than natural phospholipids.

4.3   Anti-caking or anti-agglomeration agents
These are in the main silica-based products: hydrated silica and sodium silicoaluminate. Their particular fine texture (10–20 nm) allows them to play the role of dry lubricants by coating products. The amount used is up to 2%.

The following are also used in table salt: tricalcium phosphate, magnesium carbonate, iron manganitrile. Potassium hexacyanoferrate may be used in a lower dose (5 mg/kg).

IX.   ADDITIVES OF NUTRITIONAL VALUE

These have already been studied, since these are nutrients. Three types of substances are mainly used to enrich foodstuffs:

(1) Vitamins C, B_1, B_6, B_{12}, nicotinic acid, folates, pantothenic acid, A, D, E, K (see Chapter 8).
(2) Minerals (see Chapter 6). Mostly, metals such as Fe, Zn, Cu, etc., are used, often in the form of complexes, and some metalloids such as fluorides.
(3) Amino acids in the L (natural) form. Free amino acids (Lys, Met) are often added. The use of peptides is becoming more widespread (see Chapter 5). Chemical grafting of essential amino acids onto a protein chain, by isopeptidic bonds, has also been proposed.

In Chapter 13, the enrichment of the fat in cow's milk with linoleic acid was pointed out. In Chapter 3 it was seen that increase in the fibre content of foodstuffs has also been suggested.

Index

An italic number indicates the page reference for the structure of a substance